Jacob Bigelow

Modern Inquiries: Classical, Professional, and Miscellaneous

Jacob Bigelow

Modern Inquiries: Classical, Professional, and Miscellaneous

ISBN/EAN: 9783337178550

Printed in Europe, USA, Canada, Australia, Japan

Cover: Foto ©Thomas Meinert / pixelio.de

More available books at **www.hansebooks.com**

MODERN INQUIRIES:

CLASSICAL, PROFESSIONAL, AND MISCELLANEOUS.

By JACOB BIGELOW, M.D.,

LATE PRESIDENT OF THE AMERICAN ACADEMY OF ARTS AND SCIENCES,
AND LATE A PROFESSOR IN HARVARD UNIVERSITY.

"Nullius addictus jurare in verba magistri."

BOSTON:
LITTLE, BROWN, AND COMPANY.
1870.

TO

GEORGE TICKNOR, ESQ.

My dear Ticknor, —

In a note received from you a short time since, you kindly advert to the youthful days when "we lay on the carpet, and read Homer together." Since that now distant period, you have remained loyal to your first attachment, dividing it only with the more recent literature, which you have largely cultivated and signally adorned. If I seem to be recreant to the pleasing associations of those times, it is because I am swept along with the progress of the age, and have become disciplined in some measure to replace delightful visions with more arduous and growing realities.

Your early and late friend,

JACOB BIGELOW.

Boston, April 15, 1867.

PREFACE.

THE contents of this volume are mostly reprints of occasional productions, written or spoken, in various forms and at different times, during the last fifty years. They have been the exceptional recreations of a long and busy professional life. If they have any common bond of resemblance, it is that a great part of them are innovations, or departures from opinions which were more or less prevalent at the time of their publication.

The tendency of the world, not less in modern than in former ages, has been to exaggeration. Popular sentiment on speculative subjects is docile and gregarious, and follows readily in the track of guides whose authority is previously accredited by others, and whose zeal is persistent, even if it be not always according to knowledge. But, afterwards, the effect of time is to replace excessive devotion with a corresponding distrust in public opinion; so that, sooner or later, the reign of idolaters is succeeded by that of iconoclasts.

In looking back on the existing opinions which at intervals have seemed to call for, or at least to excuse, the publication of these desultory papers, it is to be recollected that there have been times, even now not far remote, —

When the attributes of scholarship were accorded to those only who were proficients in the ancient languages, and when familiarity with profitable sciences and with modern literature was not held to constitute learning, —

When the great changes effected in European civilization about four centuries ago were ascribed to the revival of classical learning, and not to their true cause, — the discoveries made in physical sciences and arts, —

When the removal of human physical maladies was believed to be mainly, if not solely, practicable through the application of drugs and medicines, and by a resort to perturbative, and often violent, measures, —

When the introduction of pure water into cities·

was not accounted safe if it came in the now common vehicle of leaden pipes, —

When the crypt and the overcrowded churchyard, and not the forest sanctuary, were considered fitting repositories for the remains of the dead, —

When the intercourse of nations was thought to be the fruitful cause of cholera and of some other epidemics not yet known to be contagious, —

And when, as a matter of historical curiosity among the unjust judgments of mankind, Vesuvius was held accountable for the suffocation of the elder Pliny.

CONTENTS.

I.
                                                                PAGE
ON THE LIMITS OF EDUCATION   1

II.
ON CLASSICAL AND UTILITARIAN STUDIES 87

III.
ON THE LIFE AND WORKS OF COUNT RUMFORD 90

IV.
ON THE DEATH OF PLINY THE ELDER 111

V.
ON THE BURIAL OF THE DEAD, AND MOUNT AUBURN CEMETERY . 119

VI.
REPORT OF THE ACTION OF COCHITUATE WATER ON LEAD PIPES, AND THE INFLUENCE OF THE SAME ON HEALTH . . 137

VII.
ON SELF-LIMITED DISEASES 143

VIII.
On the Treatment of Disease 173

IX.
On the Medical Profession and Quackery 199

X.
Brief Expositions of Rational Medicine 216

XI.
The Paradise of Doctors: a Fable 251

XII.
Practical Views on Medical Education 263

XIII.
On the Early History of Medicine 271

XIV.
Whether Cholera is Contagious 287

XV.
Testimony on the Cattle Disease in Massachusetts . . 295

XVI.
Report on Homœopathy 326

XVII.
Address Delivered before the American Academy of Arts and Sciences 333

XVIII.
Aphorisms on the War.—I. 358

XIX.

APHORISMS ON THE WAR.—II. 362

XX.

DIALOGUE BETWEEN NAPOLEON THE FIRST, AND JEREMIAH, A LATE CITIZEN OF THE UNITED STATES 365

XXI.

THE DARK SIDE, THE BRIGHT SIDE, THE PRACTICABLE SIDE . 371

ON THE LIMITS OF EDUCATION.

AN ADDRESS READ BEFORE THE MASSACHUSETTS INSTITUTE OF TECHNOLOGY, NOV. 16, 1865.

In 1829, a volume was published in Boston bearing the name of "Elements of Technology." This name was not then in use, nor was it generally understood except by those who drew its meaning from its etymology. It was not in Johnson's Dictionary, nor yet in Rees's Cyclopedia. In Worcester's Dictionary, where it now has a place, no older authority is cited for its support than that of the volume alluded to. Its analogue, indeed, was extant in some other languages, and, fifty years ago, was published in Latin among the "Theses" of the graduating-class of Harvard College. But its revival for the use of English readers had to be justified by the assertion, that it might be found in some of the older dictionaries.

Such, less than forty years ago, was the doubtful tenure in English literature of a word which now gives name in this city to a vigorous and popular institution, a large endowment, a magnificent edifice, and at the same time a great and commanding department of scientific study in every quarter of the civilized world.

It has happened in regard to technology, that, in the present century and almost under our own eyes, it has advanced with greater strides than any other agent of civilization; and has done more than any science to enlarge the boundaries of profitable knowledge, to extend the dominion of mankind over nature, to economize and utilize both labor and time, and thus to add indefinitely to the effective and available length of human existence. And, next to the influence of Christianity on our moral nature, it has had a leading sway in promoting the progress and happiness of our race.

To appreciate what has been done by the applied sciences operating through their dependent and associate arts, we have only to go back a little more than two-thirds of a century, to the times of Franklin and Washington, and in many cases to those of our own immediate fathers. In those days of small things, men were compelled to pass their lives in a sort of destitution, which, in this age of scientific luxury, would be considered a state of semi-barbarism. The means of domestic convenience, personal neatness, easy locomotion, rapid intelligence, agreeable warmth, abundant light, physical as well as intellectual, were things wished and waited for, but not yet found.

To us, their effeminate descendants, it might be painfully interesting to witness the efforts of those hardy and much-enduring people to procure warmth in their dwellings, by the scorching and freezing of their alternate sides, under the blast that swept from many apertures towards the current of a vast open chimney; and this state of things was hardly bettered by the established zero-temperature of an unwarmed church, or the irrespirable atmosphere of a stove-heated schoolroom or country court-house. Our recent progenitors read their dusky and infrequent newspaper by the light of a tallow-candle, and groped their way through dark and unpaved streets under the guidance of a peripatetic lantern. If in summer they desired a draught of cold water, there was no ice; and, if in winter they wished for dry feet, there was no India-rubber. If in darkness they sought for light, there was neither gas nor even lucifer matches.

Men were stationary in their habits and deliberate under their necessities. He who would communicate with a friend in a neighboring State might do it in a week, provided he could devote a preparatory week to seeking a safe private conveyance. And, if any one had occasion to transport himself from one town or city to another, he could do it on a trusty saddle-horse, or, still more rapidly, in the organized relays of the Boston and New-York stage-coach, "Despatch Line," which undertook to put him through in less than a week. They who went down to the sea in ships could reach England from either of the above-named ports in from one to two months, if wind and weather were favorable. Literary productions were written out with a goosequill, and printed in a reasonable time by the labor of two men toiling at a hand-press. Housewives plied the spinning-wheel, the distaff, and the shuttle; and webs of coarse texture grew into perceptible existence with a speed which might be compared to that of a growing vegetable. Beef was roasted on a revolving spit, turned round by a man, a dog, or a smoke-jack. And, what will hereafter be accounted still more strange, garments were made by sewing slowly together their constituent parts with a needle and thread.

I have taken technology as a leading exponent of the great advance which was to be made, and has been made, during the lifetime of some of us, in certain intellectual and practical improvements of mankind, in supplying the wants, overcoming the difficulties, and increasing the elegances of life. To enumerate all these improvements would simply be to recount the great steps by which our own age has advanced to the elevated and privileged condition in which we now see it. And yet, although the practical arts, in the hands of science, have taken the lead in the great visible changes of the present century, it would be presumptuous to call technol ogy the only field from the cultivation of which mankind have obtained abundant and unlooked-for harvests. In every other walk or sphere of science, literature, and refined humanity, the civilized world, with unfaltering progress, has pushed forward, at the same time, its dominion over mind and matter.

It is the object of the present remarks to show that the amount of knowledge appropriate to civilization which now exists in the world is more than double, and in many cases more than tenfold, what it was about half a century ago; and that, therefore, no individual can expect to grasp, in the limits of a lifetime, even an elementary knowledge of the many provinces of old learning, augmented as they now are by the vast annexations of modern discovery. Still farther: education, which represents the threshold of accessible knowledge, instead of being expanded, must be contracted in the number and amount of its requirements, so that while all its doors are freely kept open to those who possess time, opportunity, and special aptitude or necessity, a part of them at least must be closed to those who do not possess those requisites. If in the days of the ancient Greeks "life was short," while "art was long," how is it now, when life is not longer, but art, literature, and science are immeasurably greater? How will it be in another half-century, when new discoveries shall have arisen, commensurate in their results with those of electro-magnetism and of solar actinism, of modern optical combinations, and geographical and geological explorations? How will it be with the discoveries of newly armed astronomers and the calculations of geometers yet to appear; with revolutions stirred up by chemists among elements that have slumbered together since the creation; with the augmented conversions of heat into other force, driving innumerable mechanisms to minister to man's pleasure and power; and, more than all, how will it be with the cumbrous, vast, and insurmountable weight of books, which shall render literary distinction a thing of chance, of uncertainty, perhaps even of impossibility.

A law which obtains in matter, obtains also in regard to the mind and its acquirements, that strength is not increased in proportion to magnitude. The static and dynamic strength of materials for the most part decreases as their bulk increases. A column or a bridge cannot be carried beyond a certain size, without crushing or breaking its substance; and a whale, if unsupported by the surrounding water, would die from the pressure of his own weight. A small animal will leap many more times his length than a large one; and the integrity of his slender limbs will not be injured by the exertion. The useful development of a tree is known to be promoted by severe pruning; and where this is impossible, as in primeval forests, the trees prune themselves, and attain greater height by the death of their under branches, the insufficient supply of sunlight being monopolized by the upper and dominant members at the expense of the lower. These examples, drawn both from inert and organic matter, may serve to illustrate the corresponding truth, that human intellect, though varying in capacity in different individuals, has its limits in all plans of enlargement by acquisition ; and that these limits cannot be transcended without aggregate deterioration in distracting the attention, overloading the memory or overworking the brain, and sapping the foundations of health.

The school system of New England is at the present moment our glory and our shame. We feel a just pride, that among us education is accessible to all, because our public schools are open to the humblest persons. But, in our zeal for general instruction, we sometimes forget that a majority of men and women must labor with their hands, that the world may not stand still, and that all may not lose by disuse the power to labor. We cannot train all our boys to be statesmen and divines, nor all our girls to be authors and lecturers or even teachers. We ought not, therefore, to drive them into the false position of expecting to attain, by extraordinary effort, a place which neither nature nor circumstances have made possible. Many unfortunate children have been ruined for life, in body and mind, by being stimulated with various inducements to make exertions beyond their age and mental capacity. A feeble frame and a nervous temperament are the too sure consequences of a brain overworked in childhood. Slow progress, rather than rapid growth, tends to establish vigor, health, and happiness. It has always appeared to me, that a desirable and profitable mode of school education would be one in which every hour of study should be offset by another hour of exercise, required to be taken in the open air.

To illustrate the impossibility of making any one what may be called a general scholar, we need but to take a slight view of the extent and recent progress of a few of the most familiar and popular sciences at the present day. Let us take geography, which treats of the earth's external structure; and geology, which treats of its internal. In the first of these, the education of many of the present generation abounded in what are now found to be errors and defects. We were taught that the Andes were the highest mountains of the globe, and the Amazon the longest river. Discoverers had then stopped a thousand miles short of the sources of the Nile and of the Missouri. The Columbia and the Sacramento were geographical myths; while a fabulous Oregon, or River of the West, was laid down on the maps on the hearsay authority of Carver, displacing what are now the Rocky Mountains, and entering the Pacific Ocean about latitude 43°. The existence of the African Niger was known to the Romans; yet the Royal Geographical Society, until 1830, did not know where it reached the ocean, though a hundred Englishmen at various times had laid down their lives in African deserts, in fruitless attempts to resolve the mysterious problem. It was not until a still later period, that the world knew that there was ·a continuous Arctic Sea, or any thing like an Antarctic Continent.

But if so much has been done in the more difficult and inaccessible parts of our globe, how much more has been achieved in the parts accessible to settlement and cultivation. The American Continent, the interior map of which was almost a blank at the close of our Revolution, is now profusely dotted with towns, cities, forts, post-offices, and rail-stations, until the most diligent compiler of a gazetteer is obliged to pause in despair at the manifest defects of his latest edition.

Geology may be considered as almost a creation of the present age. When Werner visited Paris, in 1802, it could hardly be said to consist of more than insulated observations, with a few crude and unsettled theories. But now it has become a great, organized, and overshadowing department of science. In every language of Europe it has its voluminous systems and its unfailing periodicals. Societies of special organization carry forward its labors, and every country of the globe is traversed by its observers and collectors. The shelves of museums are weighed down by its accumulations; and in its palæontology alone the Greek language is exhausted to furnish factitious names for the continually developed species of antecedent creations.

Chemistry, in a limited degree, appears to have attracted the attention of the ancients; but of their proficiency in this pursuit we know more from their preserved relics and results than from their cotemporaneous records. In modern times the chemists constitute a philosophical community, having a language of their own, a history of their own, methods, pursuits, and controversies of their own, and a domain which is co-extensive with the materials of which our globe is made. Many men, of gifted minds and high intellectual attainments, have devoted their lives to the prosecution of this science. Chemistry has unravelled the early mysteries of our planet, and has had a leading agency in changing the arts and the economy of human life. It now fills the civilized world with its libraries, laboratories, and lecture-rooms. No individual can expect to study even its accessible books, still less to become familiar with its recorded facts. Yet chemistry is probably in its infancy, and opens one of the largest future fields for scientific cultivation.

Natural history in its common acceptation implies

the investigation, arrangement, and description of all natural bodies, including the whole organized creation. If no other science existed but this, there would be labor enough, and more than enough, to employ for life the students and observers of the world. Each kingdom of organic nature already offers to our acquaintance its hundred thousand specific forms; and these are but the vanguard of a still greater multitude believed to cover the surface of countries yet unexplored, and to fill the mysterious recesses not yet penetrated by the microscope. And, as far as we know, every one of these organisms, great or small, carries with it its parasites, to which it affords habitation and food, and which may be supposed not only to double, but to multiply in an unknown ratio, its original numbers. Again, when we reflect that every one of these species has its own anatomy, its physiology, its peculiar chemistry, its habits, its sensations, its modes of reproduction, its nutrition, its duration, its metamorphoses, its diseases, and its final mode of destruction, we may well despair of knowing much of the whole, when a single species might furnish materials of study for a human lifetime.

The foregoing are examples of the claim on our attention and study advanced by a portion only of the progressive sciences. They serve to develop truths and laws appertaining to the material earth, which truths and laws must have existed had there never been minds to study them. The relations of number and figure, the laws of motion and rest, of gravity and affinity, of animal and vegetable life, must have been the same, had the dominant race of man never appeared on earth. But there is another extensive class of scientific pursuits, the subjects of which are drawn from his own nature. He has devised metaphysics to illustrate the operations of his own mind. He has introduced ethical and political science to promote order and happiness, and military science to assist, for a time at least, in destroying both. He has built up history with "her volumes vast," which volumes are as yet a small thing compared with those that are to come. Under the name of news, the press daily inundates the world with a million sheets of cotemporaneous history; for history and news, under small qualifications, are identical. The annals of the last four years may deserve as large a place in the attention of mankind as was due when the poet informed the Egyptian mummy, that, since his decease, "a Roman empire had begun and ended." The greatest part of what should have been history is unwritten, and of what has been written the greatest part is of little general value. If all that has actually been committed to papyrus, parchment, or paper had by chance been preserved from the effects of time and barbarism, the aggregate would be so vast, and the interest so little, that the busy world could hardly turn aside for its examination from more absorbing and necessary pursuits.

But the world is not contented with history which states, or professes to state, the progress, arts, dates, successes, and failures of distinguished men and nations. It requires further the supplementary aid of fiction, which finds facts, not in testimony, but in probability; not as they are recorded to have happened, but as they ought to have happened under the circumstances and with the actors. Fiction, moreover, not being restrained by the limits of circumstantial truth, is at liberty to seek embellishment from exaggeration, from ornament, from poetry, from dramatic utterance, and passionate expression. Hence it has taken the lead in modern literature, and it is not probable that at this day the most accomplished bibliographer or bookseller could point the way to one-half of its multiplied and perishable productions.

There is neither time nor inducement to refer to the pseudo-sciences, which in all ages have made serious drafts upon the limited lifetime of man; nor to the ephemeral and unprofitable issues which consume his time and labor, and wear out his strength. At the present day we have not much to fear from alchemy, palmistry, or astrology, nor yet from spiritualism, homœopathy, or Mormonism. But it is not easy to prevent men from wasting their time in the pursuit of shadows; from substituting exceptions for general laws; from believing things, not because they are probable, but because they are wonderful and entertaining. Still less can we divert them from yielding to the guidance of an excited will, from following prejudices or creating them, from adopting one side of a controversy or party strife for no better reason than that some other party has adopted the opposite.

It would be unnecessary to add to what has already been said, even an inventory of other studies which present seducing but interminable claims on the life and labor of man. It would be vain to open the flood-gates of philology, and to follow the thousand rills of language which have intersected and troubled each other ever since they left their fountains at Babel. And we pause in humility before the very portals of astronomy, which has revealed to us that we roll and revolve, and perhaps again revolve, around we know not what. And, helpless as animalcules on the surface of a floating globule, we are ever striving to see, to explore, and to mark our way through the "starry dust" of infinite space. Strong and devoted minds have piled up unreadable tomes, the result of their life-long studies and observations; yet few, save the professional and the initiated, attempt to invade the recondite sanctuary of their deposit.

Thus the immense amount of knowledge, general and special, true and fictitious, salutary and detrimental, the record of which is already in existence, has grown into an insurmountable accumulation, a *terra incognita*, which, from its very magnitude, is inaccessible to the inquiring world. Hence the economy of the age has introduced the labor-saving machinery of periodical literature, which, by substituting compendiums and reviews for the more bulky originals, has seemed to smooth the up-hill track of knowledge, and lighten the Sisyphean load of its travellers. But periodical literature, useful or frivolous as it may be, and indispensable as it undoubtedly is, has become, by its very success, inflated to an enormous growth, and bids fair in its turn to transcend the overtaxed powers of attention of those for whose use it is prepared. Like our street cars, while it helps forward to their destination a multitude of struggling pedestrians, it substitutes pressure for exercise, and does not save the fatigue of those who are still obliged to stand that they may go. In looking forward to another century, it is curious to consider who will then review the reviews, and condense, redact, and digest the compends of compendiums, from which the life has already been pressed out by previous condensation.

Since these things are so,— since, in the dying words of Laplace, "The known is little, but the unknown is immense," and —

"Since life can little more supply
Than just to look about us and to die,"—

it is a question of paramount importance how, in this short period, education can be made to conduce most to the progress, the efficiency, the virtue, and the welfare of man.

It is not presumptuous to say, that education, to be useful, must, as far as possible, be made simple, limited, practicable, acceptable to the learner, adapted to his character and wants, and brought home to his particular case by *subdivision* and *selection*. What is now called a liberal education is a term which means something and nothing. Among us it generally implies an attendance for four years upon the "curriculum," or course of studies, prescribed and pursued in some incorporated college or university. This attendance may be punctual and thorough, or it may be negligent and unprofitable; so that while one student makes a limited acquirement of multifarious knowledge, another forgets a great part of what he knew on entering the college, and prepares to forget the rest as soon as he enters upon active life.

Subdivision and selection afford the principal avenues through which men arrive at success in the humbler, as well as the more conspicuous, walks of life. The mechanical labor of artisans is best performed, and its best results obtained, by distributing its duties among a multitude of special agents; and this is more or less successfully done, in proportion as a society or a craft is more or less perfectly organized. So likewise in the higher or more intellectual pursuits of life, in which men procure bread by the labor of their heads instead of their hands, the number of learned professions has been within a short time wonderfully increased. In the days of our fathers, the learned professions were accounted three in number, — Law, Physic, and Divinity. But now more than three times that number afford means of honorable subsistence to multitudes of duly educated persons. We have now a profession of authors, of editors, of lecturers, of teachers, of engineers, of chemists, of inventors, of architects, and other artists; and to these may be added the better class of soldiers and politicians. And all these professions are again subdivided in proportion as society advances in its requirements.

For precisely the same reason that it would not be profitable for experts in a mechanical vocation to distract and dissipate their attention among pursuits alien to their tastes and qualifications, it can hardly be advantageous for pupils and neophytes in learning, to undertake to make themselves competent representatives of the various sciences, the literary studies, the languages, dead and living, which are now professedly taught in our colleges and seminaries. Every individual is by nature comparatively qualified to succeed in one path of life, and comparatively disqualified to shine in another. The first step in education should be for the parties most interested, to study, and, as far as possible, to ascertain, the peculiar bent and capacity of a boy's mind. This being done, he should be put upon a course of intellectual and physical training, corresponding, as far as possible, to that for which nature seems to have designed him. But in all cases a preparatory general elementary education, such as is furnished by our common schools, must be made a pre-requisite even to qualify him to inquire. The more thorough this preparatory training is made, the better it is for the student. But, after this is completed, a special or departmental course of studies should be selected, such as appears most likely to conduct him to his appropriate sphere of usefulness. Collateral studies of different kinds may always be allowed; but they should be subordinate and subsidiary, and need not interfere with the great objects of his especial education.

A common college education now culminates in the student becoming what is called a master of arts. But this, in a majority of instances, means simply a master of nothing. It means that he has spent much time and some labor in besieging the many doors of the temple of knowledge, without effecting an entrance at any of them. In the practical life which he is about to follow, he will often have occasion to lament, be he ever so exemplary and diligent, that he has wasted, on subjects irrelevant to his vocation, both time and labor, which, had they been otherwise devoted, would have prepared and assisted him in the particular work he is called on to do.

Young men, as well as their parents in their behalf, are justly ambitious of a collegiate education. Older men often regret that they have not had the opportunity to receive it when young. And this is because of the generally acknowledged fact, that four years, spent under the tuition of faithful, accomplished, and gentlemanly teachers, can hardly fail to improve their character, language, and bearing, as well as their store of useful knowledge. It is the habitual contact and guidance of superior minds, as well as the progressive attrition with each other, which make young men proficients in rectitude, in honor, in science, in polite literature, in tact, and in manners. And this result will appear, whether they have been taught French at West Point, or Greek in Harvard or Yale.

It is the province of the Institute of Technology, so largely and liberally sustained by the Legislature, by the munificence of individuals, and by the untiring labors of its distinguished president, to endeavor within its sphere to assist in providing for the educational wants of the most practical and progressive people that the world has seen. By its programme of instruction, a separate path is provided for all who require to accomplish themselves in any one or more of the especial branches of useful knowledge. It would not be just to ignore the fact, that the same thing has long been doing in several of our larger universities, where the practical sciences and the modern languages are extensively taught. But these time-honored institutions exceed some of their younger associates in this respect, that, under the name of classical literature, they premise and afterwards carry on a cumbrous burden of dead languages, kept alive through the dark ages, and now stereotyped in England by the persistent conservatism of a privileged order. I cannot here say much to add to the lucid, scholarly, and convincing exposition of the state of education as it now is in the great schools of England, given in a recent lecture before this Institute, by one of its professors, on the subject of classical and scientific studies.* No one who examines this discourse can fail to be impressed with the injudicious exactions made in favor of the dead languages in the English schools and universities, their insufficiency as means of intellectual training, and their limited applicability to the wants of the present advanced generation.

I would not underrate the value or interest of classical studies. They give pleasure, refinement to taste, depth to thought, and power and copiousness to expression. Any one who, in this busy world, has not much else to do may well turn over,

---

* Professor W. P. Atkinson.

by night and by day, the *exemplaria Græca*. But if, in a practical age and country, he is expected to get a useful education, a competent living, an enlarged power of serving others, or even of saving them from being burdened with his support, he can hardly afford to surrender four or five years of the most susceptible part of life to acquiring a minute familiarity with tongues which are daily becoming more obsolete; and each of which is obtained at the sacrifice of some more important science, or some more desirable language. It may not be doubted, that a few years devoted to the study of Greek will make a man a more elegant scholar, a more accomplished philologist, a more accurate and affluent writer, and, if all other things conspire, a more finished orator. But of themselves they will not make him what the world now demands, — a better citizen, a more sagacious statesman, a more farsighted economist, a more able financier, a more skilful engineer, manufacturer, merchant, or military commander. They will not make him a better mathematician, physicist, agriculturist, chemist, navigator, physician, lawyer, architect, painter, or musician. The ancient Greeks knew but little, though they knew how to express that little well. The moderns know a great deal more, and know how to express it intelligibly. Antiquity has produced many great men. Modern times have produced equally great men, and more of them.

It is common at the present day to say, that the Greek language disciplines the mind, extends the compass and application of thought; and that, by its copiousness and by its versatility of inflection and arrangement, it trains the mind to a better comprehension of words, thoughts, and things. All this is no doubt true, and might have great weight as a governing motive in education, were it not that the same ends can be more cheaply obtained by the agency of other means. Unfortunately for the supremacy of classical literature, all civilized countries are at this moment full of distinguished men and women who write well and speak well, and who have never acquired the learned languages. It is easy to say that such persons would have been more distinguished if they had known the classics. It is easy to say that Laplace would have been a better mathematician, and Faraday a better chemist, if by chance they had been duly instructed in Greek. But this is gratuitous assumption. The contrary result is more probable, inasmuch as the pursuit of classical literature would have abstracted just so much time from more pertinent and profitable investigations. At this day nobody believes that Watt would have made a better steam-engine, or Stephenson a better locomotive, if they had been taught philosophy by Plato himself.

The ancient languages, if applied to use, are not adequate to supply the wants of modern cultivation.

Truths and things have grown faster than words. Modern customs, arts, and sciences can be expressed in French or German, but not in Greek and Latin. A French writer, Professor Goffaux, has undertaken to translate Robinson Crusoe into Latin. The translation is successful, as far as easy diction and pure Latinity are concerned. But the language of the Romans is at fault in the islands of the Pacific, and new words must be coined to express, even imperfectly, things which are not coeval with the language employed. The world-renowned "man Friday" is introduced to us under the vicarious name of "Vendredi," and when Friday goes a-shooting he loads his "sclopetum" with "pulvis nitralis." If modern Greece should ever become a first-class power among the nations, it will have to complete, as it is now trying to do, a vocabulary of new terms to express the arts and commerce, the facts and fancies, the business and belles lettres, of the existing time. In other words, it must re-enforce its language with a new half, not found in the ancient classics.

The admiration of the old Romans for the Greek language and literature had its origin in the fact, that, in that age of limited civilization, they found not much else of the kind to admire. They looked to Greece as the fountain of what had been achieved in art, philosophy, poetry, and eloquence. Of consequence it was chosen as the great place of resort for educational objects, and Athens became the emporium of literary and philosophic instruction. But the Roman youth would never have been sent to Athens, had there been, as now, a railroad to take them to Paris, or a steamship to bring them to America. They would not have consumed their time in the groves of Academus, if they could have gained admittance to the Ecole Polytechnique, or to the Royal Institution.

At the present day, we relish the Greek language, from the mingled impression, not only of its own superiority, but of the pleasure it gives us and the pains it has cost us. We relish it as the musician enjoys his music, the mathematician his geometry, and the antiquarian his diggings. We are pleased that it has been preserved with its euphonious intonations, its copious expressiveness, and its noble literature. We know that the spirit of Homer cannot be translated into English, any more than the soul of Shakspeare can be done into Greek. All languages have their idiomatic expressions of thought, and in all of them translation has a killing effect on the strong points of literature. In the opera of Macbetto, the term "hell-broth," in the witch-scene, is rendered in Italian as "polto inferno." And, on the opposite page of the libretto, it is served up afresh in English as "infernal soup." It is highly probable that the half-savage accomplishments of Homer's heroes and gods cannot be made duly appreciable in the English tongue. Nevertheless, the modern world can get on without them; and we may be excused for believing, that, if the study of Greek should be abandoned as a requisite in our universities, — although it would still be cultivated, like other exceptional studies, with success and delight by many devotees, — yet our practical, bustling, and overcrowded generation would never again postpone more useful occupations to adopt it as an indispensable academical study.

In regard to success in the world at the present day, it is not an academic education, however desirable in any shape it may be, that gives a man access to the confidence and general favor of his fellow-men, or to the influential posts of society. It is native talent, reliability, perseverance, and indomitable will, that conduct him to the high places of the world. In all countries, and most of all in our own country, a contest continually goes on between academic education and self-education, — the education that comes from without and the education that comes from within. The much-cultivated boy, who, under favor of advantages, performs faithfully his allotted tasks, who fulfils the requirements of his teachers, who is accustomed to subordinate his own judgment to the dictation of others, — although he may hold a high rank in the scale of proficiency and the amount of acquisition, is liable, on arriving at manhood, to continue to lean rather than to lead, and thence to occupy a secondary place in the struggle for worldly distinction. On the other hand, the neglected but independent youth, who is brought up in the suggestive school of necessity, who becomes original and inventive because his life is a continued contest with difficulties, who balances character against opportunity, and individual vigor and patience against external guidance, — such an one, from the habit of directing himself, becomes more competent to direct others, and to wear more easily offices of trust and responsibility. It is remarkable how many of our distinguished men have been self-educated, or at least without academic education. Franklin was a philosopher, Washington a statesman, Patrick Henry an orator, but not by the grace of classical education. Henry Clay knew nothing of the Greek language, nor did probably Thomas Benton. Andrew Jackson and Andrew Johnson had rougher nursing than that of an alma mater. Rumford, Bowditch, and Fulton did not develop their intellects under the shades of academic seclusion. And, if we were to go abroad for examples, we should find that Napoleon was no classical scholar; and that Peter the Great, when he issued from his lair at Moscow to study the civilization of Western Europe, did not repair to the Universities of Cambridge and Oxford, but entered as a working mechanic in the shipyards of Saardam and Deptford.

We need not regret that our country is the field of wholesome competition between the well-taught and the self-taught; between advantage on the one side, and energy on the other; between early development under assistance, and slow maturity under difficulties. The success of either condition awakens and stimulates the zeal of the other.*

---

* Lord Jeffrey, in his review of Franklin's Works (Edinburgh Review, 1806), makes the following remarks: "Regular education, we think, is unfavorable to vigor or originality of understanding. Like civilization, it makes society more intelligent and agreeable; but it levels the distinctions of nature. It strengthens and assists the feeble; but it deprives the strong of his triumph, and casts down the hopes of the aspiring. It accomplishes this, not only by training up the mind in an habitual veneration for authorities, but, by leading us to bestow a disproportionate degree of attention upon studies that are only valuable as keys or instruments for the understanding, they come at last to be regarded as ultimate objects of pursuit; and the means of education are absurdly mistaken for its end. How many powerful understandings have been lost in the Dialectics of Aristotle! And of how much good philosophy are we daily defrauded, by the preposterous error of taking a knowledge of prosody for useful learning! The mind of a man who has escaped this training will at least have fair-play. Whatever other errors he may fall into, he will be safe at least from these infatuations; and if he thinks proper, after he grows up, to study Greek, it will probably be for some better purpose than to become critically acquainted with its dialects. His prejudices will be those of a man, and not of a schoolboy; and his speculations and conclusions will be independent of the maxims of tutors, and the oracles of literary patrons.

"The consequences of living in a refined and literary community are nearly of the same kind with those of a regular education. There are so many critics to be satisfied, so many qualifications to be established, so many rivals to encounter, and so much derision to be hazarded, that a young man is apt to be deterred from so perilous an enterprise, and led to seek for distinction in some safer line of exertion. He is discouraged by the fame and the perfection of certain models and favorites, who are always in the mouths of his judges; and, 'under them, his genius is rebuked,' and his originality repressed, till he sinks into a paltry copyist, or aims at distinction by extravagance and affectation. In such a state of society, he feels that mediocrity has no chance of distinction; and what beginner can expect to rise at once into excellence? He imagines that mere good sense will attract no attention; and that the manner is of

There are many persons who, even in this age, speak in terms of derogation of what are called utilitarian studies, in contrast with classical and ideal literature; as if pursuits which tend directly to the preservation and happiness of man were less worthy of his attention than those which may be founded in fancy, exaggeration, and passion. Poetry, art, and fiction have sought for the beautiful and sublime in creations which are imaginary and often untrue, which " o'er inform the pencil and the pen," and attract because they are mysterious and inaccessible. But, in the present age, fact has overtaken fancy and passed beyond it. We have no need to create new miracles, or to imagine them, when the appetite for wonder is more than satiated with reality, and objects of delight and amazement confront us in the walks of daily life. I know nothing in nature or art more beautiful than a railroad train, when it shoots by us with a swiftness that renders its inmates invisible, and winds off its sinuous way among mountains and forests, spanning

---

much more importance than the matter in a candidate for public admiration. In his attention to the manner, the matter is apt to be neglected; and, in his solicitude to please those who require elegance of diction, brilliancy of wit, or harmony of periods, he is in some danger of forgetting that strength of reason and accuracy of observation by which he first proposed to recommend himself. His attention, when extended to so many collateral objects, is no longer vigorous or collected; the stream, divided into so many channels, ceases to flow either deep or strong; he becomes an unsuccessful pretender to fine writing, or is satisfied with the frivolous praise of elegance or vivacity."

abysses, cleaving hills asunder, and travelling onward to its destination, steadily, smoothly, unerringly, as a migratory bird advances to the polar regions. And I know of nothing more sublime than, in the hold of an ocean steamship, to look on the mightiest enginery that has been raised by man, as it wields its enormous limbs like a living thing, and heaves and pants and rolls and plunges, urged onward by the struggling of the imprisoned elements.

The traveller passes daily by the never-ending rows of posts and wires which mark the pathway of the electric telegraph, until at length, by their very frequency, they are blended in the inert features of the landscape, and cease to attract attention. Yet, all the while, invisible thought is riding on those wires, and mind is answering to mind over a thousand miles of distance.

The half-fabulous siege of Troy has been made immortal in the epics of Homer and Virgil, and we are led by their poetry to admire the achievements of heathen gods and of heroes descended from them. We stand in awe at the exploits of primitive warriors, with the same emotions with which we afterwards mark in history the real deeds and eras of great military commanders. But, however much we may be impressed with the imagined spectacle of a host of disciplined barbarians fighting with swords and bucklers, we cannot keep out of sight that they would have been chaff before the wind in the presence of modern military science. Ulysses and Agamemnon were ten years in taking the city of Troy. Ulysses Grant with his batteries would have taken it in ten minutes. Artists, historians, and poets depict even now the memorable battles of Alexander and Cæsar. But half a dozen shells would have scattered the Macedonian phalanx, and the Roman empire could not have stood many days after a modern war-steamer should have found its way up the Tiber.

The march of military improvement has not yet halted in its course. The great war of American conservation has been eminently a war of science, and has changed by its inventions the whole face of modern conflicts. Huge forts and strong war-ships no longer protect harbors from the inroads of invulnerable enemies. The wooden walls of England, so long her defence and her boast, — like the walls of Jericho, have fallen flat before the sound of the distant crashing of rams and monitors and torpedoes. If the time shall ever come when classical readers shall tire at the monotonous championship of Trojans, Greeks, and Rutulians, they will kindle with wonder over that miracle of romance and reality, "The Bay Fight" of Mobile, by Henry Howard Brownell.

It is the duty of educational institutions to adapt themselves to the wants of the place and time in which they exist. It needs no uncommon penetration to see that we are now living in a great transition period, and that the world is resting its future hopes, and quieting its future fears, in reliance on an educated and enlightened democracy. When Andrew Johnson, at the inauguration ceremony of 1865, somewhat hastily declared himself a plebeian, dependent on the will of the people, and applied the same impeachment to his fellow functionaries,— like Paul of old, he was not mad, but spoke forth the words of truth and soberness. The last few years of history, the greatest and most momentous that the world has ever witnessed, bear testimony to the power of an educated common people to perceive and to carry forward their own true interests. Against the wiles of an astute and determined oligarchy, against the frowns of foreign privileged orders, amid the vicissitudes of good and evil fortune, this great people have advanced to their final triumph, not of revolution but of conservation, under the guidance of men like themselves, — of men who had been cleavers of wood and sewers of garments; who had wrought as farmers, as tanners, and as homely manufacturers; who knew the genius and character of their constituents, and the roads through which they were to be conducted to natural and necessary success.

At this moment, no nation of the globe can be called more truly powerful than one which has peacefully absorbed into its interior depths half a million of veterans, with discipline in their history, arms in their hands, and education in their heads. The most formidable ruler whom the world has at one time known is a self-educated man, who could hardly read and write at the age of twenty.

It is a fact so generally admitted, in this country at least, as to have become almost a truism, that prescriptive and hereditary positions are declining in social influence. Personal unworthiness or incompetency cannot be covered up by personal privilege. It is better to be the founder of a great name than its disreputable survivor. When a general of France, Duke of Abrantes and Governor of Paris, was reminded by others of the obscurity of his birth, he proudly replied, "Moi je suis mon ancêtre" (I am my own ancestor). In this great and original country, which is now treading in the van of a new reformation, we have thousands yet untaught who are to become ancestors in fame, ancestors in fortune, ancestors in science, ancestors in virtue. May their descendants be worthy of them!

These are the men who may well claim to "constitute a State." They are, as it were, the granite substratum which underlies the rich coal-fields and the arable soils of the earth's exterior surface. Like that they will last when softer and richer tracts shall have been swept away. Yet a continent as extensive and various as ours should be capable of furnishing all soils and materials for all needful and desirable productions. When the necessaries which sustain life are provided, the luxuries which adorn and gratify it must follow in their order. "In every country," says Buckle, "as soon as the accumulation of wealth has reached a certain point, the produce of each man's labor becomes more than sufficient for his support; it is no longer necessary that all should work; and there is found a separate class, the members of which pass their lives, for the most part, in the pursuit of pleasure; a very few, however, in the acquisition and diffusion of knowledge." This statement is a good exposition of the law which rules in the affairs of this country; it contains the danger and the safety, the bane and the antidote, of our social destiny. In a nation in which "the government is made for the people, and not the people for the government;" whose fundamental requisite is "the greatest good of the greatest number," — education, elementary and practical, such as common schools can furnish, must be made accessible to all who can be withdrawn, either from labor or idleness, for a sufficient time to realize its advantage. Afterwards those whom favor of fortune or strength of will has qualified to approach higher paths of intellectual culture should be encouraged, assisted, and excited to enter and occupy either one or many of the more difficult fields of literature and science, preferring those that best harmonize with the adopted path which is to be the occupation of life. And as to the residuary class, not numerous in any country, to whom is left the option of pursuing pleasure or knowledge, it is fortunate when there is judgment enough to perceive that these two objects can be identified in one pursuit. Knowledge is never so successfully cultivated as when it becomes a pleasure; and no pleasure is more permanent than the successful pursuit of knowledge, combined, as it should be, with moral progress. Natural gifts and variations of aptitude qualify men to tread with advantage the special paths of art and science; and such gifts are most frequently born in and with them, and cannot be imparted from without. A musical ear, an artistic eye, and a poetic sense, are not to be created in any man. We might as well expect to endow him with the sagacity of the hound, the quick ear of the hare, or the lightning sense of danger which preserves and insures the perilous life of the summer insect.

The man of robust though ungainly frame may make a first-rate laborer; the slender, shy, and delicate youth may shine in the walks of literature; the man of strong voice, and prompt and comprehensive intellect, may take precedence as an orator. But transpose these conditions, and we have a result of mistakes and failures. What God hath put asunder, man cannot well join together.

I have dwelt on the importance of a special and

well-selected path of study as leading to success in education, and not less in subsequent life. Nevertheless, the necessity of absolute confinement to this path is to be accepted with great modifications. A youth with vigorous and varied powers will not easily restrict himself to a beaten track; but, as his mind grows, he will become discursive in his aspirations. He will carry along with him, not only the adopted or select pursuit which has enabled him to serve, to impress, or to excel others, but he will also be prompted, both before and after he has grown up, to entertain himself and to extend his relations with those who surround him, by devoting his surplus time, which his very success has given him, to the enlargement of his sphere of occupation. Every professional man, however efficient and prosperous he may be in the discharge of his daily routine, must have, if he would not rust, some collateral pursuits, some by-play of life, in which he may recreate himself and keep up a wholesome freshness by intercourse with congenial minds, and at times with the ideal world. Our country has been called in reproach the arena of a cultivated mediocrity. Happy would it be if all mankind could be brought up even to that level. A cultivated mediocrity is the boundless soil from out of which must spring at times the vigorous and favored shoots of genius, — sparse and exceptional though they may be, yet sufficient to supply the just needs of mankind;

various and eccentric in their character, yet conspiring to dignify and ennoble our race. Men cannot all be geniuses; yet there are many in whom exist the germs of art, poetry, and eloquence, the love of beauty, the sense of the ideal, and the perception of the unseen. These are the men who, when discovered and brought out, delight, attract, and impress the world; who are generally appreciated, though not often followed; whose presence and inspiration are necessary to the enjoyment and the upward progress of the human race. They spread the sails in the adventurous and perilous voyage of life, while others hold the helm and labor at the ropes.

Our country, with its vast territory, its inviting regions, its various population, its untrammelled freedom, looks forward now to a future which hitherto it has hardly dared to anticipate. Let us hopefully await the period when the world shall do homage to our national refinement, as it now does to our national strength; when the column shall have received its Corinthian capital; and when the proportions of the native oak shall be decorated, but not concealed, by the cultivated luxuriance of vines and flowers.

ON CLASSICAL AND UTILITARIAN STUDIES.

READ BEFORE THE AMERICAN ACADEMY OF ARTS AND SCIENCES DECEMBER 20, 1866.

DURING a few centuries past, the opinions of those who seek as well as of those who distribute knowledge have been divided between the relative claims of ancient and modern studies; by which are commonly meant those intellectual pursuits which preceded, and those which followed, the vacant period of the Middle Ages. As there is no good reason for believing that the bodily or mental vigor of the Caucasian race is different now from what it was two thousand years ago, our estimate of the relative inducements to study the productions of times so remote from each other must depend, not so much upon our deference to the especial genius that produced them, as upon the power of these works to contribute to our present pleasure and advantage.

There are two points of view, in which the learning of past and present ages are usually contrasted by those who would estimate their comparative fitness as objects and vehicles of education.

The first of these is the truth of the things taught by them, and the value of these things as means of human happiness and progress. The second is their more strictly educational bearing, or the efficacy of the things taught and of the language conveying them, viewed as means of developing and strengthening the mind in young persons. Both these considerations have had their weight in forming the grounds on which preference has been awarded at different times by different parties.

The privilege of acquiring education, and of controlling the literature of their day, has, in some ages and countries, been confined to a few, whose character or position has placed exceptional advantages within their grasp. In other times, and among different people, the opportunities of learning have been more general, and the acquirement and diffusion of knowledge, of consequence, more equal. In the former case, education has tended to centre and terminate in individuals; in the latter, it has rather been the property of communities, and has tended to greater progress, extent, and stability in its results. When printed books were unknown, learning was necessarily controlled by the taste and fancy of the few; but since the introduction of the press, and the multiplication of readers, it has shaped itself more to the requirements of the many.

If the question between ancient and modern precedence were to be decided by the relative amount of talent, time, and labor which have been bestowed on the acquirement of knowledge, or personal accomplishment, by those individuals on whom the interests of science and literature have devolved, there might possibly be doubt in forming our decision. But if a comparison is based upon the amount of their progress, and the actual worth of their product, it is manifest that a few of the last generations have not only excelled, but greatly distanced, the collective performances of all those who have preceded them.

Among the ancients, the labors of gifted and cultivated men, when not expended on subjects of local and temporary interest, were extensively given to fictions, words, and profitless abstractions, rather than to the augmentation of permanent knowledge. With brilliant and fervid imaginations, with minds capable of the profoundest studies and deepest efforts of reasoning, and with extensive acquirement of all antecedent learning, the writers, orators, and sages of those times expended their powers on productions which, — although often captivating by their eloquence, sometimes noble in their morality, valuable as examples, and profitable as exercises of the mind, — nevertheless, have hardly entailed on us, their remote descendants, a debt of gratitude for any solid and lasting good, which we do not now obtain as well or better from more accessible sources.

On the other hand, the general enlightenment of mankind which exists in the present age, and the advances which have been made by our cotemporaries and immediate predecessors, in intellectual power, and its material and social results, constitute a state of civilization which lifts our own time and generation immeasurably above all that have preceded them. And the question forcibly arises, *why this progress and these advantages were not realized by our classical predecessors more than two thousand years ago*, when circumstances seem to have been equally favorable for their development. The answer is to be found in the general and unfortunate misdirection of the public taste which prevailed in ancient times, and which led men to ignore the pursuits of progressive practical science, and thus to avoid the paths which might have led them to an earlier improvement of their state. There was no want of refined literature, of trained eloquence, and of perceptive taste. Intellectual effort was prodigally lavished whenever it was necessary to persuade the judgment or to delight the fancy. But utilitarian science and studies connected with practical, tangible, material, and useful things, did not comport with the supposed dignity of the human mind. These were left to mechanics, artificers, and slaves, and were thought unworthy of cultivation by the more privileged and polished classes of society. The developments of

Pompeii show that much empirical progress had been made in arts which were not scientifically understood, nor carried to their just maturity. The machinery of luxury did not represent the machinery of use. The conquest of enemies had not been found to be the conquest of matter or of mind. Light was occasionally and fitfully kindled, but was as often suffered to go out. Discoveries were begun and abandoned in their incipient and abortive state. It is remarkable that a Roman* once got so far as to print his own name with a stamp, but was not visited with the revelation, that, by transposing his letters or types, he might print the name of another; and thus the discovery of printing was delayed for more than a thousand years.

"The admiration," says Macaulay, "which we feel for the eminent philosophers of antiquity forces us to adopt the opinion, that their powers were systematically misdirected; for how else could it be, that such powers should effect so little for mankind? A pedestrian may show as much muscular vigor on a treadmill as on a highway road. But on the road his vigor will assuredly carry him forward, and on the treadmill he will not advance an inch. The ancient philosophy was a treadmill, not a path. It was made up of revolving questions,— of controversies which were always beginning again. It was a contrivance for having much exertion and no prog-

---

* Cœcilius Hermias.

ress."—"We believe," says the same distinguished writer, "that *the books which have been written in the languages of Western Europe, during the last two hundred and fifty years, are of greater value than all the books which, at the beginning of that period, were extant in the world.*" And in another place he says, "The boast of the ancient philosophers was, that their doctrine formed the minds of men to a high degree of wisdom and virtue. This was indeed the only practical good which the most celebrated of those teachers even pretended to effect; and undoubtedly, if they had effected this, they would have deserved the greatest praise. But the truth is, that in those very matters in which alone they professed to do any good to mankind,—in those very matters for the sake of which they neglected all the vulgar interests of mankind, they did nothing, or worse than nothing. They promised what was impracticable; they despised what was practicable. They filled the world with long words and long beards, and they left it as wicked and as ignorant as they found it."*

For more than five thousand years—from the beginning of history until about three centuries ago,—the human race had made little progress in any thing which we now regard as constituting material welfare, or growth in power, knowledge, and means of happiness. A persistent spell, which had

---

* Review of Bacon's Works.

rested on society ever since its beginning, still clogged its advance, or diverted it into narrow and unprofitable paths. The classic ages which succeeded to original barbarism had provided nothing to prevent the world from relapsing into barbarism again. And afterwards, when barbarism returned, the scanty practical arts and limited literature, which held a difficult and doubtful existence through the dark ages, were controlled by an exceptional few, who from time to time assumed the precarious tenure of authority or wealth, or, still more rarely, of cultivation. But the mass of mankind grovelled on, as they had been wont to do, in ignorance and wretchedness. Human life was hardly a boon to be desired. In the words of Hobbes, it was " solitary, poor, nasty, brutish, and short." If examples of brilliant genius or effective study occasionally showed themselves at the surface of the world's stagnant bog long enough to exhibit or leave behind distinctive images, names, or monuments, they finally gravitated into the universal equilibrium of an unimproved and unprofited race, leaving the wants of that race unprovided for and its miseries unrelieved.

A " new philosophy," as it was sometimes called, which received its first great development a few centuries ago from the mighty mind of Bacon, and which is but another name for utilitarian progress, at length drew the attention of inquirers from barren studies to those which promised substantial and cumulative good. Fortunately for mankind, new objects began to attract the regard of scientific and philanthropic minds. A new interest was kindled and directed, which went on to spread until the world was filled with a blaze of light, and the sphere of intellectual vision was more than doubled. An enumeration of the tangible results which have already been achieved by this humane and practical philosophy is, from the very magnitude and growth of the subject, impossible to be made. It has, nevertheless, been attempted to embody in a picture the harvest already gathered from the beneficent and remunerative change which has taken place in intellectual pursuits.

"It has lengthened life, it has mitigated pain, it has extinguished diseases, it has increased the fertility of the soil, it has given new securities to the mariner, it has furnished new arms to the warrior, it has spanned great rivers and estuaries with bridges of form unknown to our fathers, it has guided the thunderbolt innocuously from heaven to earth, it has lighted up the night with the splendor of the day, it has extended the range of human vision, it has multiplied the power of the human muscle, it has accelerated motion, it has annihilated distance, it has facilitated intercourse, correspondence, all friendly offices, all despatch of business; it has enabled man to descend into the depths of sea, to soar into the air, to penetrate securely into the noxious recesses of the earth, to traverse the land in cars which whirl along without horses, and the ocean in ships which sail against the wind. These are but a part of its fruits and of its first-fruits. For it is a philosophy which never rests, which is never perfect. Its law is progress. A point which yesterday was invisible is its goal to-day, and will be its starting-post to-morrow."

Thus spoke the "Edinburgh Review" just thirty years ago; and since that time men have learned to write with the electric flash, to paint with the solar ray, to destroy pain, to sew without fingers, to cross the Atlantic without sails, or, even without crossing, to hold conversation on its shores.

The languages and literature of ancient Greece and Italy have for many ages engrossed the attention of scholars and educated men. In many countries, they have had a dominant and almost exclusive possession of the educational field. Libraries have been filled with the classics, and with the works of their advocates and commentators. In England, Germany, and in some parts of the United States, they now hold a controlling influence on the public mind; and a knowledge of the ancient languages is accepted as synonymous with scholarship and learning. The prominent writers of antiquity have by acclamation been received as standards of literary excellence. Like the canons of the Church, their works have been approached with traditional and unquestioning reverence. Metaphysical and philological writers have asserted for them a pre-eminence belonging to no other language and no other study. The labor of acquisition arising from their exuberance, flexibility, and complicated structure, has been claimed as an advantage, both in an æsthetic and disciplinary point of view; and we are left to wonder, that nations possessing such early and large accomplishments should ever have made a retrograde step in civilization.

Yet classical literature, copious, majestic, expressive, and musical as it is, has failed to perform its desired mission of improving or ameliorating the condition of the human race, from the want of any solid and sustaining basis of practical utility. We are compelled to decide the question of its relative importance, not by abstract and metaphysical reasoning on its intrinsic capabilities, not by the oracular declamation of its devotees, but by the simple experience of the past, taken as an exponent of the probable future.

The first three centuries of the Christian era had before their eyes the light of the classics and the wisdom of the ancients; but they went steadily from bad to worse. The last three centuries have had modern literature and the useful sciences and arts, and have gone steadily from good to better. The next coming three centuries will witness unheard-of progress and revolution in many things; and this progress and change will be greatly influenced by the character of prevailing intellectual pursuits. If the classics, which are stationary, predominate in the educational world, we may expect less progress to be made than if later literature and sciences and arts, which are progressive, should hold a controlling influence in the same field.

Great stress has been laid, by the more exclusive advocates of classical studies, on the peculiar fitness and efficacy of those studies for training the minds of young students, and developing, enlarging, and strengthening their powers, irrespectively of any application to other use. That such an efficacy does exist in these studies no one will probably deny; but it does not follow that such training is superior to all others, or that it promotes the greatest economy of the time of young persons destined to various pursuits of life. Education, in its largest and most liberal sense, involves two things. It means not only development of the mind, but also the acquirement of useful knowledge, "by which every rising generation is put in possession of the attainments of preceding generations, and becomes capable of increasing and improving this inheritance." It is not enough that the prime of youth should be spent in developing the mind, or in learning how to learn. It is much better to have combined together the instrument and the object, the process and a useful result. An ignorant man or child might develop his mind somewhat by studying the Algonquin language or the science of heraldry, or by making himself familiar with the Talmud, the Koran, or the Mormon revelation; but if, on the other hand, he should have devoted the same time to acquiring the French language, or the science of chemistry, or a salutary code of ethics, he would have a doubly valuable result to show for his labor. It is the same as in physical education, where he might develop and increase his muscular strength by continually picking up stones, and laying them down again. But if he should lay them down in some mode of useful construction, — a wall for instance, — or should remove them to another place, where they would do more good or less harm, he would have not only improved his muscles, but by the same act would have created a valuable property.

No language, probably, possesses a more copious and expressive vocabulary than the Greek. No language apparently attaches by its inflections a greater variety of modifications and shades of meaning to the same words. No language has afforded to later times such an inexhaustible mine of terms to express and define the conceptions and discoveries made by successive generations. It has been called in to complete the nomenclature of ancient and modern sciences and arts. Its euphonious combinations of mutes with liquids have fitted it alike for the stately sentences of the orator and the melodious measures of the poet. Its exhaustless wealth of words has rendered it a reservoir of expression for historians, philosophers, and dramatists. Yet it may justly be doubted whether this very exuberance of means is not sometimes, when in actual use, a superfluity and incumbrance, rather than an advantage. It has many features which most later languages do not possess, — such as a dual number, a middle voice, a first and second aorist, and still other inflective forms. Yet most of these things could have been omitted without essential deterioration in the works of those who have employed them. Or, if they are retained, other forms and tenses might in that case have been omitted as superfluous. In proof of this, we may select innumerable passages and verses, in the best orators and poets, in which these inflections do not happen to appear, and which nevertheless are equally effective with the remaining sentences and verses of the same authors. The more recent enlightened nations have not possessed them in their languages; and neither Cicero nor Chatham, Horace, Tasso, nor Milton, have suffered apparent detriment from their absence. They were elaborated by the old Greeks into graceful and pleasing results; yet none of the current languages of cultivated Europe have perpetuated the use of so cumbrous a luxury. The modern Greeks themselves have dropped a large part of these ancestral inflections, and have replaced them, like other moderns, by short periphrastic expressions.

At the present day, the study, the acquirement, and comparison of a variety of languages have, by common consent, been made part of a liberal education. The speech of all nations, having been at first invented by rude and ignorant people, is more or less imperfect, redundant, or defective, as well as crude, harsh, and unnecessarily difficult to acquire. But, like existing standards of measure and value, we are obliged to accept it as we find it; and, if a perfect language were to be invented to-morrow, the world would hardly take the trouble to learn and use it. Revolutions and substitutions of races have alone been adequate to effect a radical change of speech in a country. And though the Latin may at times have been adopted throughout some leading or philosophical communities, and the French in certain courts and cliques, and even as the currency of European intercourse, still the uneducated and practical multitude in all countries will persist in expressing their thoughts through the vehicle of the same words which their fathers had used before them.

Languages differ from each other in copiousness, euphony, flexibility, and manner of construction. It is therefore a profitable exercise for young students to make themselves acquainted with a variety of the forms, meanings, and arrangements of words by which dissimilar people have given utterance to their conceptions. Our comprehension of thoughts and things is much assisted, when we have spread before us the peculiar oral signs and combinations by which these different nations at different times have undertaken to express them.

In comparison with the rest, the two classical languages have been long and abundantly commended, not only for their beauty and expressiveness, but for their peculiar structure, and for the discipline which they impose on students of tracing out and combining remote words and members of a sentence, which, though disjoined in place, are still held in their true relations by inflections of mode, tense, degree, number, case, and gender. These preserve the connection of the scattered parts, and bring these parts finally together with precision and harmony. But the involuted and parenthetic modes of expression, which follow as results of this flexibility, although they may often please us by their euphony, and surprise us by the dexterity with which they are managed in unfolding delayed or recondite meanings, yet can hardly be welcomed when we wish to expedite or facilitate the comprehension of the things expressed. On the contrary, the mixing and deranging of clauses, epithets, and qualifications, and the postponing of essential verbs, often keep the mind of the reader in suspense, if not in confusion, until the *denouement* of a long and complicated rehearsal. To take a familiar example: in Cicero's commencing congratulation to the Roman people on the overthrow of Catiline's conspiracy, we have, announced in one sentence, the subjects and the objects, the manner and the instruments, the causes remote and proximate, the date, the description of the city, the greatness of the peril and magnitude of the deliverance, the debt of gratitude due to the immortal gods, and to the orator himself,—all to be carried along in the memory, until we at length arrive at the effective participles and the terminating verb, when we again feel at liberty to breathe.

Now, as far as the object of language is the ready communication of thought, it is at least more convenient to use those recent languages, which from poverty of inflections require short settlements of meaning, and which move directly on the main points to be expressed. But if the object be to obstruct the readiness of perception, and to strengthen the minds of hearers or pupils, by increasing their difficulties; or to obtain ornament and euphony for the entertainment of cultivated classes, at the expense of facility to them and all others,—such an end might doubtless be obtained in a variety of other ways. If the fashion of the age should happen to require that letters, advertisements, bills of sale, and deeds of conveyance, should be written out in poetry, the incumbrance would be a serious matter to those who had the writing to do, at least until by practice their minds should be educated up to the mark of enjoying the beauty and harmony of their own productions. The euphuists of Queen Elizabeth's time no doubt increased their own satisfaction, and perhaps strengthened their minds somewhat, by enlarging their vocabulary of expression. Yet neither poetry nor euphuism nor classical arrangement of words could be any substitute in our place and day for direct, plain, practical English. And human life is not so long, nor human leisure so abundant, that we can afford to involve them deeply in any exercise which does not promise a seasonable and remunerative return.

The question has been repeatedly introduced, how far the Greek and Latin languages can be satisfactorily replaced in education by living languages of European nations. Within certain limits, and in many cases, there is no doubt that such a substitution may be usefully allowed. The old languages are suited to some purposes, the modern to others. In its educational bearing, every language during its acquirement instructs and expands the mind. And, if other things are equal, the living languages have some claims which entitle them to preference over those of former times. The living languages, and not the dead, are wanted for the daily intercourse of the world. The literature of every refined nati already furnishes more desirable books than any living man can read; and the number of these books is continually increasing, because they are the necessary vehicles of cotemporaneous knowledge. The living languages of cultivated nations are, for the most part, reciprocally convertible into each other, but the dead languages do not furnish words sufficient to express things and ideas which are exclusively modern. How long the friends of classical studies will be able to uphold them as a paramount object in schools and colleges, to the partial exclusion of other necessary things, during the many susceptible years of youth, is a question which another century may perhaps determine. It may be admitted, and to a certain extent justly, that the preference which has existed for so many ages in favor of Greek and Latin studies, is caused by the intrinsic and special aptitude of these studies for exercising and strengthening the mind, and by the superiority of the old languages over later ones, in their idioms, modifications, and construction. But in reality other causes beside those named have been at work in upholding this long-continued ascendancy of the classical writings. Foremost of these causes is the prestige, the traditional and conventional reverence, which, during many scholastic and ecclesiastical generations, they have commanded in most European countries. This sentiment has covered them, as it has the Catholic religion for ages, with a shield of impenetrability, and a veil of reverential awe. A second cause is the advocacy of their trained votaries, the classically educated men, who abound in all modern communities, and who, like experts in other sciences, arts, and accomplishments, magnify their own vocation, and dwell with satisfaction on a feast of exclusive literature, which is inaccessible to the unclassical world, and which sometimes constitutes the foundation on which their own distinction is supported. A third cause is the fact, that we get our Greek and Latin, as far as we get them at all, with but a part of the peculiar labor which it costs to acquire a living language. In the former case, we get only the meaning of words; in the latter, we must get both the meaning and the pronunciation. It is true that we obtain from the metres of the old poets the quantities of their syllables. But of the sounds of their vowels and the power of their consonants we have no reliable knowledge. In modern times we know, that the sounds articulated by the vocal organs of different tribes are seldom reported alike by different discoverers and interpreters who visit those tribes. The Owhyhee of Captain Cook is now the Hawaii of the subjects of Queen Emma; and in like manner Otaheite has become Tahiti.* The lower Niger is called Quorra by the Landers, and Kowara and Kwara by Barth and others. To what precise effect the old Romans managed the position of their tongues and palates in the articulation of their words, notwithstanding the fragmentary suggestions which we get from Quintilian, and a few others, we shall never know. But we do know,

---

* It is said that the O is a prefix used by some tribes, and not by others.

that their present descendants in France, England, Hungary, and Turkey speak Latin in a manner hardly intelligible to each other. If it were possible that Cicero could at this day re-appear upon the stage, we may safely assume, that he would be astonished at the spoken jargon which we now complacently call Latin in our academic rehearsals. It is somewhat as if an Italian should undertake to declaim French or English in the manner in which those languages are spelt. If a knowledge of any Continental European living language were required for admission into Harvard College, it would be difficult, in many parts of our country, to find competent teachers to prepare the students to enter. But in Latin and Greek there is no such difficulty, because instructors are rendered competent by our acquiescence in their necessary incompetency.

Before we can be at home in the literature of the ancients, it is necessary that we should be familiar with their history, manners, and institutions, and especially that we should accept and sympathize in the machinery of their religion. The heathen mythology is always present, and frequently overshadows every thing else, in the works of the great classic writers. Abhorrent as this mythology and its superstitions are to the enlightened views of the present age, we are obliged, if we would enjoy the classics, to surrender ourselves to the temporary dominion of —

> "Gods partial, changeful, passionate, unjust,
> Whose attributes were rage, revenge, and lust."

We must train ourselves to an acceptance of beliefs the most absurd, and customs the most revolting, before we can fairly become naturalized in a "land of lost gods and godlike men." And this transition would not be easily made, if our disgust had not been previously educated down in youth. "Many things," says Lord Brougham, "with the Greeks and Romans most venerable, have not merely lost their sanctity in our eyes, but present contemptible, and even ludicrous ideas to us: hence any allusion to them, or any expression of the feelings connected with them, or even a reference to the habits of thinking which those feelings have produced, must have an operation most unpropitious."

The fictions constituting the epic poetry of Homer, Virgil, and their imitators, so far from being consonant with the taste and sense of propriety of modern readers, are, on the contrary, often annoying, from the absence of all moral or poetical justice. The chivalry of the feudal ages demanded for its champions an equality of arms, appointments, and advantage. But there is scarcely in the conflicts of the whole "Iliad" an instance of absolute fair play. Every favored and distinguished combatant is clad in supernatural armor, or else is backed up by a patron or powerful ally, commonly in the person of an unseen divinity, who officiously interferes to spoil the pending sport, by warding off a weapon, or raising a fog, which renders the obnoxious party invisible. Ajax rages, and prays to Jupiter, but cannot find his enemies; and, when a recreant like Paris is about to expiate his crimes by a merited death, he is suddenly caught up in a cloud, and conveyed away to his mistress in some safe and comfortable quarters, leaving to his wronged and disappointed antagonist simply the consolation of the baffled sheriff, — *non est inventus*.

The mystery attending the person of Homer, and the obscurity which veils the Homeric age, has given to the "Iliad" a human if not divine interest, hardly surpassed in effect and duration by that of the Pentateuch itself. A work, finished in its character and wonderful in its poetic inspiration, which preceded authentic history and failed to record its own, may well stimulate the curiosity and deep interest of the world. It appeared when society was fresh and primitive, and struck its roots deep in a soil unoccupied by competing growths. It invented, portrayed, and exaggerated things acceptable to the age in which it appeared. It sounded the depths of the human heart as it then existed, a compound of savage impulses, grasping credulity, and strong human yearnings. On this basis it constructed gods and heroes, and finished them with a completeness and individuality of character not to have been expected from the existing age and the limited materials which that age afforded. The miracle of its composition is exceeded only by that of its preservation. From obscure and shadowy beginnings, it has descended through nearly three thousand years of accumulating homage, to receive from loyal worshippers its apotheosis at the present day. It is not enough that it was applauded and held up as a model by the writers of antiquity. Its fame had not culminated till the nineteenth century; and we now see it occupying a throne in the schools and universities, at least of England, of which the steps belong to the very structure and machinery of church and state. The word "learning" now means a knowledge of Greek literature, and the name "scholar" is accorded to none but those familiar with the works of Homer and his countrymen. Within three years, at least six new metrical translations of the "Iliad"* have been added to the host previously existing. The Homeric poems have been placed, by more writers than one, by the side of the Holy Scriptures; and Mr. Gladstone, the distinguished statesman and churchman, in his voluminous work of "Studies on Homer," instructs us, that "the poems of Homer may be viewed, in the philosophy of human nature, as the complement of the earliest portion of the Sacred Records."

Such is the extraordinary devotion, if not fanati-

---

* By Lord Derby, Blackie, Herschel, Dart, Wright, Simcox, and others. Also of the "Odyssey" by Worsley, Norgate, Musgrave, &c.

cism, of the present day, which places the successful and imaginative poetry of a semi-barbarous age above all the acquirements which have since rendered our terrestrial life worth possessing. Its savage attributes, brute instincts, and exceptionable morality, override the more modern sentiments of humanity, honor, and Christian charity. The gods who preside in this scenic exhibition are tainted with every vice which has since degraded their supposed subordinates of the human race. Cruelty, revenge, deceit, hatred, unrelenting rancor, and unbridled lust, are the qualities which call for approval in a generation professing to feel and practise virtues of an opposite nature. An exterminating war is undertaken for the sake of a vacillating adulteress, and its principal heroes quarrel implacably about the possession of their female slaves. Indomitable rage exalts and apologizes for all acts of injustice and atrocity. The consummation of heroism is to upbraid and then butcher a fallen foe. Ulysses, the hero of the "Odyssey," on his return home, winds up that poem by a wholesale slaughter of his disorganized subjects, hangs up a dozen censurable females in a row, and puts Melanthius to a lingering death by gradual mutilation, much after the manner of a modern Chinese execution, by vivisection into inch-pieces.

But there are lesser improprieties, which perhaps find a parallel in more modern times. Diomede and

Glaucus meet on the field of battle, and, instead of attending to their duty, which is to fight, they fall into a long discussion about their pedigrees, and compare the generations of men to leaves,—as poets in all ages have done, from Job to Dr. Beattie. The interview ends in a trading operation, in which one party gets a set of golden arms in exchange for one of brass, the estimated value of which, by the statement, is not a tenth part of that of the former; and although the bargain appears to have been arranged by Jupiter, who took away the brains of one of the parties for the purpose, nevertheless it might at the present day have been legally accounted a swindle of the first magnitude.

Achilles, having killed Hector, drags him by the heels round the walls of Troy; and in subsequent days recreates himself by repeating the same process three times round the tomb of Patroclus. This classical tale, the stereotyped wonder of the schoolboys of Christendom, has its parallel in the story of the Oriental Caliph, who, having cut off the head of his enemy, afterwards occupied himself for twelve hours in kicking it round his courtyard.

At the present day, men speak with enthusiasm of the "revival" of classical literature as the great event, era, and landmark of intellectual progress in modern times. Yet this so-called revival of literature was not the production of any new light. The best that can be said in its behalf is, that it was a partial return to the state of things that existed in the Periclean and Augustan ages. And what men knew in either of those ages was not a tenth part of what they know now. Notwithstanding the traditional acclamation which has heralded their praise down to this time, we are not certain that these people excelled their remote descendants of the present day in any desirable acquisition or accomplishment. In their gymnastic and musical exhibitions, they seem to have driven, spoken, sung, and danced with success, if not always with propriety. Their poetry, in its power of delighting the ear or moving the passions, may have been equal to ours, but was in no respect superior. Their forensic and popular oratory was elaborate, powerful, brilliant, and effective; and so at the present day are those of every cultivated nation in Europe and America. They had popular exhibitions of the drama, both comic and pathetic. The Greeks had bacchanalian orgies, and the Romans gladiatorial combats, in which they publicly butchered captives in the presence of ferocious audiences, and threw living victims to wild beasts for the amusement of crowds of refined spectators. The untold horrors of their slavery have not often been thought of sufficient account to encumber minutely the pages of their history. In their social relations they were licentious and exquisitely depraved. In their domestic habits they were primitive, destitute, and uncleanly.

The absence of books and scarcity of writing made popular education a thing of impossibility.

It is obvious, then, that, after the fluctuating continuance of a most imperfect civilization for some thousands of years, a change, if it came at all, must come, not, as it has been wrongly supposed, in the form of a *renaissance*, or reproduction of any thing that had existed before, but in the shape of a new creation, a new laying-out of unexplored territory, a new planting of virgin soil with seeds unknown to former cultivators, of seeds pregnant with an abundant harvest, with new fruits and flowers, worthy of the acceptance and enjoyment of an improved and appreciative race.

The Reformation, the exodus of Greeks from Constantinople, the revival of letters, and the restoration of arts, are familiar words which mark the concurrent influence of different agencies in revolutionizing the social condition of men a few centuries ago. They are so many instruments by which the indispensable influence of Christianity has been truly and slowly developed to the world. But at the root of all these agencies, and deep and far beyond and above them, was the vivifying nurture of utilitarian science. The world mainly owes its present advanced and civilized state to the influence of certain physical discoveries and inventions of comparatively recent date, among which are conspicuous the printing press, the mariner's compass, the steam-engine, and the substitution of machinery for manual labor. The materials and agents for these and other like improvements have existed ever since the creation of the world; but the minds of competent and qualified thinkers, being absorbed in less profitable studies, had not been turned effectively upon them or upon their uses. There was electricity in the clouds, there were loadstones in the mountains, cataracts in rivers, and steam in household utensils. But the world rolled on; empires and dynasties and ages of barbarism passed away, and left the minds of men engaged in superstitious rites, in scholastic studies, and in fruitless or pernicious controversies. We owe the great debt of modern civilization to the enterprising, acute, patient, and far-seeing innovators who, during the last few centuries, have broken away from the prescribed and beaten track of their predecessors, and have given their energies to developing, directing, and utilizing the illimitable forces of the material world. If these very men had given up their time to the objectless controversies of the schools, or to the more easy and agreeable studies of Latin and Greek, ignoring the great and vital problem of physical science, — the dark ages would stil have prevailed in Europe, and America might have remained an undiscovered wilderness.

-The mere lapse of time furnishes nothing to human improvement. Neither does the endless inculcation, on successive generations, of the obsolete studies of their fathers. Metals might have slept in their ores, gunpowder in its elements, and steam in its inertest form, until doomsday; and mankind been none the wiser, if it had not happened that sagacious and persevering discoverers, under difficulties, persecutions, and perils, brought them successfully to light, and laid them at the feet of advancing civilization. It is not the perfected railroad train, nor the passenger who successfully rides in it, that deserves our applause; but it is the original and comprehensive minds that planned, organized, and launched into successful operation this great achievement of modern art. The telescope, the press, the compass, the chronometer, and the quadrant have wrought wonders for science and civilization; *but the greater wonder is, how these things got invented at all, after the world had run for five thousand years in the beaten track of unproductive routine.*

It has been brought as an objection to the claims of utilitarian science, that most of its alleged discoveries have been lucky accidents, often made by ignorant persons, stumbled upon by chance, and not arrived at by philosophic induction or investigation. As far as this is true, it is also true of every other step in the progress of human knowledge. No science, no development of complicated truth, no great advance in intellectual progress, has ever sprung full and finished into existence, like Adam from the hands of his Creator; but, on the contrary, they have all had their fortuitous and imperfect beginnings, their feeble glimmerings, their uncertain and fluctuating advance, — their years, or more frequently centuries, during which they have groped their way to a distant and long-deferred maturity. The first languages were made by barbarians, the first orations were spoken by savages, the first poems were probably war-songs, the first statues were hideous idols, the first histories were fabulous, unless possibly we except that part of them which is preserved for our edification in arrow-headed characters. Hundreds of years, and many introductory sciences, and many lives of labor, have been necessary to conduct almost any great discovery from its rude beginnings to its finished stages. The steam-engine was not perfected in a day, and the knowledge of the solar system was not stumbled upon in a night. Some of the greatest acquisitions of civilized life date back beyond tradition. The native country of wheat is unknown; and the inventors of the plough and the ship, if known to the ancients, are not known to the moderns. There were, doubtless, navigators who were sailing before Jason, as much as there were brave men living before Agamemnon. Antiquarians and geologists are now enlightening us in regard to things as remote as a stone age and a bronze age;

but they have not yet agreed in settling the period of the vinous age. The cultivation of the grape was a memorable step in human progress, to which we are indebted for some good and much evil. The Greeks gratefully ascribe it to Bacchus; but the Jews rather give the credit to Noah, who planted a vineyard, and drank of the wine and was drunken. Yet neither Bacchus nor Noah could have produced the genuine "article" without some antecedent knowledge of husbandry for cultivation, mechanics for presses and receptacles, and of chemistry for fermentation. But, if it really happened that the experiment and its subsidiary sciences went hand in hand, it will serve to show that education of the mind and realization of its substantial results may sometimes be usefully combined in one and the same process.

Horace says that we all write, both unlearned and learned. The same truth equally applies to discoverers. But, when sudden discoveries are made by unprepared persons, they are exceptions to the general rule of gradual growth, merely because their cardinal fact is so simple that it does not admit the consumption of time in its development. Thus a man may learn to swim in five minutes, and a gold mine or a continent may be, and has been, discovered in the twinkling of an eye.

The arts, the poetry, and the oratory of the ancients have with justice been made the subjects of laudation in all times. But, as all refined nations, ancient and modern, have had their artists, orators, and poets, and as subjects of the same class have of necessity been presented to all, it is not apparent that excellence belongs exclusively to any age or language. Nor are we authorized to exalt any one at he expense of degrading or overlooking the rest.

Eloquence is not made in schools. Its elements exist in the brain, the heart, the voice, the presence, none of which can be produced to order in academic institutions. Where they have been planted by nature, they may be raised, improved, and matured by cultivation; and, when these conditions have been all combined, their manifestation has become irrepressible, whether it has been on the Bema of Athens, in the Forum of Rome, the Parliament of England, or the forests beyond the Alleghanies. "True eloquence," says Daniel Webster, "does not consist in speech. It cannot be brought from far. Labor and learning may toil for it, but they will toil in vain. Words and phrases may be marshalled in every way, but they cannot compass it. It must exist in the man, in the subject, and in the occasion."

Poetry has been produced in all recorded ages. But not every person is qualified to judge and compare the poetical productions of different times and countries. The poet must be born; but the critic must be born and educated. Our individual capacity for pleasure and for dislike, in our estimate of poetry, varies not only in proportion to the qualities of the verse, the inspiration, and the composition, but according to our own previous acquirements and our familiarity with the language in which the poetry is expressed. Few men are equally proficient in all the languages cultivated in their time; and therefore few men are properly qualified to appreciate and compare Homer, Dante, Goethe, and Shakespeare. But a man who has been trained from childhood to study and admire any one of these poets more than the rest, will not afterwards be likely to transfer his allegiance and postpone his adopted favorite to any other. An impartial judge of poetry would, at this day, be as great a phenomenon as an impartial lover. Most refined nations have had their great and favorite poets; and fortunately there is enough to applaud in the writings of all refined nations and tongues, without invidious or exclusive verdicts of distinction accorded to any one of them.

Good statues have been made in Greece, Italy, Denmark, Germany, and other countries. The human form affords the same models for imitation now that it did two thousand years ago. It is conceded that artistic beauty, in feature, attitude, and expression, was first attained in perfection by the ancient Greeks, and has not since been surpassed by any of their successors. But the world is ever prone to exclusive man-worship and class-worship, and often gives its oracular decisions as to the relative excellence of works of art as it does on those of literature, — upon traditionary and often hair-breadth differences of merit, which may be as undefined and unimportant as the relative claims to beauty of the oak and the elm in the forest, or as the discrepancy illustrated by Swift between Handel and Bononcini. It is not probable, that, if a presentable representation of the human figure from any of the above-named countries were submitted for the first time to the most skilful critic, he could, by any power of discrimination, decide on its paternity.

The classic architecture of Greece and Rome, irrespectively of its adaptation to modern uses, has probably received a more extensive approval than any of the peculiar styles of construction yet known. As architecture, unlike to painting and sculpture, is an arbitrary art, whose forms have no prototype in nature, the widest license is allowed to its characteristic and decorative elements. Dissimilar nations have adopted styles based upon their own traditions; and these have been afterwards altered, modified, and combined by their successors, simply because monotony palls upon the eye, and fashion in architecture, like fashion in dress, is thought to require renovation. The great and typical structures of different nations, the pyramids, temples, and cathedrals, are founded on the principle of worship, either of man or deity; and, after their use has become general in a country, their features are long adhered to from mere habit and pertinacity of national or sectarian pride. Thus the Gothic style, invented in the dark ages, is claimed by Pugin and other Roman Catholics under the name of "Christian," in contradistinction from what they opprobriously call "Pagan" architecture; and the name of "English style" has in like manner been usurped for it by certain authorities, although the British cathedrals are generally later and smaller or lower than the great examples on the Continent. It is these accidents that have given it at the present day a dominating prevalence in church architecture; and a perversely bad taste has in like manner led modern copyists to select the high, sharp roofs, which, from a distance, fill half the field of vision with a blank surface of tiles or slabs, in preference to the more beautiful and almost classical low roofs of York and Gloucester Cathedrals, and King's College Chapel.

But, after all, the great practical principle of adaptation to a required purpose ultimately overrides all interfering considerations; and any style, judiciously managed, may be made to combine the desirable results of ornament, fitness, effect, and use. The Greeks had the start of other European nations in questions both of simple and decorative construction, — a vantage-ground which they also possessed in literature and in many other things. This priority of invention, added to earliness of full success, causes us justly to look back to them as the great fountains of correct and original taste. The ornaments and arrangements of classic architecture, although not always suited to purposes of Northern convenience, yet as they attended the birth, so they have survived the decadence, of pure early art. The world still pays undivided homage to the Athenian Parthenon, — a useless monument of an abandoned mythology, — and it recognizes in ruins the majesty of the shifting rows of columns which flank the so-called Basilica of Diocletian, at Palmyra. Like the epic poems of past ages, their construction is studied and admired; but their imitation is now unsatisfactory, if not impracticable.

It has most commonly happened, that national and sectarian prepossessions, quite as much as laws of beauty, have given form to the architecture of different occasions and countries. It was not without difficulty that Michael Angelo, Sir Christopher Wren, and others, replaced the mediæval Gothic with elements of the classical antique. Yet all prejudices succumb under the influence of time and moral change. If the religion of Mahomet shall ever become as obsolete as that of Jupiter now is, Christian churches of unquestioned beauty will arise with Moorish windows, towering minarets, and gorgeous Arabesques.

In its bearing on general studies, a knowledge of the etymology of words is often a convenient help in defining difficult shades of their meaning, and imprinting them on the memory. But, as people who are well versed in English literature generally write well and speak well the English language, it is not indispensable for all students that they should complicate their labor by learning the same thing twice over, in different and sometimes discrepant forms. A man who draws in his house the water which is suitable for him need not trouble himself to visit its distant fountain. The derivation of words is often curious and interesting, but not always important. A man who suffers a calamity gets neither consolation nor useful knowledge from the fact that the word "calamity" means a heap of corn; and a lady in a ball-room, who is apprised that she is the cynosure of all eyes, would not necessarily be raised in her own esteem, had she been trained to understand that the word "cynosure" means a dog's tail. Education has not retrograded since children at school ceased to learn the table of etymological meanings of proper names in the Old and New Testament.

The simple fact is, that the true meaning of words is a thing which has got to be learned, in school or out of it. Learners may arrive at this meaning directly, by familiarizing themselves with the best writers who use these words; or, circuitously, they may first study the languages of preceding nations who used the roots of these words, and afterwards attend to the vernacular writers who use the words themselves. But there can be little doubt, that a better knowledge of the English language and literature will be obtained by a person who reads carefully fifty of the best English authors, than by one who reads only half that number, and devotes a corresponding amount of time to acquiring their etymologies from older languages. All are agreed that a knowledge of primitive words facilitates a knowledge of their derivatives, and that one language is often a stepping-stone to another. A knowledge of Latin facilitates a knowledge of Italian, and the converse is equally true. Nevertheless, after we have eliminated all the derivative words, the stubborn fact still remains, that, as a labor question, two languages are harder to get than one.

There were once great warriors on our continent, whose mysterious names were by interpretation "Split-log" and "Walk-in-the-water." Few of us will ever know how sonorous and imposing were these appellations when uttered in their original tongues. But the students of affinities and derivations will perhaps find them, when properly studied, to be no less instructive and awe-inspiring than the Homeric epithets, *koruthaiolos*, *hippodamos*, and *chalkokorustes*.

The terminology of science has in modern times

given rise to a vast creation of words necessary to supply the nomenclatures which mark and preserve the discoveries of successive generations. The existing words of living languages are not well suited to this purpose, inasmuch as ambiguity results from adding new meanings to old terms. In this case, therefore, it is better to resort to the dead languages for our names, selecting such as are euphonious and pertinent, than to invent artificial words which might not possess these qualities. The smooth and often melodious sounds which we take from the Greek and Latin are more pleasing to the ear than the harsh names which we have drawn from the Arabic, German, and English. The word "alkali" always looks uncouth; and so does even the unclassical "potassium," when we call up its English origin. The boundless nomenclature of Natural History bids fair to exhaust the resources of all languages, as it has already done of most brains that have set about its amplification and its reduction to use.

In sciences as small as Pharmacy and Materia Medica, many of the authorized books keep up a double expression of names and formulas in Latin and English. This superfluous custom has its origin either in antiquated routine or in the mysterious importance which the vulgar are expected to attach to the words of an unknown tongue. But the ostentation of using a learned language is often merely a cloak for ignorance, and leads to the abbreviation in medical prescriptions of words which the writers could not always trust themselves to fill out at length. Even high pharmaceutical authorities are not always immaculate in their Latinity; and the London College of Physicians, in its "Pharmacopœia," expresses the genitive of the plant rosemary by "rosmarini," instead of the undoubted *rorismarini* of the classics.

Lord Macaulay, notwithstanding the unfavorable opinion which has been already cited from him in regard to the philosophy of the ancients, has, in some of his later writings, bestowed on the people of Athens the highest praise for their great accomplishments in oratory, poetry, the drama, and indeed every kind of artistic and literary excellence. These accomplishments, which all admit, were well suited to the sensuous, impulsive, and ardent temperament of the Athenian Greeks, who were an extraordinary people, reared and ripened in the youth of literary civilization. From their priority of culture, they became objects of admiration to ancient imitators, and have remained beacons of classical light in all succeeding time. The sublime and comprehensive eulogy bestowed on them by Macaulay, in his review of Mitford's "Greece," has itself become classical, even though the independent philosopher is, in this instance, merged in the *laudator temporis acti*. We are carried along by his imperious and sweeping assumptions, until we grow unconscious that it is the reviewer, and not his subject, that is bearing us away. It is one of those cases where the eloquence of a great advocate gives dignity, worth, and irresistible force, to any cause he may be employed to defend. No one denies that the city of Athens, within its narrow confines, held a great and wonderful people. No one is disposed to deny, that Demosthenes was a transcendent orator, Pericles a great administrator, and Homer a surpassing genius and poet. But if any one goes further, and says there have not been equally great orators, statesmen, and poets in every prominent modern nation, he commits a great mistake. It is not necessary to go into the ostentation of enumerating great names; but we do not risk much in saying, that in the present age causes are as well argued, judicial tribunals as cogently addressed, senates and popular assemblies as powerfully swayed, as they ever have been heretofore, or probably ever will be hereafter. And we may with equal safety assert, that the imaginative works, the poems, dramas, novels, and other fictions of the modern period, in their characters, scenes, narratives, and pictures, take as powerful a hold on the deepest sensibilities of our nature as any correponding productions ever did on the most cultivated and sensitive of our predecessors. The tears of Andromache, the grovelling of Priam, the wails of Hecuba, and the wrongs and revenge of Medea, wake powerfully our inmost susceptibilities. But, in deep pathos and delicate and unselfish tenderness, they are inferior to many hundreds of well-known productions which have sprung from the refined literature and the perceptive and exquisitely cultivated taste of the present age. What homage should we not pay to a newly recovered classic, which should bring to us any thing half so pure, so irresistibly touching, so deeply and passionately tender, as the lines to Thyrza, the Italian girl's hymn to the Virgin, or Thekla at her lover's grave!

If we should allow to modern productions but a part of the assumptive and gratuitous praise which is now bestowed upon the classics, we should at once say, that Grecian verse and Grecian oratory have furnished nothing which modern times have not fully equalled; and that Grecian progress in knowledge is relatively excelled a hundred times by the creative and inductive achievements even of our own century.

The advocacy by Macaulay of Athenian society is the special plea of a gifted and skilful barrister, who makes his cause acceptable by dilating on its most popular and captivating features. It must be observed, that the articles written by him on Mitford's "Greece" and on "the Athenian orators" are not dictated by a special love of Athens so much as by a proclivity for democracy and democratic principles. The cause of Athens against Sparta covers a powerful and eloquent argument for popular rights and privileges, against oligarchic usurpation. It may be considered a rebuke to the monopolists, landholders, and Tories of England, administered to the person of Mr. Mitford and the doctrines which he advocates.

The traditionary bias which has so long prevailed in England has been transmitted, in an operative degree, to the schools and colleges of the United States. It is the part of wisdom that we accept and avail ourselves of the desirable advantages of this inheritance, but, at the same time, beware of its excess.

Classical literature is the aid and the ornament, and may well enter into the foundation of the most liberal form of education. But it is not all in all that the world now requires. The foundation should not be so large that the individual owner will not live to see a superstructure; nor should the ornament be allowed to crowd out what is permanent, necessary, or useful. The knowledge of extraordinary things is not so indispensable as the knowledge of common things. A man may be highly accomplished in classic facts and quotations, and in the use of Greek particles, accents, and metres, and yet be the dupe of other men who build his house, or dictate his taste, or educate his children. Vast numbers of our college graduates, in a few years, have forgotten their Greek and Latin, and are toiling to make up their deficient French, chemistry, and mechanics, that they may understand their newspaper, manage the case of their constituents, clients, or patients, or conduct the institutions of which they are directors.

By the statements of our Latin schools, five or six years are now necessary to prepare boys for entering Harvard or Yale. When Webster and Everett entered college, two years were amply sufficient for this purpose; and this limited preparation did not prevent them and others from becoming great men. The prevailing cry, at the present day, is for raising the standard of education. Should it not rather be for providing the means of education, and of selecting, organizing, and administering existing knowledge to the best purpose and advantage? Those of us who love, and with humble proficiency delight in the solace of the classics, are in no danger of advocating their exclusion from colleges. But a more moderate proficiency than that which is now required might suffice to command entrance to the precincts of our universities, where provision is made for carrying them to any degree of desirable perfection, by those few who elect to make them afterwards a prominent pursuit. In the meanwhile, an even-handed distribution is asked of time, opportunity, and honors, for that other and more numerous class of students who would wish to obtain a corresponding proficiency in English and modern literature and languages, in progressive sciences, and in useful and elegant arts.

The sciolism which now leads incompetent men to profess a knowledge of every thing, will be unnecessary when accredited scholarship is allowed to flow in channels which are separately recognized and duly honored.

In England, probably more than in any other country at the present day, a preponderating and almost exclusive importance is given, in leading educational institutions, to the study of Greek and Latin classics. This preponderance has been made the subject of animadversion on both sides of the Atlantic, and has revived a controversy by no means new in the annals of literature. It dates back for at least two centuries. More than fifty years ago, one of the most acute scholars of the age, Sidney Smith, himself bred up in the thorough nurture of classical education, has expressed the following among many similar opinions:—

"To almost every Englishman, up to the age of three or four and twenty, classical learning has been the great object of existence; and no man is very apt to suspect, or very much pleased to hear, that what he has done for so long a time was not worth doing. This classical literature reminds every man of the scenes of his childhood, and brings to his fancy several of the most pleasing associations which we are capable of forming. A certain sort of vanity, also, very naturally grows among men occupied by a common pursuit. Classical quotations are the watchwords of scholars, by which they distinguish each other from the ignorant and illiterate; and Greek and Latin insensibly become almost the only test of a cultivated mind."

"That vast advantages may be derived from classical learning there can be no doubt. The advantages which may be derived from classical learning, by the English mode of teaching, involve another and a very different question; and we will venture to say, that there never was a more complete instance, in any country, of such extravagant and overacted attachment to any branch of knowledge, as that which obtains in this country with regard to classical knowledge. A young Englishman goes to school at six or seven years old, and he remains in a course of education till twenty-three or twenty-four years of age. In all that time, his sole and exclusive occupation is in learning Latin and Greek; he has scarcely a notion that there is any other kind of excellence; and the great system of facts with which he is the most perfectly acquainted are the intrigues of the heathen gods." . . . "These facts the English youth get by heart as soon as they quit the nursery; and are most sedulously and industriously instructed in them, till the best and most active part of life is passed away. Now, this long career of classical learning we may, if we please, denominate a foundation; but it is a foundation so far above ground, that there is absolutely no room to put any thing upon it. If you occupy a man with one thing until he is twenty-four years of age, you have exhausted all his leisure time: he is called into the world, and compelled to act; or he is surrounded with pleasure, and thinks and reads no more. If you have neglected to put other things in him, they will never get in afterwards; if you have fed him only with words, he will remain a narrow and limited being to the end of his existence.

"An infinite quantity of talent is annually destroyed in the universities of England by the miserable jealousy and ignorance of ecclesiastical instructors. It is vain to say that we have produced great men under this system. We have produced great men under all systems. Every Englishman must now pass half his life in learning Latin and Greek; and classical learning is supposed to have produced the talent which it has not been able to extinguish. It is scarcely possible to prevent great men from rising up under any system of education, however bad."

The foregoing is a part of the testimony of one of the best known and most sagacious scholars in Great Britain, on the exaggerated value attached to classical learning in that country, and the waste of time expended in its acquisition, to the exclusion of better and more necessary things. And the same authority may at least shake the stability of our faith as to the point, whether the list of great men, so frequently cited as having been educated at the classical institutions of England, have become great through the agency of their special training; or whether, on the contrary, they have become great in spite of it, as it often happens in regard to other results in other places.

With these anti-classical sentiments of Sidney Smith we may contrast those of Mr. Gladstone, long the champion and apostle of the English aristocracy and English Church, some of whose ultra-opinions have already been cited in these remarks. Mr. Gladstone has given to the world three solid octavo volumes on "Studies on Homer and the Homeric Age," as a contribution to fill partially whatever chasm may remain among the pre-existing tomes of Homeric lore and Homeric controversy. From the seriousness with which the subject is approached, it would seem as if an extensive consecration was now required to take place in human life and education, comparable to the religious dedication of monastic forms and ages. "An immense price," says he, "is already paid by the youth of this country for classical acquirement. It is the main effort of the first spring-tide of their intellectual life. It is to be hoped that this price will continue to be paid by all those who are qualified to profit by the acquisition; and that though of other knowledge much more will hereafter be gained than heretofore, yet of this there shall on no account be less. Still, viewing the greatness of the cost, which consists in the chief energies of so many precious years, it highly concerns us to see that what we get in return is good, both in measure and in quality." In viewing the magnitude of the present deficiency he says, "The study of Homer in our universities is as yet below the point to which it is desirable that it should be carried; and the same study, carried on at our public schools, neither is nor can be a fitting substitute for what is thus wanting at the universities."

It may be, that, in the progress of destiny, the world is yet to be divided into Homeric and anti-Homeric factions. The avalanche of Greek literature, which seems to be descending on the old world in the form of a new revival, may saturate that favored region with discoveries and interpretations of things unknown in the days of Pericles or Porson. Mr. Gladstone astonishes us with the labors of a certain man, who spent his whole life in endeavors to elucidate the meaning of a single Homeric word; and coolly adds, "Such a disproportion between labor and its aims is somewhat startling; yet it is hardly too much to say, that no amount of exertion spent upon the great classics of the world, and attended with any amount of real result, is really thrown away."

In regard to the impending deluge of Grecian literature, we may reasonably hope that our own hemisphere at least will be relatively spared, inasmuch as we have a Pacific Railroad to be built and a nation to be reconstructed, all which may absorb the superfluous energies of our people for some years to come. We may safely leave to our transatlantic friends the leading glory of farther investigating and expounding the old classics, hoping that no devoted student of any Grecian nodosity will be obliged hereafter to console himself with the candid yet melancholy reflection of Grotius, *Vitam perdidi operose nihil agendo.*

A seminary of learning, and especially a university, cannot be perfect unless it is adapted to the character and wants of all those whom it professes to educate. To effect this adaptation, at least in this country, it is necessary to take into view the individual position of students, their aptitude for particular studies, the amount of time which they can afford to devote to the acquirement of education, their probable sphere and destination in life,— not omitting the more general considerations of public want, and the need of men duly trained for particular professions. Above all, it is necessary to consider the changing and continually renovated state of things which grows from intellectual and social progress, the vastness of the field which is always waiting for cultivation, the impossibility of learning all that is to be learned, and the difficulty of selecting in each case what is best to be learned. And we are compelled to consider, that, in the cases of many young persons, every day spent in the study of superfluous and inapplicable classics is a day deducted from the pursuit of profitable and indispensable knowledge.

The educational loaf on which the community are fed has already increased to many times its former size. It was once so small, that classical literature might have constituted one-half of it. It is now so large, that a lifetime cannot compass it; and the same fractional ratio for an arbitrary division would be unjust and absurd. The lawgivers of education and the purveyors of learning must institute a new basis of distribution; just as they would proceed in districting anew a territory which should be found excessively or unequally populated.

Few persons now deny, that the study of the ancient languages and ancient authors assists to fill and to strengthen the mind, to enlarge the sphere of thought, and to improve, polish, and amplify the power of expression. It has also the present prestige of acquired currency in the educated world, and may well form a constituent part of the most acceptable as well as liberal culture. But it should not monopolize the room which is now too scanty for other indispensable pursuits. Classical learning, like music and painting, will refine, delight, and elevate the mind of a susceptible person; but it will not bring him up to the intellectual demands of the present period. There are other things that, in this age and country, press upon his attention and time, in comparison with which classical learning is already obliged to be subordinated. No man now quotes Greek and Latin in the pulpit or on the stage, in Congress or in a popular assembly. But it will not do for an aspirant for social influence or distinction to be ignorant of the great moving-springs and channels of modern industry and progress, of the science of government, the constitution of his own country, the laws of society and of nations, the geographical, social, and commercial relations of the world, the leading questions of finance and political economy, the properties of bodies and their values, uses, aptitudes, relations, and actions upon each other. He should not be ignorant of the laws of animal and vegetable life, or of the sources of agricultural and mineral wealth. These, with moral science, modern languages, and the vast domain of English literature, may profitably replace much of the labor and time now expended in colleges on the hypertrophy of classical learning.

The dead languages are dead. No man expects hereafter to create new Greek or Roman classics, even if such were needed. But modern sciences and studies are full of vitality, of expansion, of progress present and yet to be. A new thought, an inviting theory, or an important want, needs only to be announced, and at once a thousand eager eyes and acute minds are turned upon its development. If nine hundred fail of success, their very failure has better qualified them for future effort. If one succeeds, the world is revolutionized.

A few years ago, men witnessing the effect of an electric current on the magnetic needle wondered if a motive force could not be transmitted with electric speed to an electric distance. A few years ago, men looking at their faces in a glass wondered if such an image could not be fixed on a plane surface, by the agency of actinic rays. A few years ago, men toiling slowly and wearily on highway roads wondered if the fatigue and loss of time could not be saved by some better mode of conveyance. A few years ago, men about to undergo surgical operations wished in vain that the attendant pain might in some way be averted. The solution of all these problems is now achieved by the triumphs of utilitarian science. The nineteenth century, one-third of which is yet to come, has already converted all these wants and wonders into physical and historical facts. Would the recovery of the lost books of Livy, the orations of Hortensius, or the poems of Sappho, be any compensation for the loss of any one of these from among our own cotemporaneous revelations?

ON THE LIFE AND WORKS OF COUNT RUMFORD.

ADDRESS DELIVERED AT CAMBRIDGE, DEC. 11, 1816.

HUMAN ingenuity, in all ages of the world, has been directed to the acquisition of power. The simple bodily strength with which nature has endowed every one, the inventions which we have sought out to extend and improve our physical ability, the craft and subtlety with which we learn to operate on our fellow-beings, have been strikingly employed, at all times, for the promotion of this object. Those men have been great who have brought others under their dominion; who have swayed them by their eloquence, or influenced them by the ascendency of their character; or who, by enlarging the boundaries of human knowledge, have increased the extent of their own resources, and obtained a control over the creation around them.

Power, when acquired, may have centred and terminated with the individual; or it may have become the common stock of society, and descended from one age to another. In this respect, we find a remarkable difference between the civil and the philosophical history of the world. The power which men and nations exercise in regard to each other is temporary and transient. The greatest individuals have lived to see the decline of every thing upon which their greatness reposed. Societies and political institutions, which have been distinguished in their ascent, have been not less remarkable in their fall. Those nations and governments which in former times have subdued their competitors, and controlled for a time the destinies of a great portion of the world, are now erased from the list of empires, and perhaps recognized only in name.

In the history of philosophy, on the other hand, every thing is permanent and progressive. The triumphs of the human mind over the obstacles that oppose its progress have never been suspended in any period of the world. The ingenuity of mankind has never ceased to devise successful means of perpetuating its own empire. It has never forgotten how to subjugate the elements to its will, and to reduce all natural agents into ministers of its pleasure and power. What one age has acquired, another has not lost; but each succeeding generation have taken up the conquest where their predecessors had relinquished it; and, if they have not been able to advance into unexplored regions, they have at least sacrificed nothing of what was already won. Those sciences and arts, which give mankind an ascendency over the creation about them, have never for a moment escaped from their direction and use. The navigation of the sea and the cultivation of the earth, the forging of metals and the fashioning of wood, though their origin is beyond the memory of man, yet have continued without ceasing, even to the present day, to be extended and improved.

In the progress of philosophy we have also the consoling evidence, that its uniform tendency has been to ameliorate the condition and promote the happiness of mankind. Its effect is not merely to aggrandize the individuals who cultivate it, but likewise to benefit those who may be within the sphere of its influence. The branches of natural science in particular have this excellence, that they do not terminate in mere speculation, but that most of them have a direct bearing upon the wants of society, and tend to objects of real use. But these are not the only inviting features in their character. As they have hitherto been uniformly progressive, so they will continue to be; and the analogy of their previous growth affords an unlimited prospect for the future. Even at the present period of improvement, there is much to be learned in natural science; and the student who would be serviceable to his country may enlist himself in this department of labor, almost with the certainty of being able to contribute something to the general good. He need not despair at the amount of preparatory acquisition which seems necessary to qualify him for usefulness.

The paths to eminence are less circuitous in this than in some of the more abstract departments of knowledge. Many of the important discoveries in physics have been made by men young in life, restricted in leisure, and perhaps uninformed in the elegant branches of literature. The avenues to distinction in natural science are proportionate to the multiplicity of its objects. Independent of the general subjects of investigation, which are open in all countries alike, there are opportunities exclusively local, peculiar to the place of one's own residence, by the study and improvement of which his labors may become interesting and valuable. This remark may well be brought home to our own country. If any one here despair of successfully cultivating those branches of physical science which are pursued by learned men in other parts of the globe, with large establishments and expensive endowments, let him see if there are not subjects within the circle of his own walks which are neither arduous in their character nor expensive in their cultivation, and which lie open to his unassisted industry. A multitude of such subjects he may find in the face and features of our continent: its structure and composition; its capacity for the different branches of agriculture; the improvements of which its present appropriations are susceptible; its geography; its climate and meteorology; its influence on the human body and the human mind; its dis-cases; its natural productions, minerals, plants, and animals; the resources which it has already derived from these, and those which it has yet to discover; the local exigences and wants which may be supplied by the application of foreign inventions and known improvements, or by the contrivance and adaptation of new ones; in short, whatever may tend to increase the facilities of subsistence, and the welfare of those among whom we live.

Motives of philanthropy may urge the pursuit of subjects like these, but the calls of patriotism prefer even a stronger claim. The place of our birth and residence is the proper sphere and object of our exertions. It does not become *us* to complain of its disadvantages, and descant upon the superiority of more favored spots. We should rather consider how we may overcome its defects, and improve its real advantages. We should also see whether its irremediable faults are not, in some instances, productive to us of good as well as of evil.

The portion of country in which it is our fortune to live, is not one of exuberant soil and spontaneous plenty. The summer of New England does not elicit a second burden from our trees; nor is even our annual harvest exempt from the contingency of failure. Winter maintains here a long and late influence upon the seasons, and frosts are visiting us in the latest breezes of spring. Our territory is interrupted by extensive masses of rock, and broken by mountains intractable to cultivation. Our thin and penurious soil rests upon beds of granite, upon flint and sand, which drain it of its moisture, while themselves afford no pabulum for its vegetation. Whatever is raised from the bosom of the earth must be extorted by assiduous and painful culture; and a laborious vigilance is necessary to insure the fruits of the year.

Yet has this part of our country become the most populous and enlightened in the continent upon which we live. The very causes which seemed at variance with our prosperity have proved its most powerful promoters. A vigor and hardihood of character have grown up out of the evils which they had to combat; and a spirit of enterprise and perseverance, unknown in more luxurious climates, has become the characteristic of our population. The intelligence and the untiring application which were at first the offspring of necessity have eventually exhibited ample fruits in the features of our land. Cultivated grounds and ornamental dwellings, wealthy cities and flourishing institutions, have arisen upon a spot where nature was never lavish of her gifts. A spirit of frugality and a talent of invention have more than supplied the disadvantages of our natural situation. Around us are comfort and plenty and health. Our faculties are not exhausted by the debilitating heats of a sultry summer, nor our constitutions assailed by the miasmata of pestilential marshes. In our climate, youth is active, and manhood is hardy. A spirit of adventure carries us everywhere in pursuit of the means of living; and there is no part of the world in which the New-England character is not represented. The means of information are cherished in our humblest villages; our cities are but little infested with the crimes of the older continent; and among us, to an extent perhaps unexampled, the reign of intelligence and of principle supersedes the coercion of law.

Under advantages so distinguished, let us not complain of our lot in a country which gives us natural powers, and a climate which calls them into action. We should rather consider, that the health and alacrity which we possess, are not the common tenants of a rank and luxuriant clime; that the sultry and tepid breezes which multiply the fruits of the earth and render their qualities more exquisite, do not bring with them a keener relish, a more healthy circulation, or a more vigorous frame. Few countries can boast of being what Italy was in the time of her ancient poets, — at once the parent of fruits and of men.* Luxury and indolence are the well-known concomitants of a torrid atmosphere and an exuberant soil. If, in our northern and wintry climate, we are strangers to the rich profu-

---

* Salve, magna parens frugum, Saturnia tellus!
Magna virum!   VIRGIL. *Geor.* ii. 173.

    All hail, Saturnian earth! land loved of fame,
    Parent of fruits and men of mighty name!   SOTHEBY *var.*

sion of a southern soil, we have the consolation that this climate, while it yields us but a scanty harvest for a laborious cultivation, yields us at the same time a blessing for which there can be no equivalent, — the capacity of enjoyment that results from vigor of body and activity of mind.

In science and the arts, notwithstanding the infancy of our institutions and the embarrassment which most individuals experience from the necessity of attending to the calls of business, we have not been wholly without improvement, and are perhaps not destitute of a name. The researches of most of our ingenious men have had utility for their object. They have been performed in intervals taken from professional duties, and have been impeded by a deficiency of books and means. We have had little of the parade of operation, yet we have sometimes seen the fruits of silent efficiency and perseverance. We have had few learned men, but many useful ones. We have not often seen individuals among us spending their lives in endless acquisitions, while perhaps themselves add little to the general stock of knowledge; yet we have had men of original talents, who have been fortunate enough to discover some province in which they were qualified to be serviceable to their country and mankind. We have had ingenious mechanicians, skilful projectors, profound mathematicians, and men well versed in the useful learning of their time.

The progress of our internal improvements, and the high state of the mechanic arts among us, as well as in our sister States, has entitled us to the character of a nation of inventors. The individuals who have originated and promoted such improvements have often been men unambitious of fame, whose lives have passed in obscurity; yet there have sometimes been those among us whose labors have attracted the honorable notice of foreigners, and reflected lustre upon the country of their birth. It has even been our fortune to impose obligations on others; and there are services of our citizens which are now better known than their names. There are some things which, if gathered from the ashes of obscurity, might serve to shed a gleam upon our literary reputation, and to make known at least the light they have kindled for others. It is a fact perhaps not generally realized, that the American Philosophical Society at Philadelphia, the Royal Society of Great Britain, and the Royal Institution of London, all of them are in a measure indebted for their birth and first foundation to natives or inhabitants of New England.*

---

* John Winthrop, Governor of Connecticut, and son of John Winthrop, Governor of Massachusetts, was one of the principal founders of the Royal Society of London. In the dedication to the fortieth volume of the Philosophical Transactions, it is stated that, when he was appointed to his office, Mr. Boyle, Bishop Wilkins, and the rest, proposed to leave England to establish their society in the new colony, of which their friend and associate, Mr. Winthrop, was made governor. They were prevented in consequence of the protection and charter granted them by

Among those whom we shall longest remember, are men whose memory is associated with our own institutions, or with the sciences which they labored to promote. While we pass over the distinguished names of the Winthrops and Bowdoin, we should not forget that Franklin, the philosopher of the Western world, was a native of New England, and a son of our own metropolis. It was his fortune to live in times of political importance, and to find in science some paths untrodden by his predecessors. The great national events which he contributed to promote, and the brilliant and imposing nature of his philosophic discoveries, have been sufficient to aggrandize his character and immortalize his fame. Many men have been as learned, and many patriots as ardent; but few have left behind them a character to be summed up in a sublimer epitaph than his, who "snatched the thunderbolt from heaven, and the sceptre from tyrants." *

It is with peculiar emotions of gratitude, of patriotism, and pride, that we this day recall the memory of a son of Massachusetts, — of one who was transplanted from us at an early period, and destined to flourish under other skies than ours; but

---

Charles II. Governor Winthrop wrote many anonymous papers on various subjects. "His name," says the writer of the above dedication, "had he put it to his writings, would have been as universally known as the Boyles, the Wilkins, and the Oldenburgs."

Count Rumford was the founder of the Royal Institution of London, and Benjamin Franklin was first president of the Philadelphia Society.

* "Eripuit cœlo fulmen, sceptrumque tyrannis."

who has left us the memorial that he was not unmindful of the country of his birth, and that for us he has not lived in vain. Few among us are ignorant that Benjamin Count Rumford received his birth and education in the near vicinity of these walls.* There are now living among us those who remember the features of his boyhood, and recognized the early traits of his unfolding genius. On the present occasion, time would not suffice us to go minutely into the history of his adventurous and important life. He remained long enough on this side the Atlantic to develop those powers of mind and body, which afterwards paved his way to the distinctions of Europe. An enthusiasm in the pursuit of learning, an ardent ambition for fame, a noble and commanding person, and a fascinating address and manner, were as conspicuous in his youth as they were celebrated in his after-life. At the commencement of our Revolutionary troubles, Count Rumford having the misfortune to labor under the combined influence of disappointment and suspicion, which the qualities of his temper were ill calculated to brook, resolved to embark for England, and to intrust to fortune

---

* Benjamin Thompson, afterwards Sir Benjamin and Count Rumford, was born in 1753, at Woburn, near Boston, and not at Rumford (Concord), as stated in his European Biographies. He served a part of a mercantile apprenticeship in Salem and Boston. In 1769 he attended the lectures of Professor Winthrop on Natural Philosophy, in Harvard University. Among his early associates were the late Colonel Baldwin, of Woburn; his Excellency John Brooks, present Governor of Massachusetts; and Samuel Parkman, Esq., of Boston.

and to his own genius the allotment of his future destiny.*

Arrived in London, it was his singularly good fortune to acquire at once the confidence and esteem of men high in power. His talent for science, as well as his political and military abilities, began to display themselves. Early distinctions flowed in upon him; so that, while yet a young man, this emigrant from the Western wilds was attracting public attention, as a member of the Royal Society, as Under-secretary of State, and as a colonel in the British army.

His fondness for travelling and his passion for the military life drew him to the Continent; and at Strasburg he was so fortunate as to acquire not only the acquaintance, but the personal and intimate friendship, of the Prince of Deux Ponts, afterwards King of Bavaria. By this prince he was introduced at the court of the reigning Elector Palatine, his personal

---

* Count Rumford was decidedly attached to the cause of American liberty, and earnestly sought for a commission in the service of Congress. He was present at the battle of Lexington, and afterwards remained some time with the army at Cambridge. His expectations of promotion were disappointed, in consequence of suspicions arising from his former intercourse with Governor Wentworth of New Hampshire, and some others attached to the British cause. These suspicions it was impossible to overcome, although he demanded a court of inquiry, and was honorably acquitted of all intentions inimical to the cause of his country. After remaining some time in fruitless hope with the American army, and seeing the post of his ambition filled by a rival candidate, he retired in disgust, and embarked for England in January, 1776. While at Cambridge, he exerted himself in preserving the library and philosophical apparatus, when the colleges were occupied as barracks by the soldiery.

and mental talents procured him a reception almost unprecedented, and Munich became the seat of his subsequent residence and fame. In this capital, the qualities of his mind had full scope and opportunity to display themselves. His philosophic researches and discoveries became celebrated throughout Europe. His public and domestic improvements were acknowledged and adopted; and, though a foreigner in Germany, the highest civil and military honors became his reward.

Returned to England in the character of minister plenipotentiary, though for state reasons he was not accredited in this capacity, yet his popularity in that country was extensive and undiminished. A series of essays which he began to publish upon philosophic subjects were generally read and admired; his economic improvements became everywhere fashionable; the weight and ascendency of his character were such that they enabled him to carry into effect extensive and important innovations; and, among other things, the Royal Institution of London, a school of science which has been destined to attain the highest celebrity and to become a fountain of light to the philosophic world, owes its first existence to his individual influence and efficiency.

The paths in which Count Rumford trod were as numerous as his success in all of them was remarkable. The practical and philosophic part of his career seems to have furnished the source of his ruling passion, as well as of his most permanent distinctions in society. His scientific investigations were laborious, most of them were original, and all of them tending to purposes of practical utility. Those two universal and mysterious agents of our globe, heat and light, — so cheering and so necessary, that to procure them constitutes more than half the labor of our existence,* — were incessant subjects of his study and investigation. He experimented on the non-conducting power of different substances for heat, that he might bring them to practical use in clothing; he investigated the phenomena of radiation, and the modes of producing, detaining, and economizing heat, that the greatest result might be brought into use with the smallest expense of combustion. His improvements were carried from the fireside of the parlor into the humbler sphere of culinary operations, and their successful application has been abundantly realized in a diminution of the wants and expenses of life.

His philanthropic institutions for the support and nourishment of the poor were among the most fortunate and successful efforts of his genius. In the places of his residence he succeeded in relieving society of one of its most unprofitable burdens, and of substituting industry and comfort for profligacy and want. It was his lot to experience what does

---

* It is probable that among us, houses, clothing, fuel, and lights constitute more than half the necessary expenses of living.

not always befall the benefactors of mankind,—the real gratitude of those who were the objects of his services. He has described, in interesting language, the effect produced on his mind during a dangerous illness, by a sound under his window from a procession of the poor, who were going to church to put up prayers for the recovery of their benefactor.

It may not be expedient at this time to go into a detail of the principles upon which Count Rumford's various improvements in philosophy, and in private and political economy, were founded. In the prosecution of them, he was led to the observation of many curious phenomena of light and heat, with which the world has been made acquainted. The application of these to use, and the various contrivances he originated to increase the convenience, economy, and comforts of living, have given a character to his writings, and are everywhere associated with his name. His pursuits might even be embodied into a science, for their object is everywhere known; a science conversant with a multiplicity of details, but possessing unity of design; a science humble in the sphere of its operations, but noble in its ultimate destiny; a science which every man must practise, but which philosophers and philanthropists must extend; one which, should it ever demand a definition, would be found to be the science of clothing, of warming, and of nourishing mankind.

It will be gratifying to those who have an interest in the character of this great man, to know that the world was not insensible to his merits, and that the countries of his residence were not parsimonious of their honors and rewards. Of the scientific institutions which hastened to enroll him among their members, were the Royal Societies of London and Edinburgh, the Royal Academy of Ireland, the Academy of Sciences at Berlin, and the Imperial Institute of France. The public thanks of cities were repeatedly expressed to him in person, and monuments were erected to him during his life.*

---

* An elegant and expensive marble monument was erected in the English garden at Munich, during Count Rumford's absence from Bavaria, bearing the following inscription in German: —

Stay, wanderer.
At the creative fiat of Charles Theodore,
Rumford, the friend of mankind,
by genius, taste, and love inspired,
changed this once desert place
into what thou now beholdest.

And on the opposite side, —

To him
who rooted out the greatest of public evils,
idleness and mendicity;
relieved and instructed the poor;
and founded many institutions
for the educating of our youth.
Go, wanderer,
and strive to equal him
in genius and activity,
and us
in gratitude.

Biographical sketches of Count Rumford will be found in the Literary Miscellany, published at Cambridge in 1805-6, in Thompson's Annals of Philosophy for April, 1815, and in Cuvier's *éloge* before the Institute of France.

His political talents prepared his way to civil honors both in England and Bavaria; and in the latter place he was successively placed at the head of the departments of war and of general police, and appointed minister plenipotentiary to the Court of Great Britain. In the military line, his progress was not less remarkable; and he who commenced his career as a major in the militia of New Hampshire, ended it as lieutenant-general of the armies of Bavaria. He was successively knighted by the Kings of Great Britain and Poland; and that nobility might not be wanting to swell the sum of his distinction, he was raised to the dignity of a Count of the German empire.

Thus much of Count Rumford the world knows, and posterity will remember. To say that he possessed a character without faults would be to challenge the incredulity of both. But if he had faults they were those of ambition, and his failings were the failings of the great. They were never sufficient to diminish the admiration of mankind for his character, though they sometimes embittered the scenes of his private life. The latter part of his days, which he passed in France, does not seem to have been marked by that conciliating demeanor, and that happy superiority over circumstances, which had formerly been his passport with the world. Conscious of the importance of his services, and accustomed to the homage of those around him, his mind acquired a cast of character little suited to the levity and urbanity of the French metropolis. His schemes and suggestions were heard with respect, but not adopted with eagerness. His intercourse with the society around him was decorous and formal, but not cordial and unreserved; a second marriage had not blessed his domestic repose; and he seems at last to have retired, somewhat in disgust with the world, to his private mansion at Auteuil, near Paris.

Thus was the period at length arrived, when Count Rumford reviewed the scenes of his versatile and chequered life, and remembered the country of his birth. It was the period when the claims of ambition and the vanities of the world were to find their true place in the scale against the more ingenuous feelings and convictions of the soul. This man, who had risen into life with a success the most brilliant and unexampled; who for successive years had flourished in the sunshine of royal patronage; who had seen institutions grow up under his forming hand, which were to enlighten and improve the world; who had been hailed as the benefactor of cities, and caressed as the favorite of courts,— this man, in the twilight of his life, felt that he was a stranger in a foreign land. With the eye of desire and of gratitude, he looked back to the rocky shores of New-England,—

    " Et dulces moriens reminiscitur Argos."

The world was not indifferent to his death. His character and biography appeared in the journals of Europe; and his eulogy was pronounced in the Institute of France by one of the most learned men of the present age. "Surely," said Cuvier, "if worldly honors and renown can ever be superfluous, they must have been so to that man, who, by the fortunate choice of his career, knew how at once to acquire the esteem of the great and the blessings of the unfortunate."

To the country of his birth, Count Rumford has bequeathed his fortune and his fame. The lessons of patriotism which *we* should learn from his memorable life are important and convincing. It should teach us to respect ourselves, to value our resources, to cultivate our talents. Let those who would depreciate our native genius recollect that he was an American. Let those who would make us the dependants and tributaries of the Old World recollect that he has instructed mankind. Let those who would despond as to our future destinies, remember that his eye, which had wandered over the Continent and capitals of Europe, settled at last upon the rising prospects of this Western world. For one who is destined to labor in the path that he has marked out, and to follow with his eyes, though not with his steps, the brilliancy of such a career, it may suffice to acknowledge, that he is not indifferent to the honor that has befallen him; that he is sensible of the magnitude of the example before him; that he believes that the true end of philosophy is to be useful to mankind, and that he will cheerfully and anxiously enter upon the duties that await him; happy if by his efforts he can hope to add even a nameless stone to the monument of philanthropy and science that commemorates the name of *him*, of whom it may in truth be said, that he lived for the world, and that he died for his country.

NOTE.

It is about fifty years since the foregoing address was delivered at Harvard University, on the inauguration of the professorship founded by Count Rumford in that institution. The course of lectures which followed, on the application of the sciences to the arts, was repeated by the author during ten successive years, when, on his resigning the professorship, they were published in an octavo volume, under the title of "Elements of Technology."

The scientific reputation of Count Rumford, and his claims to be regarded as pioneer in a profound and important department of philosophy, have continually gained ground since his death; and his name, instead of being now merged among those of a crowd of competitors, rather occupies the position of their leader in priority and prominence.

In a series of "Expositions" of "the Correlation and Conservation of Forces," published in New York, by Dr. Youmans, and which embodies in a satisfactory manner the researches and reasonings of the most distinguished cotemporaneous philosophers, the following *résumé* is presented of the services of our distinguished countryman: —

"The claims of Rumford may be summarized as follows: —

"1. He was the man who first took the question of the nature of heat out of the domain of metaphysics, where it had been speculated upon since the time of Aristotle, and placed it upon the true basis of physical experiment.

"2. He first proved the insufficiency of the current explanations of the sources of heat, and demonstrated the falsity of the prevailing view of its materiality.

"3. He first estimated the quantitative relation between the heat produced by friction and that by combustion.

"4. He first showed the quantity of heat produced by a definite amount of mechanical work, and arrived at a result remarkably near the finally established law.

"5. He pointed out other methods to be employed in determining the amount of heat produced by the expenditure of mechanical power; instancing particularly the agitation of water or other liquids, as in churning.

"6. He regarded the power of animals as due to their food, — therefore as having a definite source, and not created; and thus applied his views of force to the organic world.

"7. Rumford was the first to demonstrate the quantitative convertibility of force in an important case; and the first to reach experimentally the fundamental conclusion, that heat is but a mode of motion."

ON THE DEATH OF PLINY THE ELDER.*

It is commonly represented by authors and compilers, that Pliny the elder, who died during an eruption of Vesuvius in the year of Christ 79, perished by suffocation from the exhalations of the volcano; and a great preciseness of expression on this subject has been perpetuated by most writers who have touched upon it in modern times.

In the preface of Broterius to the Life and Writings of Pliny, it is said: "Flammis et flammarum prænuntio odore sulphuris exanimatus est." Mason, in Smith's Greek and Roman Biography, says: "He almost immediately dropped down, *suffocated*, as his nephew conjectures, by the vapors." In Lemprière's Classical Dictionary the same is stated: "He soon fell down, *suffocated* by the thick vapors that surrounded him." Rees's Cyclopædia, art. PLINY, has a similar statement: "In his flight he was *suffocated*, being then in the fifty-sixth year of his age."

* From the Memoirs of the American Academy of Arts and Sciences, vol. vi., Dec. 9, 1856.

Cuvier, in the *Biographie Universelle*, thus particularizes the closing scene: "Deux esclaves seulement restèrent auprès du malheureux Pline, qui périt *suffoqué* par les cendres et par les exhalaisons sulfureuses du volcan." Simond, in his Tour in Italy, says of Pliny at Stabiæ: "Although not much nearer to Vesuvius than Naples is, he there met his death, from mere *suffocation* probably, as his body was afterwards found externally uninjured." Sir Charles Lyell, in his Principles of Geology, says of Pliny: "In his anxiety to obtain a nearer view of the phenomena, he lost his life, being *suffocated* by sulphurous vapors."

The only authentic and contemporaneous narrative extant of the death of Pliny, and that on which subsequent opinions are necessarily founded, is that contained in the letter of his nephew, Pliny the younger. After an examination of this celebrated epistle, it appears to me highly probable that the elder Pliny got his death, not from suffocation or asphyxia, as is commonly believed, but from a more specific and natural disease. The following is a part of the translation by Mr. Melmoth of this epistle: —

"In the mean while, the fire from Vesuvius flamed forth from several parts of the mountain with great violence, which the darkness of the night contributed to render still more visible and dreadful. But my uncle, in order to calm the apprehensions of his friend, assured him that it was only the conflagration of the villages which the country people had abandoned. After this, he retired to rest, and it is most certain he was so little discomposed as to fall into a deep sleep; for, being corpulent and breathing hard, the attendants in the antechamber actually heard him snore. The court which led to his apartment being now almost filled with stones and ashes, it would have been impossible for him, if he had continued there any longer, to have made his way out. It was thought proper, therefore, to awaken him. He got up, and joined Pomponianus and the rest of the company, who had not been sufficiently unconcerned to think of going to bed. They consulted together whether it would be most prudent to trust to the houses, which now shook from side to side with frequent and violent concussions, or flee to the open fields, where the calcined stones and cinders, though levigated indeed, yet fell in large showers, and threatened them with instant destruction. In this distress, they resolved upon the fields, as the less dangerous situation of the two; a resolution which, while the rest of the company were hurried into by their fears, my uncle embraced upon cool and deliberate consideration. They went out then, having pillows tied upon their heads with napkins; and this was their whole defence against the storm of stones which fell around them. It was now day everywhere else; but *there* a deeper darkness prevailed than in the blackest night, which, however, was in some degree dissipated by torches and other lights of various kinds. They thought it expedient to go down further upon the shore, in order to observe if they might safely put out to sea; but they found the waves still running extremely high and boisterous. There my uncle, having drunk a draught or two of cold water, laid himself down upon a sail-cloth which was spread for him; when immediately the flames, preceded by a strong smell of sulphur, dispersed the rest of the company and obliged him to rise. He raised himself up with the assistance of two of his servants, and instantly fell down dead, suffocated, I conjecture, by some gross and noxious vapor, having always had weak lungs, and being frequently subject to a difficulty of breathing."

Notwithstanding the elegance and general accuracy of Mr. Melmoth's translation, there is room for doubting the exactness of that part which contains the closing scene of Pliny's life. The words of the younger Pliny are as follows: "Deinde flammæ, flammarumque prænuntius odor sulfuris, alios in fugam vertunt, excitant illum. Innixus servis duobus adsurrexit, et statim concidit, ut ego conjecto crassiore caligine spiritu obstructo, clausoque stomacho, qui illi natura invalidus et angustus et frequenter interæstuans erat." The more exact translation of this passage would be as follows: "Then the flames, and the odor of sulphur premonitory of the flames, put the others to flight and aroused him. He rose, leaning upon two slaves, and immediately fell dead; his breath being obstructed, as I conjecture, by the thick mist (*caligine*), and his stomach being shut up, which in him was by nature weak, narrow, and subject to frequent commotion." The fact here is that he fell suddenly dead. The theory of Pliny, his nephew, who was not present, and who was not much versed in anatomy, is that he died from obstruction of his breath by the "caligo;" a word which means darkness, fog, mist, also metaphorically blindness, dizziness, and ignorance, but does not mean a noxious or irrespirable vapor.

That this "caligo" was not composed of materials necessarily destructive of life, there is abundant collateral evidence. Pliny had been attended to the spot by a considerable party, and two slaves were actually supporting him at the time of his death. Yet it does not appear from record that any of these persons suffered death or detriment from the inhalation of noxious gas on the occasion. The character of the "caligo" is further elucidated by the personal experience of the younger Pliny, who witnessed its effects during the same eruption, and has described its phenomena in a subsequent letter; the nephew being at Misenum, while the uncle was at Stabiæ, in the same vicinity to the mountain:—

"It was now morning, but the light was exceedingly faint and languid. The buildings all around us tottered; and though we stood upon open ground, yet, as the place was narrow and confined, there was no remaining without imminent danger. We therefore resolved to leave the town. The people followed us in the utmost consternation, and pressed in great crowds about us in our way out. Being advanced at a convenient distance from the houses, we stood still in the midst of a most hazardous and tremendous scene. The chariots which we had ordered to be drawn out were so agitated backwards and forwards, though upon the most level ground, that we could not keep them steady even by supporting them with large stones. The sea seemed to roll back upon itself, and to be driven from its banks by the convulsive motion of the earth. On the other side, a black and dreadful cloud, bursting with an igneous, serpentine vapor, darted out a long train of fire, resembling flashes of lightning. . . . Soon afterwards the cloud seemed to descend and cover the whole ocean, as indeed it entirely hid the island of Caprea and the promontory of Misenum. . . .

"The ashes now began to fall upon us, though in no great quantity. I turned my head, and observed behind us a thick smoke, which came rolling after us like a torrent. I proposed, while we had yet any light, to turn out of the high road, lest [we] should be pressed to death in the dark by the crowd that followed us. We had scarcely stepped out of the path when the darkness overspread us, — not like that of a cloudy night, or when there is no moon, but of a room when it is shut up and all the lights extinct. Nothing then was to be heard but the shrieks of women, the screams of children, and the cries of men; some calling for their children, others for their parents, others for their husbands, and only distinguishing each other by their voices; one lamenting his own fate, another that of his family, some wishing to die from the very fear of dying. . . . At length a glimmering light appeared, . . . then again we were immersed in thick darkness, and a heavy shower of ashes rained upon us, which we were obliged every now and then to shake off, otherwise we should have been overwhelmed and buried in the heap. . . . At last this terrible darkness [*caligo*] was dissipated by degrees, like a cloud or smoke, the real day returned, and even the sun appeared, though very faintly, as when an eclipse is coming on. Every object that presented itself to our eyes seemed changed, being covered with white ashes, as with a deep snow"

From these descriptions we are justified in believing that the "caligo" which pervaded the air during this eruption of Vesuvius was simply the darkness, or dark haze, existing in an atmosphere rendered nearly opaque by falling ashes. These ashes (*cinis*) appear to have consisted mainly of particles of solid substance, thrown out from the crater, or sublimed in the volcano and condensed in the atmosphere, such as now cover the ruins of Pompeii. As to the "odor sulfuris," mentioned in the first letter, it is not spoken of as a thing in itself deleterious, but merely as the forerunner (*prænuntius*) of the flames. Had the air been highly charged with sulphurous or hydrosulphuric acids, which are among the gaseous products of volcanoes, or even with the sublimed chlorides more common among volcanic gases, it is hardly probable that Pliny would have been the only sufferer on the occasion, or that eye-witnesses would have survived to be narrators of a catastrophe in which they themselves had no share, or even that the inhabitants of Herculaneum and Pompeii, which cities were buried in the same eruption of Vesuvius, would so generally have escaped as they appear to have done.

The important facts which belong to the object of the present inquiry may be summed up briefly as follows: Pliny the elder, a corpulent man, subject to laborious breathing and to other infirmities which had excited the notice, if not the apprehensions, of his friends, was, on the day and night preceding his death, exposed to unusual fatigue and anxiety. In the evening he had had himself carried to a bath, ate his supper, and went to bed, where he slept so profoundly as to be insensible to the noise and danger which kept his companions awake. At length, the danger growing more imminent, he was awakened, and with his companions fled from the house, the whole company carrying pillows on their heads to ward off the falling stones. In this way they groped their way through the darkness till the next morning (*jam dies alibi, illic nox*). He then lay down on a sail-cloth spread out for him, — a measure which, we may suppose, would hardly have been resorted to under the continuance of danger from the falling stones, except from want of strength on his part to proceed. Neither, under the same circumstances, would he have stopped repeatedly to demand cold water, unless suffering unusual thirst (*Semel atque iterum frigidam poposcit hausitque*). At length, under a fresh alarm, he raised himself up, and immediately fell dead while leaning upon his two servants.

A medical man may be excused for believing that Pliny died from apoplexy following unusual exertion and excitement, or possibly from a fatal crisis in some disease of the heart previously existing.

ON THE BURIAL OF THE DEAD, AND MOUNT AUBURN CEMETERY.

[The interest which the author has felt in the Cemetery at Mount Auburn, the first of its kind in the United States, has in a measure grown out of his personal connection with its foundation and subsequent development. The project of Mount Auburn was originally conceived, the preparatory meetings called, the land selected and engaged, and the larger public structures, the gate, chapel, tower, and iron fence, designed by himself at different times.* The pleasure of witnessing, through so many years, the progressive improvement of this beautiful spot has been enhanced by the interest and active co-operation of many of our distinguished and valued citizens.

While the subject was of recent agitation, the following Address was delivered at the hall of the Masonic Temple, before the Boston Society for the Promotion of Useful Knowledge : —]

THE manner in which we dispose of the remains of our deceased friends is a subject which, within the last few years, has occupied a greater share than formerly of the public attention in our own vicinity. It involves not only considerations which belong to the general convenience, but includes also the gratification of individual taste, and the consolation of

---

* Historical notices of Mount Auburn have been published by Thacher, Walter, Dearborn, and others, also in the Daily Advertiser, Sept. 9, 1851, and the Boston Atlas, Sept. 18, 1851.

private sorrow. Although, in a strictly philosophical view, this subject possesses but little importance except in relation to the convenience of survivors, yet so closely are our sympathies enlisted with it, so inseparably do we connect the feelings of the living with the condition of the dead, that it is in vain that we attempt to divest ourselves of its influence. It is incumbent on us, therefore, to analyze, as far as we may be able, the principles which belong to a correct view of this subject; since it is only by understanding these, that we may expect both reason and feeling to be satisfied.

The progress of all organized beings is towards decay. The complicated textures which the living body elaborates within itself begin to fall asunder almost as soon as life has ceased. The materials of which animals and vegetables are composed have natural laws and irresistible affinities, which are suspended during the period of life, but which must be obeyed the moment that life is extinct. These continue to operate until the exquisite fabric is reduced to a condition in no wise different from that of the soil on which it has once trodden. In certain cases, art may modify, and accident may retard, the approaches of disorganization; but the exceptions thus produced are too few and imperfect to invalidate the certainty of the general law.

If we take a comprehensive survey of the progress and mutations of animal and vegetable life, we shall perceive that this necessity of individual destruction is the basis of general safety. The elements which have once moved and circulated in living frames do not become extinct nor useless after death: they offer themselves as the materials from which other living frames are to be constructed. What has once possessed life is most assimilated to the living character, and most ready to partake of life again. The plant which springs from the earth, after attaining its growth and perpetuating its species, falls to the ground, undergoes decomposition, and contributes its remains to the nourishment of plants around it. The myriads of animals which range the woods or inhabit the air at length die upon the surface of the earth; and, if not devoured by other animals, prepare for vegetation the place which receives their remains. Were it not for this law of nature, the soil would be soon exhausted, the earth's surface would become a barren waste, and the whole race of organized beings, for want of sustenance, would become extinct.

Man alone, the master of the creation, does not willingly stoop to become a participator in the routine of nature. In every age he has manifested a disposition to exempt himself, and to rescue his fellow, from the common fate of living beings. Although he is prodigal of the lives of other classes, and sometimes sacrifices a hundred inferior bodies to procure himself a single repast, yet he regards with scrupulous anxiety the destination of his own remains; and much labor and treasure are devoted by him to ward off for a season the inevitable courses of nature. Under the apprehension of posthumous degradation, human bodies have been embalmed, their concentrated dust has been inclosed in golden urns, monumental fortresses have been piled over their decaying bones; with what success, and with what use, it may not be amiss to consider.

I have selected a few instances, in which measures have been taken to protect the human frame from decay, which will be seen to have been in some cases partially successful, in others not so. They will serve as preliminaries to the general considerations which are connected with the subject.

One of the most interesting accounts of the preservation of a body, the identity of which was undoubted, is that of the disinterment of King Edward I. of England. The readers of English history will recollect, that this monarch gave, as a dying charge to his son, that his heart should be sent to the Holy Land, but that his body should be carried in the van of the army till Scotland was reduced to obedience.

He died in July, 1307; and, notwithstanding his injunctions, was buried in Westminster Abbey, in October of the same year. It is recorded that he was embalmed, and orders for renewing the cerecloth about his body were issued in the reigns of Edward III. and Henry IV. The tomb of this monarch was opened, and his body examined in January, 1774, under the direction of Sir Joseph Ayloffe, after it had been buried four hundred and sixty-seven years. The following account is extracted from a contemporaneous volume of the "Gentleman's Magazine:"—

"Some gentlemen of the Society of Antiquaries, being desirous to see how far the actual state of Edward I.'s body answered to the methods taken to preserve it, obtained leave to open the large stone sarcophagus, in which it is known to have been deposited, on the north side of Edward the Confessor's chapel. This was accordingly done on the morning of Jan. 2, 1774, when, in a coffin of yellow stone, they found the royal body in perfect preservation, inclosed in two wrappers: one of them was of gold tissue, strongly waxed, and fresh; the other and outermost, considerably decayed. The corpse was habited in a rich mantle of purple, paned with white, and adorned with ornaments of gilt metal, studded with red and blue stones and pearls. Two similar ornaments lay on the hands. The mantle was fastened on the right shoulder by a magnificent *fibula* of the same metal, with the same stones and pearls. His face had over it a silken covering, so fine, and so closely fitted to it, as to preserve the features entire. Round his temples was a gilt coronet of *fleurs-de-lis*. In his hands, which were also entire, were two sceptres of gilt metal: that in the right surmounted by a cross fleure; that in the left by three clusters of oak leaves and a dove on a globe. This sceptre was about five feet long. The feet were enveloped in the mantle and other coverings, but sound, and the toes distinct. The whole length of the corpse was five feet two inches."

This last statement, it will be observed, is the only point in which the narrative appears to disagree with history. We are generally given to understand that Edward I. was a tall man, and that he was designated in his own time by the name of Longshanks. Baker, in his "Chronicle of the Kings of England," says of him that he was tall of stature, exceeding most other men by a head and shoulders. I have not been able to find Sir Joseph Ayloffe's account of the examination; and know of no other mode of reconciling the discrepancy, but by supposing a typographical error of a figure in the account which has been quoted.

Edward I. died at Burgh-upon-sands, in Cumberland, on his way to Scotland, July 7, 1307, in the sixty-eighth year of his age.

Another instance of partial preservation is that of the body of King Charles I., who was beheaded by his subjects in 1649. The remains of this unfortunate monarch are known to have been carried to Windsor, and there interred by his friends, without pomp, in a hasty and private manner. It is stated, in Clarendon's "History of the Rebellion," that when his son, Charles II., was desirous to remove and re-inter his corpse at Westminster Abbey, it could not by any search be found. In constructing a mausoleum at Windsor, in 1813, under the direction of George IV., then Prince Regent, an accident led to the discovery of this royal body.

The workmen, in forming a subterraneous passage under the choir of St. George's Chapel, accidentally made an aperture in the wall of the vault of King Henry VIII. On looking through this opening, it was found to contain three coffins, instead of two, as had been supposed. Two of these were ascertained to be the coffins of Henry VIII., and of one of his queens, Jane Seymour. The other was formally examined, after permission obtained, by Sir Henry Halford, in presence of several members of the royal family, and other persons of distinction. The account, since published by Sir Henry, corroborates the one which had been given by Mr. Herbert, a groom of King Charles's bedchamber, and is published in Wood's "Athenæ Oxonienses:" —

"On removing the pall," says the account, "a plain leaden coffin presented itself to view, with no appearance of ever having been inclosed in wood, and bearing an inscription, 'King Charles, 1648,' in large, legible characters, on a scroll of lead encircling it. A square opening was then made in the upper part of the lid, of such dimensions as to admit a clear insight into its contents. These were an internal wooden coffin, very much decayed; and the body, carefully wrapped up in cerecloth, into the folds of which a quantity of unctuous matter, mixed with resin as it seemed, had been melted, so as to exclude, as effectually as possible, the external air. The coffin was completely full; and, from the tenacity of the cerecloth, great difficulty was experienced in detaching it successfully from the parts which it enveloped. Wherever the unctuous matter had insinuated itself, the separation of the cerecloth was easy;

and, where it came off, a correct impression of the features to which it had been applied was observed. At length the whole face was disengaged from its covering. The complexion of the skin of it was dark and discolored. The forehead and temples had lost little or nothing of their muscular substance; the cartilage of the nose was gone; but the left eye, in the first moment of exposure, was open and full, though it vanished almost immediately; and the pointed beard, so characteristic of the period of the reign of King Charles, was perfect. The shape of the face was a long oval; many of the teeth remained; and the left ear, in consequence of the interposition of the unctuous matter between it and the cerecloth, was found entire.

"It was difficult, at this moment, to withhold a declaration, that, notwithstanding its disfigurement, the countenance did bear a strong resemblance to the coins, the busts, and especially to the picture of King Charles the First, by Vandyke, by which it had been made familiar to us. It is true that the minds of the spectators of this interesting sight were well prepared to receive this impression; but it is also certain that such a facility of belief had been occasioned by the simplicity and truth of Mr. Herbert's narrative, every part of which had been confirmed by the investigation, so far as it had advanced; and it will not be denied that the shape of the face, the forehead, the eye, and the beard, are the most important features by which resemblance is determined.

"When the head had been entirely disengaged from the attachments which confined it, it was found to be loose, and without any difficulty was taken out and held up to view. The back part of the scalp was entirely perfect, and had a remarkably fresh appearance; the pores of the skin being more distinct, and the tendons and ligaments of the neck were of considerable substance and firmness.

The hair was thick at the back part of the head, and in appearance nearly black. A portion of it, which has since been cleaned and dried, is of a beautiful dark-brown color. That of the beard was a redder brown. On the back part of the head it was not more than an inch in length, and had probably been cut so short for the convenience of the executioner, or perhaps by the piety of friends, soon after death, in order to furnish memorials of the unhappy king.

"On holding up the head to examine the place of separation from the body, the muscles of the neck had evidently retracted themselves considerably; and the fourth cervical vertebra was found to be cut through its substance transversely, leaving the surfaces of the divided portions perfectly smooth and even, — an appearance which could have been produced only by a heavy blow, inflicted with a very sharp instrument, and which furnished the last proof wanting to identify King Charles the First."

The foregoing are two of the most successful instances of posthumous preservation. The care taken in regard to some other distinguished personages has been less fortunate in its result. The coffin of Henry VIII. was inspected at the same time with that of Charles, and was found to contain nothing but the mere skeleton of that king. Some portions of beard remained on the chin; but there was nothing to discriminate the personage contained in it.

During the present century, the sarcophagus of King John has also been examined. It contained little else than a disorganized mass of earth. The principal substances found were some half-decayed bones, a few vestiges of cloth and leather, and a long rusty piece of iron, apparently the remains of the sword-blade of that monarch.

The rapidity with which decomposition takes place in organic bodies depends upon the particular circumstances under which they are placed. A certain temperature and a certain degree of moisture are indispensable agents in the common process of putrefaction; and, could these be avoided in the habitable parts of our globe, human bodies might last indefinitely. I shall be excused for dwelling a short time on the influence of some of these preservative agents. Where a certain degree of cold exists, it tends powerfully to check the process of destructive fermentation; and, when it extends so far as to produce congelation, its protecting power is complete. Bodies of men and animals are found in situations where they have remained frozen for years, and even for ages. Not many years ago, the bodies of some Spanish soldiers were found in a state of perfect preservation among the snows of the Andes, where they were supposed to have perished, in attempting to cross those mountains, nearly a century ago; their costume and some historical records indicating the probable period of their expedition. At the Hospice of the Grand St. Bernard in the Alps, some receptacles of the dead are shown to travellers; in which, owing to the effect of perpetual frost, together with the lightness of the atmosphere, but little absolute decay has taken place in the subjects deposited during a lapse of years. But the most remarkable instance of preservation by frost of an animal body, is that of an elephant of an extinct species, discovered in 1806 in the ice of the polar sea, near the mouth of the river Lena, by Mr. Michael Adams. This animal was first seen by a chief of the Tonguse tribe, in the year 1799; at which time it was imbedded in a rock of ice, about one hundred and eighty feet high, and had only two feet, with a small part of the body projecting from the side so as to be visible. At the close of the next summer, the entire flank of the animal had been thawed out. It nevertheless required five summers, in this inclement region, to thaw the ice so that the whole body could be liberated. At length, in 1804, the enormous mass separated from the mountain of ice, and fell over upon its side, on a sandbank. At this time it appears to have been in a state of perfect preservation, with its skin and flesh as entire as when it had existed antecedently to the deluge, or during that condition of the globe which placed animals apparently of the torrid zone in the confines of the Arctic circle. The Tonguse chief cut off the tusks, which were nine feet long, and weighed two hundred pounds each. Two years after this event, Mr. Adams, being at Yakutsk, and hearing of this event, undertook a journey to the spot. He found the animal in the same place, but exceedingly mutilated by the dogs and wolves of the neighborhood, which had fed upon its flesh as fast as it thawed. He, however, succeeded in removing the whole skeleton, and in recovering two of the feet, one of the ears, one of the eyes, and about three quarters of the skin, which was covered with reddish hair and black bristles. These are now in the museum at St. Petersburg.

The foregoing facts are sufficient to show that a low degree of temperature is an effectual preventive of animal decomposition. On the other hand, a certain degree of heat combined with a dry atmosphere, although a less perfect protection, is sufficient to check the destructive process. Warmth combined with moisture tends greatly to promote decomposition; yet, if the degree of heat, or the circumstances under which it acts, are such as to produce a perfect dissipation of moisture, the further progress of decay is arrested. In the arid caverns of Egypt, the dried flesh of mummies, although greatly changed from its original appearance, has made no progress towards ultimate decomposition during two or three thousand years. It is known that the ancient Egyptians embalmed the dead bodies of their friends, by extracting the large viscera from the cavities of the head, chest, and abdomen, and filling them with aromatic and resinous substances, particularly asphaltum, and enveloping the outside of the body in cloths impregnated with similar materials. These impregnations prevented decomposition for a time, until perfect dryness had taken place. Their subsequent preservation, through so many centuries, appears to have been owing, not so much to the antiseptic quality of the substance in which they are enveloped, as to the effectual exclusion of moisture.

In the crypt under the cathedral of Milan, travellers are shown the ghastly relics of Carlo Borromeo, as they have lain for two centuries, inclosed in a crystal sarcophagus, and bedecked with costly finery of silk and gold. The preservation of this body is equal to that of an Egyptian mummy, yet a more loathsome piece of mockery than it exhibits can be hardly imagined.

It will be perceived that the instances which have been detailed are cases of extraordinary exemption, resulting from uncommon care, or from the most favorable combination of circumstances, such as can befall but an exceedingly small portion of the human race. The common fate of animal bodies is to undergo the entire destruction of their fabric, and the obliteration of their living features, in a few years, and sometimes even weeks, after their death. No sooner does life cease than the elements which constituted the vital body become subject to the common laws of inert matter. The original affinities, which had been modified or suspended during life, are brought into operation; the elementary atoms re-act upon each other; the organized structure passes into decay, and is converted to its original dust. Such is the natural, and I may add the proper, destination of the material part of all that has once moved and breathed.

The reflections which naturally suggest themselves, in contemplating the wrecks of humanity which have occasionally been brought to light, are such as lead us to ask, of what possible use is a resistance to the laws of nature, which, when most successfully executed, can at best only preserve a defaced and degraded image of what was once perfect and beautiful? Could we by any means arrest the progress of decay, so as to gather round us the dead of a hundred generations in a visible and tangible shape; could we fill our houses and our streets with mummies, — what possible acquisition could be more useless, what custom could be more revolting? For precisely the same reason, the subterranean vaults and the walls of brick — which we construct to divide the clay of humanity from that of the rest of creation, and to preserve it separate for a time, as it were for future inspection — are neither useful, gratifying, nor ultimately effectual. Could the individuals themselves, who are to be the subjects of this care, have the power to regulate the officious zeal of their survivors, one of the last things they could reasonably desire would be that the light should ever shine on their changed and crumbling relics.

On the other hand, when nature is permitted to

take its course, when the dead are committed to the earth under the open sky, to become early and peacefully blended with their original dust, no unpleasant association remains. It would seem as if the forbidding and repulsive conditions which attend on decay were merged and lost in the surrounding harmonies of the creation.

When the body of Major André was taken up a few years since, from the place of its interment near the Hudson, for the purpose of being removed to England, it was found that the skull of that officer was closely encircled by a network, formed by the roots of a small tree which had been planted near his head. This is a natural and most beautiful coincidence. It would seem as if a faithful sentinel had taken his post, to watch till the obliterated ashes should no longer need a friend. Could we associate with inanimate clay any of the feelings of sentient beings, who would not wish to rescue his remains from the prisons of mankind, and commit them thus to the embrace of nature?

Convenience, health, and decency require that the dead should be early removed from our sight. The law of nature requires that they should moulder into dust; and the sooner this change is accomplished, the better. This change should take place, not in the immediate contiguity of survivors, not in frequented receptacles provided for the promiscuous concentration of numbers, not where the intruding light may annually usher in a new tenant to encroach upon the old. It should take place peacefully, silently, separately, in the retired valley or the sequestered wood, where the soil continues its primitive exuberance, and where the earth has not become too costly to afford to each occupant at least his length and breadth.

Within the bounds of populous and growing cities, interments cannot with propriety take place beyond a limited extent. The vacant tracts reserved for burial-grounds, and the cellars of churches which are converted into tombs, become glutted with inhabitants, and are in the end obliged to be abandoned, though not perhaps until the original tenants have been ejected, and the same space has been occupied three or four successive times. Necessity obliges a recourse at last to be had to the neighboring country; and hence in Paris, London, Liverpool, Leghorn, and other European cities, cemeteries have been constructed without the confines of their population. These places, in consequence of the sufficiency of the ground and the funds which usually grow out of such establishments, have been made the recipients of tasteful ornament. Travellers are attracted by their beauty, and dwell with interest on their subsequent recollection. The scenes which, under most other circumstances, are repulsive and disgusting, are, by the joint influence of nature and art, rendered beautiful, attractive, and consoling.

The situation of Mount Auburn, near Boston, is one of great natural fitness for the objects to which it has been devoted. Independently of its superior size, it may be doubted whether any spot, which has been set apart for the same purposes in Europe, possesses half the interest in its original features. In a few years, when the hand of taste shall have scattered among the trees, as it has already begun to do, enduring memorials of marble and granite, a landscape of the most picturesque character will be created. No place in the environs of our city will possess stronger attractions to the visitor. To the mourner it offers seclusion amid the consoling influences of nature. The moralist and man of religion will —

> "Find room
> And food for meditation, nor pass by
> Much, that may give him pause, if pondered fittingly."

We regard the relics of our deceased friends and kindred for what they have been, and not for what they are. We cannot keep in our presence the degraded image of the original frame; and, if some memorial is necessary to soothe the unsatisfied want which we feel when bereaved of their presence, it must be found in contemplating the place in which we know that their dust is hidden. The history of mankind, in all ages, shows that the human heart clings to the grave of its disappointed wishes; that it seeks consolation in rearing emblems and monuments, and in collecting images of beauty over the disappearing relics of humanity. This can be fitly done, not in the tumultuous and harassing din of cities, not in the gloomy and almost unapproachable vaults of charnel-houses, but amidst the quiet verdure of the field, under the broad and cheerful light of heaven, where the harmonious and ever-changing face of nature reminds us, by its resuscitating influences, that to die is but to live again.

REPORT OF THE ACTION OF COCHITUATE WATER ON LEAD PIPES, AND THE INFLUENCE OF THE SAME ON HEALTH.*

The committee appointed by the Society of Medical Improvement in Boston, for investigating the question of the occurrence of any diseases attributable to the presence of lead in the aqueduct water introduced into the city from the Cochituate Lake, report as follows: —

That from an extensive inquiry among physicians, and also from the bills of mortality, they are led to believe that the health of the city of Boston has been uncommonly good during several years, since the introduction of Cochituate water; and they have not learned that any well-marked cases of the diseases usually attributed to lead have occurred, which were not traceable to some other cause than the use of Cochituate water drawn from leaden pipes.

It appears, from the experiments of Professor Horsford, that the water of the Schuylkill and Croton rivers, and of Jamaica and Cochituate lakes, acts

* From the American Journal of Medical Sciences for 1852.

upon the surface of lead so as to take up a small portion of that metal during the first two or three days of its contact. But, after a few days, the surface of the lead becomes coated with an insoluble compound, which protects the lead for the most part from the further action of the water. Nevertheless, traces of lead are reported to have been found by various chemists in specimens of some of these waters, when greatly reduced by evaporation.

In consequence of the extensive use made of lead for various economical purposes, no person in civilized society can expect to escape from the reception of that metal in minute quantities into the body. The presence of lead in the paint of dwelling-houses and furniture, of water-buckets and other culinary apparatus, in vessels made of leaden alloys or soldered with the same, in the lining of tea-chests, in flint-glass, and in the glazing of coarse pottery, furnishes but a part of the examples which indicate our exposure to receive this metal in our daily food. To these examples it may be added, that physicians give lead to their patients sometimes for weeks successively, and apply solutions and solid compounds of the metal to absorbing surfaces for longer periods; that persons are known to carry shot and bullets in their flesh during a long life; and, finally, that reliable chemists testify that lead naturally exists in the solids and fluids of man, and in those of some of the animals on which he feeds.

From all these facts we are authorized to draw the conclusion, that, in the present state of our knowledge, the existence of lead in a very minute amount, like the presence of other substances in infinitesimal quantities, is inoperative upon the living body.

It is a general law known to medical men, and to which there are not many exceptions, that diseases and symptoms produced by specific metallic agents, such as mercury, lead, and arsenic, do not cease until after the withdrawal of those agents. But it appears from the records of the Massachusetts General Hospital during the last twenty years, as well as from the private experience of physicians, that many cases of lead colic and paralysis, acquired by persons who work in that metal, have got well under the daily use of water delivered from leaden pipes. This would not probably have been the case, did the water contain any deleterious amount of lead in solution or suspension.

The principal diseases ascribed by Tanquerel, and some subsequent writers, to the presence of lead, are colic, paralysis, arthralgia, and encephalopathy. Of these the committee have not been able to learn that there has been any sensible increase in this city since the introduction of Cochituate water. Of lead colic, but one case has entered the hospital during the last two years, which is a smaller proportion than the average of the preceding twenty years.

Of lead paralysis there have been but two cases within the same period, both occurring to workmen in lead. Of arthralgia, or pain in the joints or limbs, directly traceable to lead, it is believed there have not been a sufficient number of cases at any time to attract extensively the notice of our physicians. As to encephalopathy, — a general term used by some writers to express cerebral disease, and including coma, delirium, convulsions, &c., — there is apparently no more reason for attributing it to lead, than consumption, fever, or any other common disease which may happen to occur among lead workmen.

It is obvious to a medical reader, that many of the cases detailed by writers on lead diseases are coincidences rather than consequences; and therefore do not furnish a ground for general laws. Such is the case when persons have been supposed to have contracted lead diseases by sleeping in newly-painted apartments, where, unless the lead were volatile, it could not leave the walls to enter the bodies of the patients. It is also the case when solitary examples of common diseases are ascribed to lead, when it is known that they more frequently result from different causes. It is also often the case when the reports of credulous and incompetent observers are received as scientific authority.

In a late English Report by the Government Commissioners, on the Chemical Quality of the Supply of Water to the Metropolis of London, made in 1851, by Drs. Th. Graham, W. A. Miller, and A. W. Hoffman, men of high standing in the scientific world, an investigation is made of the condition of the various waters now supplied to that city. In this Report, the Commissioners state (page 32) that " no recent or authenticated case can be cited of the health of any of the numerous towns, lately supplied with soft water, being affected by the use of leaden-distributing tubes." Again, on page 33, the Commissioners say: " We are disposed, therefore, to conclude that the danger from lead, in towns supplied with water, has been overrated; and that, with a supply from the water companies not less frequent than daily, no danger is to be apprehended from the use of the present distributing apparatus, with any supply of moderately soft water which the metropolis is likely to obtain."

On the present occasion, it is by no means intended to deny the well-known fact, that certain acid liquors, also that the water of certain springs and wells, may and do act upon and even dissolve lead in such quantities as to prove injurious to human health. It is also possible, that, at certain seasons and under certain circumstances, the soft water of lakes and rivers may contain organic or other products, which may take up in solution a minute portion of the pipes through which they pass. And it may even be conceded as possible, that a few susceptible and predisposed individuals will get lead diseases while using this water. Nevertheless, lead is a very convenient material to be used in aqueducts. It is more cheaply manufactured, more conveniently applied, and more readily repaired, than any other material; and, while this is the case, mankind will not be prevented from employing it. The general law derived from the experience of the large cities of this country and of Europe is, that its employment for the conveyance of soft water is safe. To this law the few recorded cases of disease, if genuine, must be regarded as exceptions. And it should be borne in mind, that nearly all the great agents which minister to the physical happiness and improvement of man are fraught with more or less danger. Ships and railroads, fire and water, food, drink, and medicine, destroy annually multitudes of our species. Nevertheless, all these agents increase every year in use, with the increase of wealth and civilization. And, as a humble example under the same law, it is not probable that the leaden aqueduct will be abandoned on account of the inconsiderable risk which it may involve of occasioning disease. From the present state of our knowledge, we are authorized to conclude that the insurance on a citizen of Boston, New York, Philadelphia, or London, against lead colic, is probably worth much less than his insurance would be on a voyage across the Atlantic, or on a railroad for twenty miles.

ON SELF-LIMITED DISEASES.

A DISCOURSE DELIVERED BEFORE THE MASSACHUSETTS MEDICAL SOCIETY, AT THEIR ANNUAL MEETING, MAY 27, 1835.*

THE death of medical men is an occurrence which eminently demands our attention; for it speaks to us of our science and of ourselves. It reminds us, that we, in our turn, are to become victims of the incompetency of our own art. It admonishes us that the sphere of our professional exertions is limited at last by insurmountable barriers. It brings with it the humiliating conclusion, that while other sciences have been carried forward, within our own time and almost under our own eyes, to a degree of unprecedented advancement, Medicine, in regard to some of its professed and most important objects, is still an ineffectual speculation. Observations are multiplied, but the observers disappear, and leave their task unfinished. We have seen the maturity

---

* At the beginning of this discourse, the customary obituary notice was taken of eminent members of the Society, deceased during the previous year

of age and the ardent purpose of youth called off from the half-cultivated field of their labors, expectations, and promise. It becomes us to look upon this deeply interesting subject with unprejudiced eyes, and to endeavor to elicit useful truth from the great lesson that surrounds us.

In comparing the advances which have been made during the present age, in different departments of Medical science, we are brought to the conclusion, that they have not all been cultivated with equally satisfactory success. Some of them have received new and important illustrations from scientific inquiry, but others are still surrounded with their original difficulties. The structure and functions of the human body, the laws which govern the progress of its diseases, and more especially the diagnosis of its morbid conditions, are better understood now than they were at the beginning of the present century. But the science of therapeutics, or the branch of knowledge by the application of which physicians are expected to remove diseases, has not, seemingly, attained to a much more elevated standing than it formerly possessed. The records of mortality attest its frequent failures; and the inability to control the event of diseases, which at times is felt by the most gifted and experienced practitioners, gives evidence that, in many cases, disease is more easily understood than cured.

This deficiency of the healing art is not justly

attributable to any want of sagacity or diligence on the part of the medical profession. It belongs rather to the inherent difficulties of the case; and is, after abating the effect of errors and accidents, to be ascribed to the apparent fact, that certain morbid processes in the human body have a definite and necessary career, from which they are not to be diverted by any known agents with which it is in our power to oppose them. To these morbid affections, the duration of which, and frequently the event also, are beyond the control of our present remedial means, I have, on the present occasion, applied the name of *Self-limited diseases;* and it will be the object of this discourse to endeavor to show the existence of such a class, and to inquire how far certain individual diseases may be considered as belonging to it.

By a self-limited disease, I would be understood to express one which receives limits from its own nature, and not from foreign influences: one which, after it has obtained foothold in the system, cannot, in the present state of our knowledge, be eradicated or abridged by art, but to which there is due a certain succession of processes, to be completed in a certain time; which time and processes may vary with the constitution and condition of the patient, and may tend to death or to recovery, but are not known to be shortened or greatly changed by medical treatment.

These expressions are not intended to apply to the palliation of diseases, for he who turns a pillow, or administers a seasonable draught of water to a patient, palliates his sufferings; but they apply to the more important consideration of removing diseases themselves, through medical means.

The existence of a class of diseases like those under consideration is, to a certain extent, already admitted, both by the profession and the public; and this admission is evinced by the use of certain familiar terms of expression. Thus, when people speak of a "settled disease," or of the time of "the run of a disease," it implies, on their part, a recognition of the law, that certain diseases regulate their own limits and period of continuance.

It is difficult to select a perfectly satisfactory or convincing example of a self-limited disease from among the graver morbid affections; because, in these affections, the solicitude of the practitioner usually leads him to the employment of remedies, in consequence of which the effect of remedies is mixed up with the phenomena of disease, so that the mind has difficulty in separating them. We must, therefore, seek for our most striking or decisive examples among those diseases which are sufficiently mild not to be thought to require ordinarily the use of remedies, and in which the natural history of the disease may be observed, divested of foreign influences. Such examples are found in the vaccine disease, the chicken-pox, and the salivation produced by mercury. These are strictly self-limited diseases, having their own rise, climax, and decline; and I know of no *medical* practice which is able, were it deemed necessary, to divert them from their appropriate course, or hasten their termination.

It may appear to some, that the distinction of these diseases from others is the old distinction of acute and chronic. Yet, on due inquiry, such an identification is not found to be sustained: for there are some acute diseases which, we have reason to believe, are shortened by the employment of remedies; while, on the other hand, certain chronic cases of disease are known to get well spontaneously, after years of continuance.

If the inquiry be made, why one disease has necessary limits while another is without them, the reply is not uniform, nor always easy to be made. Sometimes the law of the disease may be traced to the nature of the exciting cause. Thus the morbid poison of measles or of small-pox, when received into the body, produces a self-limited disease; but the morbid poisons of psora and syphilis may give rise to others which are not limited, except by medical treatment. Sometimes, also, the cause being the same, the result will depend on the part, organ, or texture which is affected. Thus, if we divide with a cutting instrument the cellular or muscular substance, we produce a self-limited disease; which, although it cannot by any art be healed within a certain number of days or weeks, yet in the end gets well spontaneously, by one process if the lips are in contact, and by another and slower process if they are separated.* But if, on the other hand, we divide a considerable artery, we have then an unlimited disease; and the hemorrhage or the aneurism which follows does not get well, except through the interposition of art.

The class of diseases under consideration comprehends morbid affections, differing greatly from each other in the time, place, and nature of their spontaneous developments; so that they may admit of at least three general subdivisions. These may be called, 1st. The *simple;* in which the disease observes a continuous time, and mostly a definite seat; 2d. The *paroxysmal;* in which the disease, having apparently disappeared, returns at its own periods; and, 3d. The *metastatic;* in which the disease undergoes metastasis, or spontaneous change of place. In the present state of our knowledge, we have no difficulty in finding examples of each of these subdivisions. There are also other examples, in which the disease, although capable of being in part influenced by medical treatment, still retains a portion of its original intractability, and has strong relations to the class in question.

---

* In one case, the disease is a solution of continuity; in the other, a solution of continuity and contact.

As a mode of directing our inquiries toward these diseases, we may suspect those complaints to be self-limited in which it is observed that the unwary and the sceptical, who neglect to resort to remedies, recover their health without them. We may also suspect diseases to be of this character when we find opposite modes of treatment recommended, and their success vouched for, by practitioners of authority and veracity. We may, moreover, attach the same suspicion to cases in which the supposed cure takes place under chance applications or inconsiderable remedies; as in the empirical modes of practice on the one hand, and the minute doses of the homœopathic method on the other. Lastly, we may apprehend that cases are fatally self-limited,* when enlightened physicians die themselves of the diseases which they had labored to illustrate, — as in the case of Corvisart, Laennec, Armstrong, and others.

In proceeding to enumerate more precisely some of the diseases which appear to me to be self-limited in their character, I approach the subject with diffidence. I am aware that the works of medical writers, and especially of medical compilers, teem with remedies and modes of treatment for all diseases; and that, in the morbid affections of

---

* In the following article, "On the Treatment of Disease," it has been found convenient to divide diseases into the curable, the self-limited, and the incurable. In a general sense, however, the last term falls within the second

which we speak, remedies are often urged with zeal and confidence, even though sometimes of an opposite character. Moreover, in many places, at the present day, a charm is popularly attached to what is called an active, bold, or heroic practice; and a corresponding reproach awaits the opposite course, which is cautious, palliative, and expectant. In regard to the diseases which have been called self-limited, I would not be understood to deny that remedies capable of removing them may exist; I would only assert that they have not yet been proved to exist.

Under the simple self-limited diseases, we may class *hooping-cough*. This disease has its regular increase, height, and decline, occupying ordinarily from one to six months, but in some mild cases only two or three weeks. During this period, medical treatment is for the most part of no avail. Narcotic appliances may diminish the paroxysm, but without abridging the disease. After hooping-cough has reached its climax, change of air sometimes appears to hasten convalescence. Also if inflammatory or other morbid affections supervene upon the pure disease, they may become subjects for medical treatment. With these exceptions, hooping-cough appears to be a self-limited disease.

Most of the class of diseases usually denominated eruptive fevers are self-limited. *Measles*, for example, is never known to be cut short by art, or abridged of its natural career; neither can this career be extended, or the disease kept in the system beyond its natural duration, by the power of medicine. *Scarlet fever*, a disease of which we have had much and fatal experience during the last three years, is eminently of the same character. The reasons which induce me thus to regard it are the following. The writings of medical observers agree in assigning to it a common or average period of duration, and this is confirmed by the observations of practitioners at the present day. From this average duration and character there are great natural deviations; the disease being sometimes so slight as to attract the notice of none but medical eyes, and sometimes so malignant that treatment is admitted to be hopeless. The modes of treatment which have had most testimony in their favor are various and opposite. By Dr. Fothergill, stimulants were relied on; by Dr. Currie, cold water; by Dr. Southwood Smith, and others, blood-letting. But it is not satisfactorily shown that either of these modes of practice has been particularly successful; for, where the writers have furnished us any thing like definite or numerical results, it does not appear that the mortality was less in their hands than it is among those who pursue a more expectant practice. The post-mortuary appearances, which in many diseases furnish useful lessons for practice, are in scarlet fever extremely various and uncertain; and sometimes no morbid changes, sufficient to account for death, can be discovered in any of the vital organs or great cavities.

Small-pox is another example of the class of affections under consideration, its approach and disappearance being irrespective of medical practice. It may, at first view, appear that inoculation has placed artificial limits on this disease. But it must be recollected, that inoculated small-pox is itself only a milder variety of the same disease, having its own customary limits of extent and duration, which are fixed quite as much as those of the distinct and confluent forms of the natural disease.

Erysipelas is an eruptive fever, having strong analogies with those which have been detailed. It is not certain that art can very materially affect either the duration or the extent of this malady. If a physician is called to a case of erysipelas, which is beginning to be developed upon a part of the face; and if he is asked, whether the disease will extend to the crown or the neck, or to the right ear or the left,— he cannot tell. And if he is asked to prevent it from visiting either of these places, I know of no satisfactory evidence that he can do it.

Erysipelas, however, in a great number of simple or exanthematous cases, in subjects previously healthy, gets well without any treatment; and in a great number of deep-seated and phlegmonous cases, as well as those in which vital organs are affected, it proves fatal under the most approved methods of medical and surgical practice. It is true that patients have recovered under punctures, incisions, and cautery. It is also true that they have died under the same operations: so that it may be submitted as a doubtful point, whether we yet possess adequate evidence that erysipelas is not also a self limited disease.

It is a question of great interest to the medical profession, to determine whether *typhoid fever* is a disease susceptible of control from medical means. On this subject no one now doubts that, if the disease is once fairly established in the system, it cannot be eradicated by art; but must complete a certain natural course, before convalescence can take place. But a question still exists, whether this disease is capable of being jugulated or broken up, at its outset, by the early application of remedies.

It must be allowed that attacks of disease resembling those of typhoid sometimes speedily disappear during the use of remedies; but it is by no means certain that such cases are actually cases of typhoid. The diagnosis of this disease, during the first day or two, is extremely difficult, its character being simulated by different febrile and inflammatory affections; so that if a patient, under the use of remedies, succeeds in avoiding protracted disease, we are not justified in saying that the disease he has escaped was typhoid or typhus fever. Andral, whose experiments on the different modes of treatment in continued fever are very extensive, has stated that in a number of cases observed by him, in which the fever was sufficiently intense, the disease ceased in twenty-four or forty-eight hours without any treatment except that of rest and a regulated diet.*

Moreover, in weighing the influence of treatment, it ought to be recollected, that during the existence of any prevailing epidemic, mild cases, partaking of a similar character to that of the reigning disease, continually appear among the less susceptible part of the community. Thus cholera is attended by diarrhœa or cholerine, influenza by mild catarrh, small-pox by varioloid, scarlet fever by slight sore throats or ephemeral eruptions, &c. Now, although these cases are in reality modified examples of the grave diseases which they accompany, yet I believe that no well-informed physician will attribute the mildness or shortness of their character to his own particular practice.

On the other hand, it is certain that cases of real typhoid do often come under active treatment at an early stage, without being broken up or disarmed of their appropriate consequences. This particularly happens when the disease is endemic in families; so that successive cases begin, as it were, under the eye of the attending physician, who has every

---

* Clinique, iii. 619.

possible inducement to detect and prevent them, if he can. In such families, indeed, it will sometimes happen that febrile attacks of different kinds, consequent upon fatigue and anxiety, and perhaps partaking of the typhoid character, will take place among the friends and attendants of the sick; and these may disappear speedily under rest and evacuations. But that grave and specific typhoid fever will thus disappear is a point of which we as yet want proof. That it sometimes fails to disappear we have abundant proof.

Typhoid fever has, in many respects, a marked affinity with the class of eruptive fevers, which are supposed to depend on a specific morbid poison, and which no one pretends to intercept after the body has become infected with them. Scarlet fever and measles, for example, when once established, require a certain number of days to finish their course; so also does typhoid. Scarlet fever and measles can, in most cases, be had but once during life; but to this general rule there are exceptions. The same is precisely true in regard to typhoid. The contagiousness of scarlet fever is a point of dispute among physicians; and so is that of typhoid. Scarlet fever is attended by an eruption on the skin. Typhoid fever also has for one of its most constant symptoms a red, lenticular eruption, consisting of a few scattered rose-colored pimples, appearing chiefly on the trunk, from about the sixth to the nineteenth day of the disease. There also occurs, in most subjects, a minute, vesicular eruption of *sudamina*, about the neck and elsewhere. In scarlet fever, moreover, certain portions of the mucous membrane undergo morbid alterations, particularly on the tonsils and other parts of the fauces; and these frequently degenerate into ulcers, affecting the subjacent textures. In like manner, in typhoid fever, the mucous membrane of the granular patches in the small intestines, which have been named after the anatomist Peyer, undergo morbid changes; and these changes are followed by ulcerations, and sometimes perforations, of the intestine. This fact, established by the researches of Louis and other pathologists in Paris, has been abundantly confirmed by post mortem examinations made in this country during the last few years.* If it be objected to the proposed classification of this fever, that the *taches* are sometimes few in number, or wholly absent: it is equally true, that the pustules of inoculated small-pox are likewise often very few, or absent; and that the eruption of scarlatina sometimes wholly fails to appear. The sore throat also in the latter disease is wanting quite as often, to say the least, as the morbid affection of Peyer's glands.

Before quitting the subject, I beg leave to introduce the opinion of one or two medical writers, in regard to the possibility of interrupting or breaking

---

* 1835.

up this disease by means of art. M. Louis, of whose researches in regard to typhoid fever it is but small praise to say that they are more exact and comprehensive than those of any living writer, is of opinion that the disease cannot be thus interrupted. "Experience," says he, "has shown that a well-marked typhoid affection is not capable of being broken up." * To this testimony of one of the most eminent teachers in the French metropolis, it may not be amiss to add that of an American physician, whose opportunities for observing the disease in different parts of New England were extensive, and whose "Essay on Typhus Fever" well merits an attentive perusal. The late Dr. Nathan Smith, in the course of some remarks on the possibility of interrupting this disease at commencement, observes, "During the whole of my practice, I have never been satisfied that I have cut short a single case of typhus that I knew to be such." †

Having said thus much, I leave the subject of the tractability of typhus and typhoid fever to the light

---

* "L'experience ayant montré, que l'affection typhoide bien caractérisée, n'est pas susceptible d'etre jugulée, ce qui n'est guere moins vrai, d'ailleurs, suivant toutes les apparences, de la peripneumonie et des autres maladies inflammatoires." — LOUIS, *Gastro-entérite*, ii. 512.

Andral says, in regard to the different modes of treatment in typhus, "Quelles que soient les méthodes employées, il est un certain nombre de cas où, sans que ces méthodes y prennent part, la nature conduit la maladie à une terminaison heureuse ou funeste." — *Clinique*, i. 651.

† At the time of the publication alluded to, the distinction between typhus and typhoid fevers had not been well made out. The distinction is good, though writers of authority differ on the subject.

of future investigation. It is but justice to state, that numerous and highly respectable authorities are declared in favor of the efficacy of art in shortening and mitigating these diseases; and it will be a source of gratification to the friends of humanity and science, should it ultimately be settled, that the active treatment now usually pursued at the commencement of cases is instrumental in lessening their duration, severity, or danger.

Among the morbid affections which have now been enumerated may be found sufficient examples of continued diseases which receive limits from their own nature, and not from the interference of art. Whether the number of these diseases may not be augmented by additions from among other fevers and acute inflammations, I am not prepared to decide. It is difficult, however, to withhold the belief, that a more extended inquiry must probably serve greatly to multiply, rather than diminish, the number of maladies to which this character will be found appropriate.*

We come next to a second order of self-limited diseases, of which the term *paroxysmal* is sufficiently descriptive. This term applies to certain morbid affections, which occur in fits or paroxysms, leaving

---

* There is not room here to discuss the question whether pneumonia and other acute inflammations fall under the category of self-limitation. Blood-letting, in proper cases, apparently lessens the severity and danger of these diseases. But it is not apparent that it abridges their duration. Dysentery may be accounted a self-limited disease.

the patient comparatively well in the intervals; at the same time that the paroxysms themselves can neither be foreseen, prevented, nor, as far as we know, materially abridged in their duration. At the head of this subdivision stands *Epilepsy*, a disease which has long been eminent as an opprobrium of medicine, and for which it is believed the healing art has not yet devised a cure. The first attacks of epilepsy, especially while there is any doubt as to the nature of the malady, are usually made the subjects of active and various treatment. But, after the recurring paroxysms have established the character of the disease, if active medical practice is persevered in, it is rather to satisfy the anxiety of friends than the judgment of the practitioner.

Angina pectoris, appropriately called by Dr. Good, *Sternalgia*, is a paroxysmal disease, which in many cases controls its own movements. The anatomical character of this disease is not uniform; and, I may add, the same is true of its medical treatment. And in this place it may be proper to state, that various incurable lesions of the heart, lungs, brain, and other viscera, do not apparently destroy life by a regular, undeviating march; but that, as far as their outward phenomena afford evidence, they seem to proceed by alternate fits and pauses, undergoing in their progress all states except that of retrogradation. This is apparently true in regard to tubercle, carcinoma, ossification, hypertrophy, and some other morbid alterations. It is also even true in regard to old age itself.

Thirty years ago we might have added *gout* to the opprobrious list under consideration. But as we may now be said to possess the means of shortening the paroxysms by the use of certain acrid narcotics, and as an abstemious life goes far towards lessening the frequency and violence of the recurrence, we may be justified in withdrawing gout from the place it would otherwise occupy.

The diseases of mania and melancholy, asthma when it depends on emphysema of the lungs, gravel in the kidneys, and the symptoms produced by ascarides in the rectum, furnish other examples of maladies which manifest themselves in unforeseen paroxysms. Cases which bear the names of all the above diseases are undoubtedly relieved, and sometimes even removed, by medicine; but it is equally true that other cases are wholly intractable, both as to their recurrence, their duration, and their susceptibility of much change from medical treatment. And it will come to the recollection of many practitioners, that they have, in the course of their lives, believed themselves to have cured these diseases, when in fact they have only witnessed the spontaneous subsidence of a paroxysm.

The last subdivision of our subject includes what may be called *metastatic* diseases. By this term I wish to express certain morbid affections, which pass by metastasis from one part of the body to another, for the most part independently of artificial influence. Of this kind are certain *cutaneous* affections, more especially some which are chronic and hereditary. Many persons pass a considerable portion of their lives in alternate annoyance from a disease of the skin, and from its vicarious substitute in some internal organ. Others again are afflicted with hemorrhagic or purulent *discharges*, which at times disappear only to be succeeded by equally troublesome affections in a different part. *Gonorrhœa* cannot be prevented from occasional metastasis of inflammation; and *mumps* are sometimes found to undergo the same transition. But perhaps the most remarkable example of a metastatic disease is found in *acute rheumatism*. This morbid affection often begins to discover itself in a limited and comparatively unimportant part of the system. From thence, in grave cases, it travels by successive migrations from joint to joint, and from limb to limb, till it has visited nearly all the great articulations of the body. It also attacks organs of sense, and viscera which are essential to life. During the course of these migrations, the attending physician cannot foretell at any given stage what part will be next invaded by the disease, neither can he protect any part from being thus invaded; nor can he control the period during which the disease will reside in any particular part previously to its next metastasis. Nevertheless acute rheumatism is susceptible of great palliation though of little abridgment, and, after having run out its career, terminates in spontaneous recovery; not, however, in some cases, until it has laid the foundation of serious organic derangements, especially of the heart.

I forbear to dilate on the structural lesions of different organs, many of which can only be cured by the extirpation of the part in which they reside, thus sacrificing the integrity of the body to the preservation of life; and in which extirpation cannot avail, when the seat of the disease is in a vital part. I also pass over the pestilential epidemics of plague, yellow fever, malignant dysentery, and cholera; diseases about which the medical profession have great differences of opinion, and of which thousands die annually, though hundreds of volumes have been written for their preservation.

It may perhaps appear that the views which have now been taken of the power of medicine, in so large a class of diseases, are gloomy and discouraging; and that an unworthy tribute is paid to the labors of those physicians who have patiently studied and ardently acted for the benefit of humanity. Such views, however, are far from being the object of the present discourse. Were it permitted by the compass of the subject under consideration, it would be a very grateful task to enumerate those maladies of the human frame over which we have reason to believe that medicine has obtained decisive influence. To a medical audience, it is unnecessary to recall the instances of pain relieved, spasms controlled, inflammations checked, and diseased associations broken up, under limitable diseases, by the agency of the healing art. Were there no other trophy for the medical profession to boast, it is sufficient to know that the diseases of small-pox and syphilis alone would have entailed misery and extermination on a large portion of our species, had not medical science discovered the prevention of the one, and the successful management of the other.

But that the usefulness of our profession may extend, our knowledge must go on to increase; and the foundation of all knowledge is truth. For truth, then, we must earnestly seek, even when its developments do not flatter our professional pride, nor attest the infallibility of our art. To discover truth in science is often extremely difficult; in no science is it more difficult than in medicine. Independently of the common defects of medical evidence, our self-interest, our self-esteem, and sometimes even our feelings of humanity, may be arrayed against the truth. It is difficult to view the operations of nature, divested of the interferences of art; so much do our habits and partialities incline us to neglect the former, and to exaggerate the importance of the latter. The mass of medical testimony is always on the side of art. Medical books are prompt to point out the cure of diseases. Medical journals are filled with the crude productions of aspirants to the cure of diseases. Medical schools find it incumbent on them to teach the cure of diseases. The young student goes forth into the world, believing that if he does not cure diseases, it is his own fault. Yet when a score or two of years have passed over his head, he will come at length to the conviction, that some diseases are controlled by nature alone. He will often pause, at the end of a long and anxious attendance, and ask himself how far the result of the case is different from what it would have been under less officious treatment than that which he has pursued; how many, in the accumulated array of remedies which have supplanted each other in the patient's chamber, have actually been instrumental in doing him any good. He will also ask himself whether, in the course of his life, he has not had occasion to change his opinion, perhaps more than once, in regard to the management of the disease in question; and whether he does not, even now, feel the want of additional light.

Medicine has been rightly called a conjectural art; because, in many of its deductions, and especially in those which relate to the cure of diseases, positive evidence is denied to us. We are seldom justified in concluding that our remedies have promoted the cure of a disease, until we know that cases exactly similar in time, place, and circumstances have failed to do equally well under the omission of those remedies;. and such cases, moreover, must exist in sufficient numbers to justify the admission of a general law on their basis. Nothing can be more illogical than to draw our general conclusions, as we are sometimes too apt to do, from the results of insulated and remarkable cases, for such cases may be found in support of any extravagance in medicine; and if there is any point in which the vulgar differ from the judicious part of the profession, it is in drawing premature and sweeping conclusions from scanty premises of this kind. Moreover, it is in many cases not less illogical to attribute the removal of diseases, or even of their troublesome symptoms, to the means which have been most recently employed. It is a common error to infer, that things which are consecutive in the order of time have necessarily the relation of cause and effect. It often happens that the last remedy used bears off the credit of having removed an obstruction, or cured a disease; whereas in fact the result may have been owing to the first remedy employed, or to the joint effect of all the remedies, or to the act of nature, uninfluenced by any of the remedies. We see this remarkably exemplified in recoveries from amenorrhœa and from various irregularities of the alimentary canal.

An inherent difficulty, which every medical man

finds to stand in the way of an unbiassed and satisfactory judgment, is the heavy responsibility which rests upon the issue of his cases. When a friend or valuable patient is committed to our charge, we cannot stand by, as curious spectators, to study the natural history of his disease. We feel that we are called on to attempt his rescue by vigorous means, so that at least the fault of omission shall not lie upon our charge. We proceed to put in practice those measures which on the whole have appeared to us to do most good; and, if these fail us, we resort to other measures, which we have read of or heard of. And, at the end of our attendance, we may be left in uncertainty whether the duration of sickness has been shortened or lengthened by our practice, and whether the patient is really indebted to us for good or evil. In the study of experimental philosophy, we rarely admit a conclusion to be true, until its opposite has been proved to be untrue. But in medicine we are often obliged to be content to accept as evidence the results of cases, which have been finished under treatment; because we have not the opportunity to know how far these results would have been different, had the cases been left to themselves. And it too frequently happens, that medical books do not relieve our difficulties on this score; for a great deal of our practical literature consists in reports of interesting, extraordinary, and successful results, published by men who have a doctrine to establish or a reputation to build. "Few authors," says Andral, "have published all the cases they have observed; and the greater part have only taken the trouble to present to us those facts which favor their own views."* A prevailing error, among writers on therapeutics, proceeds from their professional or personal reluctance to admit that the healing art, as practised by them, is not, or may not be, all-sufficient in all cases; so that on this subject they suffer themselves, as well as their readers, to be deceived. Hence we have no disease, however intractable or fatal, for which the press has not poured forth its asserted remedies. Even of late we have seen unfailing cures of cholera, successively announced in almost every city in which that pestilence, unchecked, has completed its work of devastation!

It is only when, in connection with these flattering exhibitions, we have a full and faithful report of the failures of medical practice, in similar and in common cases, setting forth not only the truth but the whole truth, that we have a basis sufficiently broad to erect a superstructure, in therapeutics, on which dependence may be placed. Such, it must give the friends of science gratification to observe, is a part of the rigid method which characterizes the

---

* Bien peu d'auteurs ont publié tous les cas qu'ils ont observés, et la plupart ne se sont empressés de nous transmettre que les faits que caressaient leurs idées. — *Clinique*, iii. 618.

best examples of the modern French school; and such, it is not difficult to foresee, must ultimately be the only species of evidence on this subject to which the medical profession will pay deference.

It appears to me to be one of the most important desiderata in practical medicine, to ascertain, in regard to each doubtful disease, how far its cases are really self-limited, and how far they are controllable by any treatment. This question can be satisfactorily settled only by instituting, in a large number of cases which are well identified and nearly similar, a fair experimental comparison of the different active and expectant modes of practice, with their varieties in regard to time, order, and degree. This experiment is vast, considering the number of combinations which it must involve, and even much more extensive than a corresponding series of pathological observations; yet every honest and intelligent observer may contribute to it his mite. Opportunities for such observations, and especially for monographs of diseases, are found in the practice of most physicians; yet hospitals and other public charities afford the most appropriate field for instituting them upon a large scale. The aggregate of results, successful and unsuccessful, circumstantially and impartially reported by competent observers, will give us a near approximation to truth, in regard to the diseases of the time and place in which the experiments are instituted. The *numeri-*

cal method employed by Louis in his extensive pathological researches, and now adopted by his most distinguished contemporaries in France, affords the means of as near an approach to certainty on this head, as the subject itself admits. And I may add, that no previous medical inquirer has apparently submitted to the profession any species of evidence so broad in its foundations, and so convincing in its results, as that which characterizes the great works of this author on Phthisis and Typhoid fever.

In regard to acknowledged self-limited diseases, the question will naturally arise, whether the practitioner is called on to do nothing for the benefit of his patient; whether he shall fold his hands, and look passively on the progress of a disease which he cannot interrupt. To this I would answer,—by no means. The opportunities of doing good may be as great in these diseases as in any others; for, in treating every disease, there is a right method and a wrong. In the first place, we may save the patient from much harm, not only by forbearing ourselves to afflict him with unnecessary practice, but also by preventing the ill-judged activity of others. For the same reason that we would not suffer him to be shaken in his bed, when rest was considered necessary to him, we should not allow him to be tormented with useless and annoying applications, in a disease of settled destiny. It should be remembered, that all cases are susceptible of errors of commission as well as of omission; and that, by an excessive application of the means of art, we may frustrate the intentions of nature when they are salutary, or embitter the approach of death when it is inevitable. What practitioner, I would ask, ever rendered a greater service to mankind than Ambrose Paré and his subsequent coadjutors, who introduced into modern surgery the art of healing by the first intention? These men with vast difficulty succeeded in convincing the profession, that, instead of the old method of treating incised wounds by keeping them open with forcible and painful applications, it was better simply to place the parts securely in their natural situation, and then to let them alone. In the second place, we may do much good by a palliative and preventive course, by alleviating pain, procuring sleep, guarding the diet, regulating the alimentary canal, — in fine, by obviating such sufferings as admit of mitigation, and preventing or removing the causes of others which are incidental, but not necessary, to the state of disease. In doing this, we must distinguish between the disease itself, and the accidents of the disease; for the latter often admit of relief when the former does not. We should also inquire whether the original cause of the disease or any accessory cause is still operating, and, if so, whether it can in any measure be prevented or removed; as, for example, when it exists in the habits of life of the patient, in the local atmosphere, or in the presence of any other deleterious agent. Lastly, by a just prognosis, founded on a correct view of the case, we may sustain the patient and his friends during the inevitable course of the disease; and may save them from the pangs of disappointed hope on the one side, or of unnecessary despondency on the other.

It will be seen that, in the foregoing remarks, a low estimate has been placed on the resources of art, when compared with those of nature. But I may be excused for doing this in the presence of an audience of educated men, and the members of a society whose motto is, *Naturâ duce.* The longer and the more philosophically we contemplate this subject, the more obvious it will appear that the physician is but the minister and servant of nature; that, in cases like those which have been engaging our consideration, we can do little more than follow in the train of disease, and endeavor to aid nature in her salutary intentions, or to remove obstacles out of her path. How little, indeed, could we accomplish without her aid! It has been wisely observed, by Sir Gilbert Blane, that "the benefit derivable to mankind at large, from artificial remedies, is so limited, that, if a spontaneous principle of restoration had not existed, the human species would long ago have been extinct."*

---

* Medical Logic, p. 49.

The importance and usefulness of the medical profession, instead of being diminished, will always be elevated exactly in proportion as it understands itself, weighs justly its own powers, and professes simply what it can accomplish. It is no derogation from the importance of our art, that we cannot always control the events of life and death, or even of health and sickness. The incompetency which we feel in this respect is shared by almost every man upon whom the great responsibilities of society are devolved. The statesman cannot control the destinies of nations, nor the military commander the event of battles. The most eloquent pleader may fail to convince the judgment of his hearers, and the most skilful pilot may not be able to weather the storm. Yet it is not the less necessary that responsible men should study deeply and understandingly the science of their respective vocations. It is not the less important, for the sake of those whose safety is, and always will be, committed to their charge, that they should look with unbiassed judgment upon the necessary results of inevitable causes. And while an earnest and inquiring solicitude should always be kept alive, in regard to the improvement of professional knowledge, it should never be forgotten, that knowledge has for its only just and lasting foundation a rigid, impartial, and inflexible requisition of the truth.

ON THE TREATMENT OF DISEASE.

AN INTRODUCTORY LECTURE, DELIVERED BEFORE THE MEDICAL CLASS AT THE MASSACHUSETTS MEDICAL COLLEGE IN BOSTON, NOV. 3, 1852.

OF the sciences which have most occupied the time and labor of mankind, a certain number lead, by their investigations, to clear and positive results; and enlarge the amount of human knowledge, by the discovery and promulgation of absolute truth. Another portion lead only to results which are probable or presumptive in their character, and which furnish to mankind rules of action, in cases where better lights cannot be obtained. To the former class has been given the name of exact sciences, and to the latter the name of presumptive or conjectural sciences. Mathematics form an exact science, on the conclusions of which, when once known, there can be no difference of opinion. In like manner, chemistry and mechanics, astronomy and portions of natural history, are examples of exact sciences; the demonstrations of which, when once made clear, may afterwards be modified and enlarged, but are never fundamentally shaken. On the other hand, the important sciences of ethics and politics, of commerce and finance, of government and speculative theology, are inexact in many of their principles, as is proved by the widely different constructions under which men receive them and apply them to practice.

It would at first seem that the exact sciences were those most worthy the cultivation of intelligent minds, inasmuch as they lead to satisfactory, and therefore to gratifying, results; and because, in their more elevated departments, they involve and require some of the highest reaches of the human intellect. But in the opinions of mankind, as evinced by their practice, the opposite judgment prevails; and probably nine tenths of the labor of educated and intellectual men are employed on studies which are, in their nature, uncertain and conjectural.

The cause of this great ascendency in the attention given to the inexact sciences is to be found in the vast and paramount importance of their subjects, and also in the difficulty of consummating their great ends. It is much more important to mankind to know how to avoid anarchy and crime, war, famine, poverty, and pestilence, than it is to know that the planet Saturn has a ring, or that a lily has six stamens, that light can be polarized, or that potass can be decomposed. Yet, while the latter propositions are susceptible of absolute demonstration, the former processes, which bear directly on human happiness or misery, are frequently removed beyond our foresight or control. The wisest men often fail to influence the destinies of states, families, and individuals; and the shrewdest calculators are baffled in regard to a coming crop, a pecuniary crisis, a glut in the commercial market, or a change in the public morals. Nevertheless, the wise man, conscious of superior talent, and the philanthropist, desirous of the public weal, and even the interested man, who looks to his personal advantage and progress, must give themselves and their energies to studies which involve the immediate wants of their fellow-men, even though their best-directed efforts should fail of the desired results. And the simple reason is, that, if the best-qualified minds decline to undertake this task, it will most assuredly be assumed by the ignorant and presumptuous.

Pre-eminent among the inexact and speculative sciences stands *practical medicine*, a science older than civilization, cultivated and honored in all ages, powerful for good or for evil, progressive in its character, but still unsettled in its principles; remunerative in fame and fortune to its successful cultivators, and rich in the fruits of a good conscience to its honest votaries. Encumbered as it is with difficulty, fallacy, and doubt, medicine yet constitutes one of the most attractive of the learned professions. It is largely represented in every city, village, and hamlet. Its imperfections are lost sight of in the overwhelming importance of its objects. The living look to it for succor; the dying call on it for rescue.

The greatest boons and the most important objects presented to our aspirations in this life are not to be approached through paths which are straight and unmistakable. The avenues to most of them are shadowed by doubts, or clogged with incessant obstacles. Next to the spiritual welfare of men, the preservation of their lives, the peace and safety of their communities, the acquirement and preservation of their worldly goods are among the objects which take strongest hold on their desires. Yet grave doubts are justifiable, whether any precise means have yet been agreed upon by which these desirable ends can with certainty be attained. And if any one deems it a reproach on medicine, that its cultivators have not arrived at a common faith and practice, let him consider whether the laborers in other fields, however honest their intentions, are agreed in their theological creeds and political platforms.

Considering the great importance of the objects of medicine, the frequent and earnest appeals made for its assistance, and the vast sums annually expended in its remuneration, it is not surprising that disappointment and complaint often follow the failures, necessary or unnecessary, of medical practice.

"Man is of few days, and full of trouble." Yet, in the face of this acknowledged truth, he requests and expects that his physician will provide him with many days, and remove at least his bodily troubles. This expectation on his part is reasonable or otherwise, according to the circumstances under which it is made. It is unreasonable, if his case is helpless, and he is merely paying the debt of suffering and death which his mortal nature exacts. But it is reasonable and proper, if his complaint is of a curable kind; or if, whether curable or not, his physician has claimed and vaunted the power to remove it.

Most men form an exaggerated estimate of the powers of medicine, founded on the common acceptation of the name, that medicine is the art of curing diseases. That this is a false definition, is evident from the fact that many diseases are incurable, and that one such disease must at last happen to every living man. A far more just definition would be, that medicine is the art of understanding diseases, and of curing or relieving them when possible. Under this acceptation, our science would at least be exonerated from reproach, and would stand on a basis capable of supporting a reasonable and durable system for the amelioration of human maladies.

Every young man, who proposes to become a member of the medical profession, should ask himself whether he considers medicine a liberal and honorable science, to be followed for the good it may do to mankind; or as a dishonest trade, to be pursued for the purpose of profiting himself by the deception of his fellow-men. If he accepts his profession in the first sense, he will strive to understand his science in all its bearings, and practise it with conscientiousness and fidelity; if in the latter, he will put his conscience aside, and study only the low arts which entrap the credulous and unwary.

With the trade of medicine I have nothing to do. Knowing that I address an ingenuous and cultivated audience, composed mainly of young men who are looking forward to an honest and honorable place in professional life, I make no apology for proceeding to express my belief of the manner in which medicine should be practised and disease treated, for the reciprocal benefit of him who gives and of him who receives its aids.

Let no one deceive himself by believing that success, stable, permanent, honorable success, can be attained without knowledge of the great principles of the profession and science of medicine. This knowledge must consist in an accurate acquaintance with the structure and offices of the human body, and the laws of its healthy condition. After these follows the science of pathology, involving the great and fundamental art of diagnosis, by which the diseases of the human body are detected, and distinguished rightly from each other. The power of distinguishing diseases lies at the root of all correct and enlightened practice, and without it all medical action is empirical and fortuitous. There is no more pernicious error than for a physician to believe that he can prescribe safely for the symptoms of a sick man, without understanding, in some measure, the nature of his disease. Symptoms are of various import, according to the seat of their origin and the nature of their causes; and if taken alone, without a correct interpretation of these attendant considerations, they often lead to a wrong result, or to no result at all. A patient not unfrequently sends for a physician on account of a certain symptom which is distressing him, and which may be, for example, a pain in the abdomen or in the head. Now, a pain in the abdomen may arise from colic or peritonitis, from rheumatism or neuralgia, from dysentery, from calculus, carcinoma, or strangulation. And, in like manner, a pain in the head may arise from a multitude of different and even opposite causes. Now it is well known that the kind of treatment which is effectual in one case is pernicious in another; and he who prescribes for the symptom irrespectively of the cause, is quite as likely to do mischief to his patient as good, and quite as likely to destroy life as to save it.

If the question be asked, what makes a great physician, and one who is appealed to by his peers, and by the discerning portion of the public, for council in difficult cases, I would answer, that *he is a great physician who, above other men, understands diagnosis.* It is not he who promises to cure all maladies; who has a remedy ready for every symptom, or one remedy for all symptoms; who boasts that success never fails him, when his daily history gives the lie to such assertion. It is rather he who, with just discrimination, looks at a case in all its difficulties; who, to habits of correct reasoning, adds the acquirements obtained from study and observation; who is trustworthy in common things for his common sense, and in professional things for his judgment, learning, and experience; who forms his opinion, positive or approximative, according to the evidence; who looks at the necessary results of inevitable causes; who promptly does what man may do of good, and carefully avoids what he may do of evil. Examples are rare of this perfection; yet, for an approach to such a standard of professional excellence, I would venture to direct your remembrance to the venerable ex-professor, fortunately yet among us, of the theory and practice in this University.

Every citizen, whose capacity is able to reach the ordinary affairs of life, is aware that the persons most capable of discharging the common offices, or of exercising the common arts and duties of life, are the individuals who have, by talents, education, and practice, become EXPERTS in those arts and duties; and that, on the other hand, those persons who profess to have acquired knowledge by intuition, to have become learned without labor, and to have arrived by short cuts at results and qualifications which demand years of preparatory training, must be incompetent and treacherous sources of reliance. And it is the general admission of this truth which gives support and confidence to the various professions, arts, and callings to which men devote their lives.

A little machine, called a watch, is carried about by most persons; and, when this machine has stopped or is out of order, they do not lay their own ignorant hands upon it, but submit the case to the skill of an expert, who is known to be qualified to judge and act in such cases. It is the duty of this artist, when applied to, to examine the interior of the watch; to ascertain, by the use of his skill, in what part the disease is situated; and to apply to that part the appropriate remedy. If a spring or a chain is broken, it must be restored; if the wheels are out of gear, they must be put in place; if the hands only have caught, they have only to be liberated, and if the pivots are dry and rough, they must be oiled or cleaned; and, lastly, if the watch has had a destructive fall, if it has been crushed by being trodden on, if it has lain a month in the salt water, or if it is worn out by running steadily for threescore years and ten, then the case is incurable; and the only palliative advice which the practitioner can render is, that the owner should procure a new watch, or reconcile himself to do without one.

But suppose there resides in the place a watch-doctor who prescribes for symptoms, and who, among other things, has a remedy for the symptom of stopping; and that this remedy consists in a certain kind of friction, shaking, or manipulation, an ointment applied to the outside, or an invisible particle of some nugatory substance inserted into the inside; and suppose that one or two watches in a hundred, which had stopped by accident, should by accident resume their motions under such treatment,—could any thing but the most unmitigated folly draw the inference, that such a person is entitled to become the accredited horologer to the community?

What is so conspicuously true in the common business of life, is only an example of what is more vitally true in the practice of medicine. If a man has had the misfortune to get a shot or a stab in his body, he does not need a doctor who administers a specific dose or a sovereign plaster for holes in the body: he wants a man who can tell him whether the wound has passed inside or outside of his peritoneum, and whether it is requisite for him to make his will or to make arrangements for pursuing his journey.

But the prescribing for symptoms in the dark is not the only instance in which false logic has entered into medical reasoning. It is not less absurd to suppose, that disconnected events, which have closely followed each other, have therefore a necessary dependence upon each other. Shrewd, practical men do not thus govern themselves in the common affairs of life. A merchant, about to send a ship to sea, endeavors to find a captain to take charge of her who understands navigation, who can keep his run and determine his place, who studies the weather and is on the look-out for a lee shore, and who in emergencies can judge whether it is necessary or not to cut away the masts or throw over the cargo. But suppose a man appears, and such have been, who announces that he has a specific bottle of oil with which he cures tempests, and by pouring a teaspoonful of which upon the waves the storm is speedily made to cease! Would any prudent owner intrust his vessel to such a man and on such grounds, even though he should produce a hundred certificates that storms had stopped in half a day or half an hour after the application of his remedy? For these certificates, if true, would only prove, that, in a certain number of cases, a result had followed by accident, which common sense, and if necessary a thousand opposite cases, would show had nothing to do with the pretended cause.

What would be true of the apparent or alleged cure of a tempest at sea, is no less true of the pseudo-cures which every day take place in diseases which are self-limited, paroxysmal, or recidivous in their character. There are doubtless living many men who believe themselves to have been cured half a dozen times of various diseases, of fevers and inflammations, of neuralgia, rheumatism, gout, and asthma, and each time perhaps by a different remedy; but who, on the next imprudence or returning period, are destined to find themselves feverish, neuralgic, gouty, or asthmatic still.

Deceptions in medicine are occasioned not only by the dishonesty of charlatans, but quite as often by the well-meaning credulity of other practitioners, whose intellect is impulsive or whose education has been unduly curtailed. It is so flattering to a man's self-love to believe that his chance shots have sometimes taken effect, that physicians of regular position may pass their lives in mere speculative and random efforts at curing diseases, shutting their eyes against their own failures, and not allowing themselves to consider, that, in a certain portion of successful cases which they had failed to understand, the disease in truth got well without, or perhaps in spite of, their misdirected and embarrassing practice.

Medicine is a great good, and an unquestionable blessing to mankind, when it is administered by discriminating and intelligent hands with sincerity and good judgment. It disappoints expectation, and fails to accomplish its mission, when the agent who dispenses it falls into the mistaken resource of professing infallibility, and of raising hopes which he knows not how to accomplish. No man is deemed to be safe in his worldly affairs who is afraid to look into his own pecuniary condition. Neither is a physician safe in his practice or his reputation who is afraid to face the case of his patient in all its bearings. That man is most to be relied on who looks calmly and understandingly at the emergency before him; who knows the import of signs, and deduces from them the probable tenor of coming events; who is aware of the great truth, that all men must die, but is also aware of the more gratifying truth, that most sick men recover; and who, in particular exigencies, inquires of his reason and his knowledge in which of these two immediate categories his patient is placed, and how far the event of the case is within his control. He will then interfere or he will wait, he will act or he will forbear, as he only knows how who can form a correct verdict from the evidence before him, and who knows the immeasurable good or harm which hangs on medical practice.

The vulgar standard of medical character depends very much on the supposed successful result of cases. But this is not the true standard, for the best physicians as well as the most popular practitioners often lose their patients, and even their own lives, from common diseases; while, on the other hand, the most injudicious treatment and the most reckless exposures are not unfrequently survived. Laennec and Bichat, two of the most distinguished lights of modern medicine, died of the very diseases they were themselves investigating. Priessnitz, the prince of modern empirics, himself a robust peasant, died of premature disease at the age of fifty-two, in the midst of his own water-cure. It is well known that the most thronged and popular places of resort for grave, difficult, and intractable cases, are those from which there are most funerals. On the other hand, men support life in certain cases under every extreme of opposite treatment, under ultra-depletion and ultra-stimulation, under heroic practice and nugatory practice, under "hot drops" and cold douches, under drachm doses of calomel and imponderable doses of moonshine. Clot Bey, and his two or three associate Frenchmen, entered a plague hospital at Cairo in the height of the epidemic. They shut themselves up in the concentrated atmosphere of the infection, they remained in bed in contact with dying patients, they wore the shirts of those who had just expired, they inoculated themselves with the secretions of pestilential buboes,—and all to no purpose. They were alive some years afterwards, and quarrelling with each other for the glory of their hair-brained enterprise. Four thieves in the plague at Marseilles freely prosecuted their robberies in the infected houses of the dead and dying; and the aromatic vinegar, which has immortalized their prophylactic practice, was very probably an impromptu invention got up by them to procure their exemption from punishment.

The humility which we may learn from the limited influence of our art on the health and lives of mankind, is probably a far safer guide to a correct practice than the fanatical confidence with which unenlightened ultraists of every sect carry out their respective dogmas. In a sphere of action where some good may always be done, and where much harm often is done, and "fools rush in where angels fear to tread," it is well to consider some of the rules which may lead an honest inquirer after truth to the nearest attainment of a correct judgment and practice.

Supposing, what I would fain wish might always happen, that the physician is duly and thoroughly imbued with knowledge of his science, the first great question, which presents itself in every case or emergency, is that which involves the diagnosis. This being established, the practitioner is enabled to avail himself of the lights of reason and experience in regard to a correct course of therapeutic proceeding. But it often happens that the nature of the case cannot be made out in one, or two, or three interviews with the patient; and we are obliged to wait for the gradual development of diagnostic symptoms, as a judge and jury in a like case would be expected to postpone, or wait for the arrival of witnesses. It is a mistaken pride which leads physicians to commit themselves by an oracular guess at first sight, which the events of the succeeding day may show to have been erroneous. Moreover, if, from the obscure character of the case or the imperfection of our science, diagnosis is impossible, we should then so generalize our treatment that we may include what is possible of good, and exclude what is probable of harm.

Having settled, as well as our means admit, the pathological condition of our patient, the next question is that which regards the probable tendency of the disease if left to itself. Attention to this point is of high importance; since it will prevent us from neglecting our patients in grave and dangerous affections, as well as from annoying them with useless appliances in short, safe, or unimportant cases. Many diseases are insidious in their origin. The nervous imbecility which has its foundation laid in modern schools, the slight cough and evening flush which herald approaching phthisis, soon get beyond the reach of medical means, unless seasonably detected by the wary eye of the practitioner. A simple discharge from the ear may terminate in deafness, and an ulcer of the cornea in loss of sight. A protracted intermittent at length undermines the health, and neglected syphilis ends in a miserable death. Cases like these require prompt and energetic interference on the part of the practitioner. On the other hand, diseases which are light in themselves, and tend to speedy recovery, as common catarrh, hooping-cough, varicella, and a host of other things, if they occur in healthy subjects, and are not complicated with graver affections, may safely be left to themselves, or treated with the mildest remedies and cautionary measures.

Another most important question, exercising the hopes and fears of every practitioner, from its connection with reputation, safety, and life, is that which relates to the curability of diseases. Is the disease amenable to medical treatment, or not? If the case is of a recoverable character, and happily a great majority of our cases are so, the physician should anxiously and carefully have recourse to the recorded authorities of his science, and to his own personal experience. In doing this, he should beware of implicitly trusting those who have published only the favorable side of their practice, preferring to build up a temporary reputation rather than to promulgate unpopular truths. And, in analyzing his own experience, he should equally beware of hasty generalizations, of impressions made by remarkable examples, rather than by aggregates of well-observed and duly arranged cases, from which alone impartial and correct inferences are to be drawn.

In accordance with such views, we shall find

many cases which are, for the most part, capable of being arrested or broken up by the interposition of remedies. Thus, the grave and various symptoms which result from an overloaded stomach are at once removed by the action of an emetic, or sometimes of a laxative; colic in like manner yields to opium or to purgatives; syphilis is cured by mercury, and sometimes without it; and certain inflammatory attacks apparently yield to seasonable depletion. Moreover, in other cases which cannot be thus arrested, but which, from their nature, must run a destined course, it is generally admitted that the safety of the patient may be promoted, or perhaps the duration of the case abridged, by remedial treatment. This is believed to be true in regard to evacuations at the commencement of febrile and inflammatory diseases, and to a multitude of other remedies applicable in various cases. But on this subject it is extremely difficult to obtain decisive and satisfactory knowledge. It involves a question, the settlement of which is to be approached by extensive and contrasted numerical observations, a large portion of which yet remain to be made, although we have valuable contributions and examples on many subjects.

On the other hand, when we know that a case is self-limited or incurable, we are to consider how far it is in our power to palliate or diminish sufferings which we are not competent to remove. Here is a most important field for medical practice, and one which calls for an exceedingly large portion of the time and efforts of every physician. When we consider that most diseases occupy, from necessity, a period of some days or weeks; that many of them continue for months, and some for years; and finally that a large portion of mankind die of some lingering or chronic disease, — we shall see that the study of palliatives is not only called for, but really constitutes one of the most common, as well as the most useful and beneficent, employments of a medical man.

In the use of efficient remedies, much depends upon deciding the proper stage or time to which their employment is applicable. Some curative agents can with propriety be used only at the outset of the diseases; and, if this opportunity is lost, the remedies are afterwards less effectual, and perhaps even injurious. Venesection, in the early stage of certain acute diseases, may be productive of great good; in the middle stages it is of less benefit, or of none at all; and in the latter stages it is injurious and inadmissible. On the other hand, wine and opiates, which are strongly contra-indicated in the first stage, are afterwards not only tolerated with impunity, but in certain cases are taken with decided benefit.

But, gentlemen, the agents which we oppose to the progress of disease may, by excessive or ill-timed application, become themselves the pregnant sources of disease. Every prudent practitioner is bound to consider the effect and tendency of the remedy he is using, and to inquire whether the means employed to counteract the existing disease are not, in their turn, likely to produce evil to the patient; and, if so, whether the evil will be greater or less than the disease for which they are administered. The sudden healing of an old ulcer, issue, or eruption, may be followed by symptoms more serious in their character than those which have been removed. Many remedial processes, if employed in excess or with injudicious frequency, result in permanent injury to the patient. The habitual use of active cathartics, although attended with temporary relief, seldom fails to bring on or aggravate a permanent state of costiveness. Large and often-repeated blood-letting tends to the establishment of debility and anemia in some subjects, or of re-action and plethora in others. Opium and other narcotics are in themselves, if abused, fertile sources of disease. The modern crying evil of polypharmacy and over-medication is profitable to the druggist, habitual to too many physicians, and annoying, if not detrimental, to most patients.

On account of these and similar considerations, much discretion is needed on the part of the physician to enable him to judge rightly of the kind of treatment which it may be safe and proper to employ, and of the degree and amount of that treatment, and of the requisite length of time for its continuance. Medical practice, in many cases, points to the direct substitution of a positive good for a positive evil; but unfortunately, in other cases, it admits only of a choice between evils; and in these cases not only the knowledge and experience, but also the judgment and common sense, of the practitioner, are put in indispensable requisition to lead him to a correct issue.

It is wrong to suppose, as is often done, that the opportunities for doing good in medicine are limited to the effect of specific remedies, or to the application of drugs and instruments. The enlightened physician surveys the whole ground of his patient's case, and looks for the presence of any deleterious agencies or unremoved causes of disease. Many morbid affections, which have resisted powerful remedies, cease speedily on the discovery and removal of their sustaining cause. This is the case with various specific complaints produced by particular drugs and stimulants, when habitually used. A child is often sick from an error in the diet, health, or habits of the nurse or mother. An individual frequently suffers from the quality and quantity of his habitual food or drink, or of his exercise, air, occupation, or clothing. The starved infant and the overfed gourmand, the drunkard and the ascetic, the pale student and the emaciated seamstress, require removal and reform, not drugs and medicines. A patient dies of phthisis in a confined office or a damp northern climate, who might have enjoyed long life in an active occupation or a more pure and temperate atmosphere. On the other hand, men fall victims to the fevers and abdominal diseases of the South and West, who might have escaped disease by a timely removal to the North. It is as necessary in many cases that the physician should inquire into the situation, diet, habits, and occupation of the patient, as that he should feel his pulse or explore his chest. It often happens that the disordered state of the one cannot be corrected until the other has been previously set right; and a little dietetic instruction, or even moral advice, is more serviceable than a technical prescription.

In regard to their duration, their probable issue, and their susceptibility of relief, the physician may profitably divide his cases into three classes; those which are curable, those which are temporarily self-limited, and those which are incurable.* In the first class, or that of curable diseases, are to be included those morbid affections which we know, or have reason to believe, are under the control of remedies, so that they can be arrested, or abridged in duration. For the most part, acute inflammatory diseases, when not of fatal intensity, are mitigated by depletion and the antiphologistic regimen, more

---

* See note, page 149.

or less actively enforced, according to the degree of violence. Spasmodic diseases, on the contrary, are influenced by opiates, antispasmodics, and tonics, and by the removal of their cause, when it can be discovered and remedied, as in the case of dentition, indigestible food, &c. Sympathetic diseases are to be addressed through the medium, organ, or texture, which is primarily affected. Thus, a headache depending upon a disordered stomach, or an hysteric affection upon irregularity of the uterine function, are to be treated under this view of the subject. Hemorrhages and other morbid discharges are to be dealt with by removing the cause when practicable, by diminishing vascular activity, or by quieting the discharging surfaces with opiates, or contracting them with astringents. There is one class of curable diseases which are controlled chiefly by specific remedies, — being in some instances suspended, in others radically removed. Thus, gout is relieved by colchicum; and intermittents, it is believed, by quinine. Scabies is cured by sulphur; syphilis by mercury; goitre, as we are informed, by iodine; and various chronic eruptions by arsenic and corrosive sublimate. The foregoing examples will serve to illustrate, not only the power of medicine, but also the great variety of grounds which should govern medical practice, and the importance of an intelligent diagnosis, as well as a knowledge of therapeutic means.

In the next subdivision, or that of self-limited diseases, we include those "which receive limits from their own nature, and not from foreign influences; and which, after they have obtained foothold in the system, cannot, in the present state of our knowledge, be eradicated or abridged by art, but to which there is due a certain succession of processes, to be completed in a certain time; which time and processes may vary with the constitution and condition of the patient, but are not known to be shortened by medical treatment." Examples are abundant, and are found in typhus and typhoid fever, measles, small-pox, hooping-cough, dysentery, and many other diseases of lighter or graver character.*

It is with regret that we are obliged to acknowledge the existence of a third class, that of incurable diseases, which has been recognized in all ages as the *opprobrium medicorum*. It includes the long train of internal morbid degenerations, malignant and chronic, by tubercle and granulation, by atrophy and hypertrophy, softening and hardening, scirrhus, encephalosis, ossification, concretion, contraction, and dilatation, with their various consequences of phthisis, emphysema, dropsy, epilepsy, paralysis, and a multitude of intractable disorders, in which organs are disabled, functions destroyed, and life itself rendered incapable of continuance.

---

* See marginal note, page 157.

It is obvious that in the three foregoing classes of disease very different modifications of treatment are required. In curable diseases, our remedial measures should be prompt and energetic in proportion to the emergency of the case, and the certainty of benefit which is to follow their employment. In self-limited diseases, our treatment must be of the expectant character. It consists in doing what we can for the comfort and safety of the patient, avoiding useless and troublesome applications, watching against accidents and complications, and waiting for the salutary operations of nature. In those maladies which are in their nature incurable, we are obliged to confine ourselves to the palliation of suffering, and the removal of causes which may aggravate the disease.

Such, I believe, is the true exposition of the powers and duties of every medical man. The dignity of our science, and the responsibility of our profession, require that we should form just views of the extent of our capacity and duty, and that we should not shrink from avowing them to the world. Our science, imperfect as it is, has achieved as much as any similar science for the prevention, alleviation, and removal of the evils which it combats. Let us not bring it into disrepute, by pretending to impossibilities, by asserting what cannot be proved, and by professing what human art is unable to accomplish. A new era will dawn upon medicine, when its faithful and enlightened cultivators shall more constantly devote their time and their efforts to enlighten the public mind in regard to the true mission and powers of their science, and when they shall leave to charlatans and fanatics the doubtful and dishonest game of unfounded professional pretension.

ON THE MEDICAL PROFESSION AND QUACKERY.

AN INTRODUCTORY LECTURE, DELIVERED AT THE MEDICAL COLLEGE, BOSTON, NOV. 6, 1844.

I AM about to address myself to an audience of young men, — a class of persons who, in our new and active country, assume an influence and wear a responsibility unknown in the older communities of Europe. The sparse character of our population, the call for active and efficient men, the sure market which exists for talents, and even for common ability and prudence, have given a national precocity to our youth, and a readiness in adapting themselves to new and difficult spheres of action. I have heard foreigners speak with surprise of the arrival, in distant ports of Europe or India, of American ships commanded, not as is usual by weather-beaten veterans, but by beardless striplings. The signs of our mercantile houses bear often the names of very young men; and the avenues of our professions are so crowded with them, that perhaps no regulation is more liable to be infringed than that which requires that professional candidates shall be twenty-one years of age. Young men command the ranks of our military corps and swell our political meetings. Their voice is heard among us in the periodical press and in the halls of legislation.

These precocious habits of our country have of course been felt in the medical profession. In most of the schools of Europe, medical honors are not conferred until after a novitiate of four, and more frequently five, years; during which an extensive circle of sciences is obliged to be mastered, and to be approved by a series of strict examinations. Not only are the essential branches of medicine required to be fully understood, but they must be preceded by a knowledge of the subsidiary sciences, and must also be confirmed by practical and clinical experience.

With us, on the other hand, the short period of three preparatory years devoted to regular study and lectures may be said to constitute nearly the sum total of a medical education; for the collateral requirements are so small, that their acquisition is often effected during the same three years which are applied to the other branches. And a young man, who has learned to read and write, issues from the village school, or perhaps from the counter or the plough, and in three years is licensed, and declared competent to exercise the multifarious profession of medicine and surgery in all its departments. As it often happens in this and similar cases, the newly approved candidate sends forth his anxious glance, directed not always to his own deficiencies or the means of supplying them, but to that common goal and object of a young man's inquiry, which is to fill up the measure of his practical aspirations, — an opening. By the timely decease of some elderly practitioner, or by the fortunate discovery of a rising settlement, in some distant State or on some promising water-power, he finds himself, perhaps at short notice, installed, under virtue of the acquiescent silence of the small community in which he lives, the constituted physician of the place. In one month, perhaps in one week, he may be called upon to diagnosticate organic lesion in a case of life and death, or to treat the most formidable convulsive disease. He may be summoned to tie the femoral artery, or to decide and act in a case of placental presentation. There may be no consulting physician within many miles, — at least none who can arrive in season for the emergency.

The safety, then, and probably the lives, of the unfortunate constituents of this young man will depend upon the question whether he has or has not been truly educated, — whether his mind and hand have been adequately trained for the great occasions that await him. It is not enough that he has suffered three years to expire while taking his ease in the office of a city physician, nor that he has passed a corresponding time in following the rounds of a country practitioner. It is not enough that he has carelessly read the works of approved authors, and has squeezed through the customary academic examination. If he has done only this, it is more than probable that failure awaits on himself and disaster upon his patient. But if his studies have been methodical, and conducted with an eye to practical application; if he has concentrated his attention upon necessary points; if he has felt the earnest interest which, more than any thing else, imprints truth on the remembrance; if he has gathered up and arranged his resources in reference to coming emergencies; if he has gone over in anticipation the difficulties of his profession, and planned his own mode of extrication, — then he will find that inexperience does not involve failure, and that youth is not an insurmountable barrier to success. He will recollect that the most eminent physicians and the most successful operators have had their first cases. He will perhaps also remember that some of the most distinguished men in history have emerged from obscurity while yet in youth; that not only warriors like Alexander and Napoleon, but statesmen like Pitt and Fox, and philosophers like Davy and Bichat, had achieved some of their proudest laurels at the very entrance of manhood.

Let it not be supposed, however, that I am an advocate for the premature assumption, by young men, of the responsibilities of our profession. Every medical student is to be considered unfortunate, who, by reason of poverty or the stress of other circumstances, is obliged to hurry his probationary period to an early termination. Too much time and attention are not often bestowed on the business of preparation for practice. The oldest and the best physicians have had frequent cause to regret that they were not better educated. But the superficial student, who rarely has the time and the will to repair his early deficiencies, is haunted through life by a round of perplexity and embarrassment, and degraded by a sense of his own incompetency.

It should be borne in mind, that there is no period of life in which time can be so conveniently spared from lucrative pursuits as in youth. After a man has attained to the age of thirty, it is commonly of very little consequence to him, as far as his fame and yearly receipts are concerned, whether he had commenced practice at the age of twenty-one or of twenty-four. But as far as he may prize a quiet conscience and freedom from anxiety, the later age is incomparably the most secure. I would advise any young man who has completed his education at the end of his minority, that he should devote two additional years, and, if practicable, a still longer period, to availing himself of such advantages, both in study and practice, as may prepare him for his future duties. And when, as it often happens in our community, narrow circumstances require that a young man should live by his own exertions, this state of things, instead of being a motive that he should crowd himself prematurely into the ranks of the profession, encumbered with debt and bare of acquirements and of means, is rather an imperative reason that he should at once begin by resolving to devote twice the customary number of years, if necessary, to the double purpose of keeping himself in an independent position, and of placing himself at length, in point of maturity of knowledge, on a par with his more favored competitors.

It may not be improper, in this place, to offer you some suggestions as to the mode in which students may advantageously appropriate the time of their pupilage in reference to the science which they expect to acquire. Medical literature has become so vast a subject, that the undirected student is apt to be lost in the maze of books and sciences which seem equally to press upon his attention; and he is likely to fall into the pernicious error of thinking that he must read a great deal, even though he remembers little. The true object of a medical pupilage should be, not to read, but to study, to observe, and to remember; not to pass superficially over the writings of celebrated men, but to select those compendiums of the several sciences which contain a condensed view of their essential and elementary facts, which separate the wheat from the chaff, and offer what is fundamental and useful, within a compass which is capable of being impressed on the memory. Most of the constituent sciences which are nominally included in a modern medical education are now so extensive, that the cultivation of any one of them may afford abundant occupation for a common lifetime. Passing over the more elementary branches, I may instance the theory and practice of medicine, the literature of which is a vast magazine of rubbish, with a few gems imbedded in it, accumulated in all time since the origin of writing; and in such excess, that no country in Europe could probably furnish even a catalogue of its own modern books. The history of this extensive science contains a mixture of much that is bad with much less that is good. And although in medical research the still small voice of truth has from time to time made itself heard for a season, yet it has as often been drowned by the dogmas of the visionary and the clamors of the interested. During the present century, a host of theorists and gratuitous reformers have replaced each other on the arena of medical controversy. But we have seen that while a truth in medical science, like the import of the physical signs for example, struggles its way through opposition and distrust into general adoption, an unfair and unfounded assumption rarely survives long the life of the individual whose own eloquence and obstinacy were necessary to force it for a time upon the public attention.

If we could purge the sciences of pathology and therapeutics from the writings of men who wrote merely because they had a reputation to acquire or a doctrine to establish; and could confine these sciences to the results attained by those who sought directly and impartially for the true and the useful, — it is probable that the whole subject would be brought within the comprehension, not only of every physician, but of every medical student. And from the recent mode of conducting medical investigations, which has commenced and is gradually gaining foothold in all civilized countries, we may hope, in our own day, to see near approaches to this desirable result.

Every medical man, whether student or physician, owes a threefold duty, — to himself, to his competitors, and to his patients. To himself he owes the cultivation of habits of order and perseverance, a love of honesty, and a desire of knowledge. No man is successful in a learned profession who does not cultivate a methodical disposition of his time. The neglect of an hour, the omission of an engagement, and the postponement of what is necessary for what is unimportant, have ruined many a good intention and many a promising prospect. Lord Chesterfield says that the Duke of Newcastle lost half an hour in the morning, and spent the whole day in running after it. This is a true expression of the career of a busy but inefficient man. He who is always driven, always in a hurry, always late, and always with deficiencies to be made up, is very likely to be always a failure. It is well known that the responsibilities of society are best and most easily discharged by those who estimate the value of small portions of time, who do things strictly in their proper season and place, who provide against contingencies, and distribute their day in reference to what is, as well as to what may be, required of them.

But the best-ordered arrangement of time, and the most punctual habits of attention, do not always succeed in our profession, except through perseverance, and often through long suffering. The public, especially in cities, are slow in giving their confidence to strangers and to young men. The late Dr. Physick, of Philadelphia, asserted that, during the first three years of his practice, he did not pay for his shoe-leather; and a late very eminent physician of this city once informed me, that he did not earn his own board during three times that period. The conservative principle which retards the reception of young men into lucrative business, is the foundation of their security in after life; for medical practice would not be worth having in a community whose love of change should lead them to desert their former friends and counsellors, to run after every newcomer. Physicians usually come on to the stage and move off of it in company with the generation to which they belong. In a large city, a young physician, except under circumstances of peculiar patronage or necessity, does not usually obtain employment from families who are much in advance of himself. But these families and their medical attendants pass away, and he and his cotemporaries become the standing practitioners of their time. A preparatory period in the meantime elapses, during which the candidate for future honors has usually enough to do to perfect his knowledge, to fill the gaps in his experience, and to give proofs to the community around him that he possesses aptitude for the common affairs of life.

Every physician is an inquirer during life, and continues to learn something up to the last year in which he may happen to study or practise. As the science advances, moreover, every intelligent practitioner is obliged to replace some of his former opinions with others which he finds to be better substantiated. We should be careful, therefore, not to pledge ourselves unnecessarily to medical opinions which are founded on equivocal or imperfect testimony. The public sentiment attaches a kind of disgrace to frequent changes and recantations; and it ought also to do the same to the course of any man who, for the sake of consistency with himself, continues to maintain an erroneous and exploded opinion. Both these extremes are avoided by the physician who reserves his assent to any new opinion until the evidence of the case is satisfactorily made out.

One of the most difficult virtues for a physician to cultivate is a just and proper deportment towards his professional brethren. As in all professions in which men live by their heads rather than their hands, business is liable to be overdone; and a candidate who has not acquired all the occupation that he wishes is apt to regard his competitors as stumbling-blocks, to be gotten rid of by fair means or foul. Hence arise the jealousies, calumnies, and open hostilities so often entertained, which injure all the parties concerned, and lower the estimation of the profession with the public. Harmony and a proper *esprit du corps* may uphold the dignity of even an inferior profession; but the public rarely respect any class of men, the members of which have no respect for each other. A friendly intercourse with those whom we approve is productive of pleasure and advantage; and a gentlemanly forbearance towards those with whom we do not agree will show that we are above jealousy. A man is always to be suspected who tells you that he is surrounded with enemies; and one who is an habitual calumniator of others forces upon his hearers the conviction, that they in their proper turn are to come in for their share of his animadversions.

I doubt if physicians do not sometimes injure themselves and their cause by showing too great a sensitiveness in regard to the temporary inroads of irregular practitioners. Quackery, whether carried on by the audacious enterprise of an individual impostor or upheld by the trumpeting of a fanatical sect, is to be considered a necessary evil, inherent in the constitution of society. It exists in every walk and occupation of life by the exercise of which men procure bread. The pettifogger in law, the Millerite lecturer in theology, the demagogue in politics, the system-monger in education, and the wonder-worker upon the brains and bowels of infatuated audiences, — what are all these but quacks moving in their respective spheres, and fattening upon the credulity of dupes? A certain portion of mankind are so constituted, that they require to be ridden by others; and if you should succeed in unhorsing a particular impostor, it is only to prepare the saddle for a fresh and more unflinching equestrian. It is not good policy to say or to write too much in regard to the pretensions of impostors. A celebrated author observes, that "many a popular error has flourished through the opposition of the learned."* By throwing the gauntlet at an insignificant man, you at once raise him to the dignity of being your competitor,

---
* Macintosh.

and acknowledge him as a "foeman worthy of your steel." And if you discover uneasiness, resentment, or ill-temper, the public conclude that you are influenced by your private interests. Besides, when you have entered the arena of controversy, you will probably find that the quack, who has his all at stake, can afford more breath and time than you can conveniently spare from your other occupations; and, in an active warfare, he may acquire two partisans to your one. It is not long since the exhibitor of a stuffed mermaid succeeded in drawing down the popular indignation on an unfortunate naturalist, who had ventured to declare that it was made of a fish and a monkey. The public generally require time to get disabused of a favorite error; and, if too abruptly assailed, they will sometimes hold on to it, as the traveller did to his cloak when attacked by the north wind.

In your demeanor in regard to quacks, you should keep aloof from them, and trouble yourselves little about them. Admit the general fact, that the race always do and must exist in society; that they are wanted by the credulity of a particular class of minds; that the fall of one dishonest pretender, or one visionary sect, is sure to be replaced by the elevation of another; therefore it little concerns you to know what particular imposition has the ascendency at any given time. When you are interrogated in regard to a specific subject of this kind, you should make a reasonable, cogent, and dispassionate answer, always avoiding the appearance of warmth, and especially of self-interest; and you may be sure that a majority of the public will be on the side of truth. As far as my observation extends, three quarters at least of the families in Boston and New England are in the hands of regular practitioners. The remaining fraction, more or less, consists partly of minds so constituted, that they require the marvellous as a portion of their necessary food, and partly of unfortunate beings, suffering the inevitable lot of humanity; who, having failed to obtain relief from the ordinary resources of medicine, seek for temporary encouragement in the dishonest assurances of any who will promise to cure them. The first class is the dog in the fable, catching at shadows; the last is the drowning man, catching at straws.

Above all, if you would discountenance quackery, take care that you become not quacks yourselves. Charlatanism consists not so much in ignorance, as in dishonesty and deception. In your intercourse with patients, cultivate a spirit of fidelity, candor, and truth. Endeavor to understand yourselves and your science, weigh justly your own powers, and profess only what you can accomplish. If you announce to your patients that you will cure incurable diseases, or cut short those which have a necessary period of duration, you do not speak the truth; you merely blind your patient, while you throw the die for a fortuitous result, — a game at which the veriest mountebank may at any time beat you. The profession as a body are often unpopular with a large and sagacious part of the community, because they so frequently disappoint the expectations they have allowed themselves to raise. You may safely undertake and promise to cure diseases which you know to be curable, to alleviate others which you know to be not so, and to perform what art and science can do towards conducting doubtful and dangerous cases to a happy issue. But this is all you can accomplish or promise. The skilful mariner may steer his ship through a dangerous navigation, but he cannot control the wind nor arrest the storm. Nor would he gain reputation by professing to do so.

It is hardly necessary that I should counsel you not to neglect your patients, when you can do any thing for their welfare and security. Neglect of outward attentions is not, I think, a very frequent sin of physicians, inasmuch as their interest very obviously lies in a different course. But some practitioners fall into the opposite error of over-attention to their patients; of making them long, tedious, or superfluous visits; of hampering them with strict and complicated instructions; and especially of over-drugging them with remedies. There are some patients, it is true, who like to be bled, blistered, and physicked; but the number is small:

and, in most cases, both the instinct of the child and the discretion of the grown man cause them to revolt against nauseous and painful inflictions. When, therefore, you are called to take charge of patients, ask yourselves how great is the danger, and what is the probable tendency of the disease, if left to itself. If life is in question, and you have reason to believe that the patient may be rescued by prompt and energetic remedies, you should not hesitate to employ them. But in common, trivial, and safe cases, such as afford a large part of a physician's occupation, you should not allow a habit or a hobby to lead you into the blind routine of always thinking that you must make your patients worse before they can be better. I believe that much of the medical imposition of the present day is sustained in places where practice has previously been over-heroic, and because mankind are gratified to find that they and their families can get well without the lancet, the vomit, and the blister, indiscriminately applied; and because the adroit charlatan transfers the salutary influences of time and nature to the credit of his own less disagreeable inflictions.

It is the duty of physicians to elevate their profession, by maintaining in their individual character a high moral rectitude, a just and honorable conduct, a devotedness to the welfare of their patients, and an unceasing effort to improve themselves and their science. If this course is pursued by medical men, they can hardly fail of becoming useful and respected members of society. There is no country in the world in which the avenues to respectability and distinction, to competency and even to wealth, are more open to physicians than in the United States. It has been observed, that in England no medical man is ever permitted to attain the aristocratic rank, which belongs to birth, and which is occasionally accorded to eminence in the military, political, legal, and financial professions. In this country, however, there is no post of honor or emolument, and no situation of influence and distinction, which our history does not show to be within the reach of our profession. But it is not to political or extra-professional preferment that the true physician should look. He should rather be contented to build up his own character within his own sphere, as a man of knowledge, fidelity, and honor. The respect of the community, and the attachment of friends, will always attend on him who loves truth for its own sake, pursues knowledge that he may be able to benefit others, and deals justly with his fellow-men, consenting that they, in turn, should deal justly with him.

BRIEF EXPOSITIONS OF RATIONAL MEDICINE.*

THE tendency to ultraism, which influences public opinion in great social questions, particularly of politics and theology, has been also prevalent in the affairs of practical medicine. No age has been exempt from diversity of opinion among physicians on the speculative subjects of their art; and the

---

* The following Dedication was prefixed to the first edition of this article, published in 1858:—

TO SIR JOHN FORBES, M.D., F.R.S.,

FELLOW OF THE ROYAL COLLEGE OF PHYSICIANS, LONDON, PHYSICIAN OF THE QUEEN'S HOUSEHOLD, ETC., ETC.

MY DEAR SIR,— The distinguished and influential position which you hold in regard to principles, many of which are advocated in this little publication, renders it proper that I should present it to your notice as an humble auxiliary in the promotion of a just, and I hopefully trust a growing, conviction in the public mind, as to the true mission and powers of the medical art.

It is known to you that it was my intention to have published in this country an edition of your very able volume entitled "Nature and Art in the Cure of Disease," in connection with some other publications of like tendency which have appeared on this side of the Atlantic, and to have embodied the whole under the title of "Rational Medicine." Of this plan, as well as name, I had the pleasure to receive your approval and your concurrence in its execution. But, after the whole was prepared and placed in the publisher's hands here, the unforeseen appearance of a

present period appears to be more marked than preceding ones, by the opposite methods, of treatment pursued by medical men in the management of disease. These methods consist, for the most part, in a vehement, officious, and over-drugging system on the one hand, and an inert, evasive, and nugatory practice on the other. Between these extremes, the intermediate truth meets with less consideration than it ought to receive from unbiassed and enlightened inquirers.

Extreme doctrines in practical subjects often arise from the self-interest of those who originate and first promote them. But the vehemence and fanaticism with which they are afterwards pursued are as often owing to the creation of false issues, which

---

New-York edition of your work rendered superfluous the proposed undertaking.

The world will duly appreciate the labor and learning which, during half a century, you have brought to the aid of true medical philosophy; and, in a particular manner, the impartial investigations which you have lately made in regard to the part performed by nature in the cure of diseases. Convictions in a measure similar to your own have, at the same time, found their way into other minds, and generally in a near proportion to the testimony afforded by prolonged experience. Twenty-three years ago, I read, before the Medical Society of this State, a Discourse on Self-limited Diseases, which, I have reason to believe, was not without some influence at the time and since on the minds of the profession here. This discourse was afterwards incorporated, with other essays, in a volume entitled "Nature in Disease." I now hope that the crowning and convincing testimonies afforded by your noble work, on the comparison of nature and art in the cure of disease, will be instrumental in causing the extravagances of a so-called heroic and over-active practice on the one hand, and of a nugatory and ignorant practice on the other, to be replaced by something which may deserve the name of RATIONAL MEDICINE.

divert public attention from the substance to the shadow, and mystify the general question with minor, partial, and frequently irrelevant considerations.

The introduction into the English language, for example, of the term "allopathy," and its adoption by some medical writers, has had the effect to mislead superficial readers in regard to the true issue of questions connected with the treatment of disease. This word was designed by its zealous, but weak and incompetent, inventor to express the employment of remedies which produce phenomena *different* from those produced by the disease treated; whereas the term homœopathy indicated a mode of treating diseases by employing medicines which are supposed to produce effects *similar* to those which it is desired to remove. This theoretical and absurd generalization, wholly unsupported by general facts on either side, so far as the cure of diseases is concerned, has acquired currency among the less enlightened part of the public; so that, at the present day, many persons consider homœopathy a sort of general law, to which allopathy is an exception. And, strange to tell, many otherwise sensible physicians have assumed the cloak thus offered to them; without perceiving that the propriety of so doing is the same as if the whole Protestant world were to style themselves heretics, because the church of Rome, in former ages, saw fit to apply to them that appellation. Allopathy is, in fact, a worthless term, which either means nothing real, or else embodies so many dissimilar and discordant elements, that it serves no purpose as a descriptive or distinctive name. The occasion still exists for terms which may definitively express the dogmas of modern practice.

Anatomy, physiology, and to a certain extent pathology, may be considered, so far as our discoveries have advanced, to be entitled to rank with the exact sciences. But therapeutics, or the art of treating diseases, like ethics and political economy, is still a conjectural study, incapable of demonstration in many of its great processes, and subject to various and even opposite opinions in regard to the laws and means which govern its results.

The methods which, at the present day, are most prevalent in civilized countries, in the treatment of disease, may be denominated the following: —

1. The *Artificial* method; which, when carried to excess, is commonly termed heroic, and which consists in reliance on artificial remedies, usually of an active character, in the expectation that they will of themselves remove diseases.

2. The *Expectant* method. This consists simply in non-interference; leaving the chance of recovery to the powers of nature, uninfluenced by interpositions of art.

3. The *Homœopathic* method. This is a counter-

feit of the last, and consists in leaving the case to nature, while the patient is amused with nominal and nugatory remedies.

4. The *Exclusive* method; which applies one remedy to all diseases, or to a majority of diseases. This head includes hydropathy, also the use of various mineral waters, electrical establishments, &c. Drugs newly introduced, and especially secret medicines, frequently boast this universality of application.

5. The *Rational* method. This recognizes nature as the great agent in the cure of diseases, and employs art as an auxiliary, to be resorted to when useful or necessary, and avoided when prejudicial.

The foregoing methods, with the exception perhaps of the last, have had their trial in various periods and countries, and have given rise to discussions and controversies which are not terminated at the present day. The subject is too complicated to obtain from inquirers, out of the profession, the amount of attention requisite for understanding its merits; while, among medical men, consistency to pledged opinions, defects of knowledge, and considerations of interest, not unfrequently warp the judgment of otherwise honest and discerning persons. It is certain, moreover, that medical opinion on the treatment of disease changes much between the time of one generation and another. Any person who will take the trouble to inspect the medical journals, published thirty or forty years ago, will find many things, then laid down as medical truths, which are now generally admitted to be medical errors. The length of a common professional life is sufficient to disabuse most physicians of many convictions which they had received on trust, and once considered unchangeable. Yet it does not always happen that error is replaced by truth, and it is fortunate if the delusions of ill-balanced minds are not succeeded by newer and greater delusions.

It is, nevertheless, right that intelligent and reasonable physicians should receive the confidence of the community, since they are, or should be, more qualified than other persons to undertake the care and conduct of the sick. And even if it had happened that their power was limited to merely understanding the nature of the existing disease, and the import and probable tendency of symptoms which occur from day to day without any attempt at curative interference, still their attendance would be solicited to throw light on the grave questions of pain, sickness, and recovery, and still more of life and death. The public, however, expect something more of physicians than the power of distinguishing diseases, and of predicting their issue. They look to them for the relief of their sufferings, and the cure or removal of their complaints. And the vulgar estimate of the powers of medicine is founded on the common acceptation of the name, that medicine is the art of curing diseases. That this is a false definition, is evident from the fact that many diseases are incurable, and that one such disease must at last happen to every living man.* A far more just definition would be, that medicine is the art of understanding diseases, and of curing or relieving them when possible. If this definition were accepted, and its truth generally understood by the profession and the public, a weight of superfluous responsibility on one side, and of dissatisfaction on the other, would be lifted from the shoulders of both. It is because physicians allow themselves to profess and vaunt more power over disease than belongs to them, that their occasional shortcomings are made a ground of reproach with the community, and of contention among themselves.

It is now generally admitted by intelligent physicians, that certain diseases, the number of which is not very great, are at once curable by medical means. Yet there is probably no curative agent, applied to such diseases, the efficacy and even safety of which has not been warmly contested by sectarian practitioners. It is also beginning to be admitted in this country, that certain diseases are *self-limited*,†

---

* See the author's "Nature in Disease," page 64.

† This term was first introduced by the writer in a discourse in 1835, already alluded to, with the following definition: "A self-limited disease is one which receives limits from its own nature, and not from foreign influences; one which, after it has obtained foothold in the system, cannot, in the present state of our knowledge, be eradicated or abridged by art;

incurable now by art, yet susceptible of recovery under natural processes, both with and without the interference of art. To this class belong a great portion of the diseases usually called acute, and likewise some, the character of which is decidedly chronic. Lastly, a vast tribe of incurable diseases takes precedence in the lists of mortality, and holds, in some form, its final sentence over the heads of all mankind. Yet so reluctant are physicians to acknowledge these universal truths, or to admit their own incompetency, that incurable and unmanageable diseases have been complacently called *opprobria medicinæ*, as if they were exceptions to a general rule.

The great objects which medical practice professes to effect, and which there can be no doubt that it frequently does effect, are the following: 1. The cure of certain diseases; 2. The relief or palliation of all diseases; 3. The safe conduct of the sick. In all these objects it sometimes fails; yet instances of its success are sufficiently numerous to establish the necessity of the existence of medicine as a profession.

No one doubts that morbid affections, occasioned by the presence of an offending or irritating cause,

---

but to which there is due a certain succession of processes, to be completed in a certain time, which time and processes may vary with the constitution and condition of the patient, and may tend to death or to recovery, but are not known to be shortened, or greatly changed, by medical treatment."

are often speedily cured by the discharge or removal of that cause. And here drugs are among the principal agents which we employ. Again, no one doubts that many of the diseases of civilized life, brought on by luxury, intemperance, sedentary and intellectual labor, unhealthy residence, occupation, &c., are often wholly or partially cured by change of life, including habits, and perhaps residence. And here drugs are, for the most part, of little avail. So that it may happen that the chance of cure shall depend upon the judgment with which active drugs are administered, on the one hand, and avoided or superseded, on the other.

The palliation of diseases is another great practical end of medical science, and really occupies a large portion of the time and efforts of every medical man. When it is considered that most diseases last for days, and some of them for years, and that a large portion of mankind eventually die of some chronic or lingering disease, it will readily be seen that the palliation of suffering is not only called for, but really constitutes one of the most important, as well as beneficent, objects of medical practice. The use of anodynes and anæsthetics, the obviation of various painful and distressing symptoms, the removal of annoyances, the just regulation of diet, of exertion and repose, of indulgence and restriction, the direction of moral agencies, which make up so large a part both of suffering and relief, may well afford employment to the most earnest and philanthropic physician, and obtain from the public a just appreciation of the value of his services.

The safe conduct of the sick, as will be seen from the last head, consists much more in cautionary guidance than in active interference. In the management of sickness, the rein is needed to direct, quite as much as the spur to excite. People sometimes suffer from neglect, but more frequently from ill-judged and meddlesome attention. One of the most cogent necessities of a sick man is to be saved from the excessive and officious good-will of his friends. The kindest impulses and the most benevolent intentions are liable to show themselves in ill-timed visits, fatiguing conversations, and injudicious advice or action. Intelligent and discreet physicians are sometimes driven, by the importunity of friends, to the adoption of active measures, or at least the semblance of them, which their own judgment informs them would be better omitted. And the case is still worse when the impulsive temperament of the physician himself, or the influence of his early education, or the dominant fashion of the place in which he resides, is so exacting in regard to activity of treatment, as to make him believe that he cannot *commit* too many inflictions upon the sick, provided that, in the end, he shall be satisfied that he has *omitted* nothing.

The foregoing desiderata, the cure, the relief, and

the safe conduct of patients, involve the great objects for which medicine has been striving for thousands of years. Yet, even in the present advanced state of science, physicians are not agreed as to the means by which any one of them is to be accomplished or attempted; and a man who falls sick at home or abroad is liable to get heroic treatment or nominal treatment, random treatment or no treatment at all, according to the hands into which he may happen to fall. It is, therefore, desirable that physicians themselves, and the public also, should obtain a satisfactory understanding of the various diversities of practice which have been already mentioned as occupying the greatest share of attention at the present day.

1. THE ARTIFICIAL METHOD.—This mode of treatment is founded on the assumption, that disease can be removed by artificial means. From the earliest ages, a belief has prevailed that all human maladies are amenable to control from some form of purely medical treatment; and although the precise form has not yet been found, so far as most diseases are concerned, yet, at this day, it continues to be as laboriously and hopefully pursued as was the elixir vitæ in the middle ages. Within the present century, books of practice gravely laid down "the indications of cure," as if they were things within the grasp of every practitioner. It was only necessary to subdue the inflammation, to expel the mor-

bific matter, to regulate the secretions, to improve the nutrition, and to restore the strength, and the business was at once accomplished. What nature refused, or was inadequate to do, was expected to be achieved by the more prompt and vigorous interposition of art. The destructive tendencies of disease, and the supposed proneness to deterioration of nature herself, were opposed by copious and exhausting depletion, followed by the shadowy array of alteratives, deobstruents, and tonics. Confinement by disease, which might have terminated in a few days, was protracted to weeks and months; because the importance of the case, as it was thought, required that the patient should be artificially " taken down," and then artificially " built up."

When carried to its " heroic " extent, artificial medicine undermined the strength, elicited new morbid manifestations, and left more disease than it took away. The question raised was not how much the patient had profited under his active treatment, but how much more of the same he could bear. Large doses of violent and deleterious drugs were given, as long as the patient evinced a " tolerance " of them, that is, did not sink under them. The results of such cases, if favorable, like the escapes of desperate surgery, were chronicled as professional triumphs; while the press was silent on the disastrous results subsequently incurred in like cases by deluded imitators. If diseases proved fatal, or even if they were not jugulated or cut short at the outset, the misfortune was attributed to the circumstance of the remedies not being sufficiently active, or of the physician not being called in season. So great at one time, and that not long ago, was the ascendency of heroic teachers and writers, that few medical men had the courage to incur the responsibility of omitting the active modes of treatment which were deemed indispensable to the safety of the patient. This timidity on the score of omission has now, in a great measure, passed away, yet is still promoted in most cities by some heroic doctors, and still more by interested specialists, who inflict severe discipline, and levy immense contributions, on credulous persons, who are suitably alarmed at denunciations which involve the loss of sight, of hearing, or even of beauty.

A considerable amount of violent practice is still maintained by routine physicians, who, without going deeply into the true nature or exigencies of the case before them, assume the general ground, that nothing is dangerous but neglect. Edge-tools are brought into use as if they could never be any thing more than harmless playthings. It is thought allowable to harass the patient with daily and opposite prescriptions; to try, to abandon, to re-enforce, or to reverse; to blow hot and cold on successive days; but never to let the patient alone, nor to intrust his case to the quiet guidance of nature. Consulting physicians frequently and painfully witness the gratuitous suffering, the continued nausea, the prostration of strength, the prevention of appetite, the stupefaction of the senses, and the wearisome days and nights, which would never have occurred had there been no such thing as officious medication. What practitioner has not seen infants screaming under the pangs of hunger, or of stimulants remorselessly applied to their tender skins, and whose only permitted chance of relief was in the continued routine of unnecessary calomel and ipecacuanha?

There is one great exception in favor of artificial and even heroic practice, well known and fully demonstrable in the art of surgery. Many defects, injuries, and diseases of the body, are, unquestionably, cured by surgical processes, which never could have got well without them. And the skilful and humane surgeon has more frequent opportunities to reflect with satisfaction on the immediate and positive results of his art than the most able physician. Yet even this satisfaction can only be measured by the fidelity with which he has performed his duty, and the conscientiousness with which he has avoided useless and hopeless operations. Happily the experience and statistical results of the best modern surgeons have had the effect to diminish greatly the amount of gratuitous suffering which was imposed by their predecessors on the unhappy subjects of their art. We see much less than was formerly seen of the cruel but unavailing operations of fanciful and interested surgery; the infliction of pain without corresponding good, the useless extirpation of malignant growths, the mutilation of miserable bodies already doomed by tuberculous and other irrecoverable conditions; deeds which have converted hospitals into inquisitions, and left the Bastile and the Hotel Dieu to contend for the palm of supremacy in the production of human suffering.

2. THE EXPECTANT METHOD.—This method, when fully carried out, admits no medication or interference of art, but waits on time, and commits the chance of recovery to the restorative power of nature alone. The expectant practice has not been without its advocates, and volumes have been published in its favor, at different times, chiefly on the continent of Europe. That there is some basis for the doctrine of expectation, is made apparent by the spontaneous recovery of animals and savages; of careless, obstinate, and incredulous persons in civilized life; and of those who, in consequence of their isolated or otherwise unfavorable position, are unable to procure " medical aid," or who, if they do procure it, obtain only that which is inoperative or absolutely detrimental. I sincerely believe that the unbiassed opinion of most medical men of sound judgment and long experience is made up, that the amount of death and disaster in the world would be less, if all disease were left to itself, than it now

is under the multiform, reckless, and contradictory modes of practice, good and bad, with which practitioners of adverse denominations carry on their differences at the expense of their patients. But there is no probability that expectant medicine will ever prevail in its character as such. The amount of positive good which, in fifty centuries, art has brought to the assistance of medicine, although far more limited than we could desire, is nevertheless both sufficient and worthy to employ the talents of the best and most enlightened physicians.

3. THE HOMŒOPATHIC METHOD. — Homœopathy may be defined as a specious mode of doing nothing. While it waits on the natural progress of disease and the restorative tendency of nature on the one hand, or the injurious advance of disease on the other, it supplies the craving for activity, on the part of the patient and his friends, by the formal and regular administration of nominal medicine. Although homœopathy will, at some future time, be classed with historical delusions, yet its tendency has undoubtedly been to undermine the reliance on heroic practice which prevailed in former times, both in this country and in Europe. There was, perhaps, needed a popular delusion to institute the experiment on a sufficiently large scale, to show that the sick may recover without the use of troublesome and severe medication. There are not wanting in history similar instances of good re-

sults flowing from questionable sources. The French Revolution has eventually bettered the social condition of the French people; and the Mormons have brought the wilderness of the Salt Lake to a state of productive cultivation. Yet no judicious person vindicates the doctrines of those who were prime movers in these innovations, or holds them up as worthy examples for imitation. Sir Kenelm Digby produced a beneficial reform in English surgery, and was able to banish the prevalent mode of dressing incised wounds with painful applications, by speciously going from the effect to the cause, and applying the active medicament, not to the wound, but to the weapon that did the mischief; thus giving to the former a chance to heal by the first intention.

There is great reason to believe, that, at the present day, homœopathic faith is not always kept up in its original purity by its professors. Traces of the occasional use of very heroic remedies are often detected among the most unsuspected of its practitioners. And it must not be concealed, that there are instances in which the temptation is very great, even for the most resolute convert, to come to the aid of the sick with reasonable and efficient doses of real medicine. The man must be somewhat of a stoic who can look upon a case of severe colic, or of the multiform distresses which result from overtasked organs of digestion, and quiet his conscience with administering inappreciable globules, instead of remedies.

4. THE EXCLUSIVE METHOD. — This, like the heroic system, is various in its means of treatment, but differs from it in the professed universality of its peculiar applications. Hydropathy applies one remedy, cold water, to all cases. Yet, like homoeopathy, it combines with its special agent a strict course of life, including exercise, temperance, regular hours, and a diet in the main simple and wholesome, though somewhat fanciful in its exclusions. The same was done, so far as was proper, in the previous practice of all judicious physicians. The use of cold bathing is not new, having been employed as a hygienic process from time immemorial by the civilized world. As a therapeutic agent, cold affusion was resorted to more than half a century ago, and has been practised ever since in a greater or less degree. But the peculiar mode of applying water by packing appears to be original with Priessnitz, an ignorant German, to whom it owes its popularity. Like the Russian bath, in which alternate approaches to scalding and freezing are said to be followed at last by very delightful sensations, the hydropathic discipline, in those who have soundness of constitution sufficient to insure a healthy re-action, is followed by agreeable and often salubrious results. Yet the ineffective character of hydropathy is seen in the multitude of disappointed invalids

who return unrelieved from its establishments. I have been told, by persons who have resided at Graefenberg, that funerals at that place were of constant occurrence; and it is well known, that Priessnitz, himself a robust peasant, died in the prime of life, in the midst of his own water-cure.

The greatest benefit at hydropathic establishments is obtained by those who reform their mode of life by submitting to the restraints of the place. The luxurious, the indolent, the sedentary, and the erratic, improve most under a return to regular, natural, active, and temperate habits. Accordingly it is found, that gout, dyspepsia, lost appetite, hysteria, and the various forms of nervous irritability, furnish the most hopeful subjects for such institutions. The same patients might, in many cases, obtain the same relief in another place, by pursuing the water-cure without the water.

The universality of hydropathic application has been somewhat diminished by prolonged experience. Priessnitz himself, although ignorant of science, and incapable of distinguishing one disease from another, at last became cautious in his selections, and nominally excluded diseases of the lungs from his institution.

It is not necessary to dwell upon the various exclusive modes of practice, more or less universal in their application, with which the columns of newspapers are daily filled. Mineral waters, taken at the fountain, are often of great use to those who require a journey or a change of scene. Particular springs also appear to exert a beneficial effect on particular maladies, though not panaceas for all ills. Watering-places, which combine amusement with exercise, are the temporary safety-valves of over-taxed physicians, and happily afford arks of refuge to multitudes of chronic valetudinarians. Electricity supports one or more establishments in all large cities, both in its simple form, and combined with all other imponderable agencies of mind and matter. Few persons go uncured of chronic maladies without having given it a sufficient and satisfactory trial. Finally, the host of empirical remedies, which fill the attention of a very considerable portion of this quack-ridden world, leave no human maladies out of the catalogue of subjects to their mysterious power. The drug aloes, in its hundred pill combinations, levies incessant contributions on those who purchase the privilege of being slaves to its use. Opium, variously disguised with aromatics to conceal its presence, gives temporary but fallacious respite to fatal diseases, under the deceptive names of pectorals and pulmonics.

It is superfluous to prolong the consideration of general and exclusive remedies. No person accustomed to witness the various morbid conditions which invade and occupy the human frame, active and passive, partial and general, trivial and dangerous, can ever consider them proper subjects for the same kind of treatment; unless, with Dr. Rush and Dr. Brandreth, he happens to be a believer in the unity of disease.

5. THE RATIONAL METHOD. — If no alternative were left to the physician and patient but the extreme and frequently irrational methods which have now been briefly described, practical medicine might well take its rank as a pseudo-science by the side of astrology and spiritualism. But the labors of earnest and philanthropic men, during many centuries, though often speculative, misguided, and terminating in error, have nevertheless elicited enough of general truth to serve as the foundation for a stable superstructure. And, that such truth may hereafter go on to accumulate, it must be simply and honestly sought, even when its developments do not at once promote the apparent interest of physicians, nor flatter their professional pride of opinion.

It is to sincere and intelligent observers, and not to audacious charlatans, that we are to look as the ultimate lawgivers of medical science. Our present defect is, not that we know too little, but that we profess too much. We regard it as a sort of humiliation to acknowledge that we cannot always cure diseases; forgetting that in many other sciences mankind have made no greater advances than ourselves, and are still upon the threshold of their respective structures. Medical assumption may well feel humbled by the most insignificant diseases of the human body. Take, for example, a common furunculus or boil. No physician can, by any internal treatment, produce it where it does not exist. No physician can, by any science, explain it, and say why it came on one limb, and not upon another. No physician can, by any art, cure it after it has arrived at a certain height. No physician can, by any art, delay or retain it after it has passed the climax assigned to it by nature. And what is true in regard to a boil is equally true of common pneumonia, of typhoid fever, of acute rheumatism, of cholera, and many other diseases.

In the present state of our knowledge, the truth appears to be simply this: Certain diseases, of which the number is not very great, are curable, or have their cure promoted, by drugs, and by appliances which are strictly medicinal. Certain other diseases, perhaps more numerous, are curable in like manner by means which are strictly regiminal, and consist in changes of place, occupation, diet, and habits of life. Another class of diseases are self-limited, and can neither be expelled from the body by artificial means, nor retained in the body after their natural period of duration has expired. Finally, a large class of diseases have proved incurable from the beginning of history to the present time, and under some one of these the most favored members of the human race must finally succumb; for even curable diseases become incurable when they have reached a certain stage, extent, or complication.

It will be seen that the divisions last mentioned cannot be strictly reduced under the nomenclature of nosologies; for cases, and groups of cases, may begin in one category and end in another.

It is the part of rational medicine to study intelligently the nature, degree, and tendency of each existing case, and afterwards to act, or to forbear acting, as the exigencies of such case may require. To do all this wisely and efficiently, the practitioner must possess, first, sufficient knowledge to diagnosticate the disease; and, secondly, sufficient sense, as well as knowledge, to make up a correct judgment on the course to be pursued. In the first of these, if properly educated and experienced, he will be able to make an approximation to the truth sufficient for practical purposes. In the second he will have to depend mainly on his well-ordered and logical powers of self-direction; for he will find, in the recorded evidence of his predecessors, quite as much to mislead as to guide him rightly. He will find many existing cases, in which for a time he will know not what to do, and in which his safest course will be not to do he knows not what. It is better to resort to a little expectancy, than to rush into blind and reckless action. Nature, when not encumbered with overwhelming burdens, and when not abused by unnatural and pernicious excesses, is, after all, "the kindest mother still." Art may sometimes remove those burdens, and regulate those excesses; but it is not by imposing new burdens, and instituting new excesses, that an end so desirable is to be attained. Before commencing any contemplated course of treatment in a given case, two questions should always be asked: 1. Will it do good? 2. Will it do harm? A right answer to these questions will not fail to produce a right practice.

It is the part of rational medicine to alleviate the sufferings of the sick. And for this end alone, were there no other, physicians would be necessary as a profession. For this end alone, any person knowingly about to encounter the confinement of a self-limited fever, or the lingering decay of a cancer or consumption, would invoke the guidance of a medical man whose judgment and skill were better than his own. The power of the medical art to palliate diseases is shown in a multitude of ways, active, cautious, and expectant. The pain of acute pleurisy is relieved by venesection; that of pleurodynia, by anodynes and external applications. The pain of acute rheumatism is postponed by opium; that of gout, by colchicum. Synovitis is favorably affected by rest; chronic rheumatism, more frequently by exercise. Demulcents, opiates, and even astringents, have their use in various irritations of the mucous membranes. Cathartics, laxatives, emetics, leeches, counter-irritants, cupping, hot and cold applications, &c., are of benefit in various local and general maladies. Yet these remedies, especially the more energetic of them, are often employed when not necessary, and become, by their degree and frequency, rather sources of annoyance than of relief. Violent cathartics are followed by increased constipation, when milder laxatives or enemata would not have induced that evil. Blisters, antimonial ointments, salivation, &c., may continue to afflict the patient long after the disease is gone. The effects of powerful depletion are felt for months, and sometimes for years. Excessive stimulation by vinous liquids may create or renew disease, or give rise to pernicious artificial wants. To prescribe blindly for symptoms, irrespectively of their cause, is often in the highest degree injudicious. The alvine discharges of dysentery and typhoid fever are the natural ventings of an inflamed, perhaps ulcerated, membrane: the pain and the excess may be abated by the gentlest anodynes; but the attempt to check them altogether would be like the drying up of an external ulcer, of equal dimensions, by the sudden application of astringents. The object might be attained for a day, but the result would be pernicious. Having already touched upon this subject, I have only to add, that if many of the troublesome appliances and severe exactions of modern practice were superseded by gentler, more soothing, and more natural means, a good would be done to the human race comparable to the conversion of swords into ploughshares.

It is the part of rational medicine still to strive and study for the cure of diseases; not to assume fallaciously as practical truth what has never been shown to be true, but rather to search and labor for new truth, for which it is never too late to hope. The rational physician will ever be ready to weigh and examine, candidly and carefully, new practical questions and proposed modes of treatment, whether introduced for the alleviation or the removal of diseases; and he will recollect, that although nineteen out of every twenty of the new methods proposed may be worthless, yet the twentieth may perhaps possess some valuable quality. It is known that the most established laws of science cease to be such when their exceptions have been detected and made out. Some of the most important advances in human knowledge have been among the latest in date. The great American discovery of artificial anæsthesia has been wished and waited for by mankind ever since the Flood; yet the effectual conquest of pain is, as it were, a thing of yesterday.

It is the part of rational medicine to require evidence for what it admits and believes. The cumbrous fabric now called therapeutic science is, in a great measure, built up on the imperfect testimony of credulous, hasty, prejudiced, or incompetent witnesses, such as have afforded authorities for books like Murray's "Apparatus Medicaminum," and Hahnemann's "Organon." The enormous polypharmacy of modern times is an excrescence on science, unsupported by any evidence of necessity or fitness; and of which the more complicated formulas are so arbitrary and useless, that, if by any chance they should be forgotten, not one in a hundred of them would ever be re-invented. And as to the chronicles of cure of diseases that are not yet known to be curable, they are written, not in the pages of philosophic observers, but in the tomes of compilers, the crudities of journalists, and the columns of advertisers.

It is the part of rational medicine to enlighten the public and the profession in regard to the true powers of the healing art. The community require to be undeceived and re-educated, so far as to know what is true and trustworthy from what is gratuitous, unfounded, and fallacious. And the profession themselves will proceed with confidence, self-approval, and success, in proportion as they shall have informed mankind on these important subjects. The exaggerated impressions now prevalent in the world, in regard to the powers of medicine, serve only to keep the profession and the public in a false position, to encourage imposture, to augment the number of candidates struggling for employment, to burden and disappoint the community already over-taxed, to lower the standard of professional character, and raise empirics to the level of honest and enlightened physicians.

I AM not willing to leave the subject of Rational Medicine without more earnestly calling the attention of the profession in the United States, to the admirable work of Sir John Forbes, already alluded to, on "Nature and Art in the Cure of Disease," of which an American edition has recently appeared. No testimony of mine can be needed to make known the claims of one of the most accomplished medical scholars of Europe, of whose philosophic mind, vigorous perceptions, and clear, discriminating, and impartial judgment, this volume is a legitimate product and a convincing evidence.

Neither is it necessary to inform the public, that, as one of the pioneers in the reform now in progress, the same author published, in 1846, in the "British and Foreign Medical Review," an elaborate article, bearing the title of "Young Physic," which, though somewhat startling in the novelty of its positions, and by many disapproved for the credit given to statements of questionable parties, had, nevertheless, the effect, both in England and this country, to increase public attention to inquiries which the present volume is so well adapted to satisfy. Some of the concluding propositions of this able article, not everywhere accessible to American readers, are reprinted as an Appendix to this article. It appeared nine years after the treatise on "Self-limited Diseases" was published in this country.

In France, perhaps more than any other country, the natural history of disease has been studied irrespectively of artificial influences. When the modes of rigorous investigation, to which in that country the laws of morbid affections have been submitted, shall have been carried as far as possible into the more complex and difficult subject of therapeutics, they will at least help to guard it from the errors of premature and speculative generalization, to which the medical world has in all ages been prone.*

Of the contributions to rational medicine which have been made in this country, it gives me gratification to refer to various able, just, and eloquent

---

* The numerical method, so advantageously applied by Louis and his successors to determine approximately the pathological character of diseases, cannot be well applied to the more complex subject of medical treatment, without great caution and reserve on the score of inference. Things submitted to this ordeal must be such as have some obvious connection with each other: otherwise we are liable to be led into error by the most careful observation and analysis. Such would be the case if we were to attempt to settle numerically the questions, whether medicine applied to a weapon promoted the cure of a wound, — whether the hanging of witches had favorably affected the duration of epidemics, — whether it is safe for sailors to go to sea on Friday, &c. These are questions which are settled by the common sense of an enlightened age, and not by numerical analysis. The extensive numerical trials, made in different countries, on the effect of bleeding in pneumonia, have not yet afforded results fully satisfactory to inquirers. It is worthy of notice, that ques-

discourses and essays, by my friends and others, which have appeared at different times. Among these should be distinguished a Discourse " On the Condition, Prospects, and Duties of the Medical Profession," by Edward Reynolds, M.D., published in 1841; a Discourse entitled " Search out the Secrets of Nature," by Augustus A. Gould, M.D., 1855; a Discourse on " Nature in Disease," by Benjamin E. Cotting, M.D., 1852;* a Prize Essay on " Rational Therapeutics," by Professor Worthington Hooker, of New Haven, 1857; also a previous volume, by the same able and intelligent writer, entitled " Physician and Patient," 1849.

If it be permitted to refer to an extra-professional authority, bearing, nevertheless, the marks of much intelligent observation, I would cite, in behalf of the same cause, " The Rational Doctor," in the " Household Words " of Charles Dickens.

---

tions of relief are more promptly settled than questions of duration and of safety. A man suffering the orthopnœa of pleurisy will lie down and breathe with comparative ease after venesection; and this is sufficient motive for the reasonable use of that remedy. But the length and safety of the disease, under different modes of treatment, afford questions yet to be settled, if at all, by a vast amount of observation, by competent persons, under the various differences of constitution, degree, complication, season, age, &c.

* Since the publication of the above, a very able address, by Cotting, has been delivered at the annual meeting of the Massachusetts Medical Society in 1866, on Disease as a Part of the Plan of Creation. It has been translated into French in Paris, and bids fair to be the introduction to a novel and interesting branch of inquiry.

APPENDIX TO EXPOSITIONS OF RATIONAL MEDICINE.

The following are the principal remarks of Sir J. Forbes, appended, as a sort of recapitulation, to his article in the "British and Foreign Medical Review," vol. xxi. p. 262. They are there submitted by him as things to be reflected and acted on by the medical profession. A great portion of them, though perhaps not all, are applicable in this country as well as in England.

"1. To endeavor to ascertain, much more precisely than has been done hitherto, the natural course and event of diseases, when uninterrupted by artificial interference; in other words, to attempt to establish a true natural history of human diseases.

"2. To reconsider and study afresh the physiological and curative effects of all our therapeutic agents, with a view to obtain more positive results than we now possess.

"3. To endeavor to establish, as far as is practicable, what diseases are curable, and what are not; what are capable of receiving benefit from medical treatment, and what are not; what treatment is the best, the safest, the most agreeable; when it is proper to administer medicine, and when to refrain from administering it, &c., &c.

"4. To endeavor to introduce a more philosophical and accurate view of the relations of remedies to the animal economy and to diseases, so as to dissociate in the minds of practitioners the notions of *post hoc* and *propter hoc*.*

"The general adoption by practitioners, in recording their experience, of the system known by the name of the *Numerical*

---

* Subsequent and consequent.

Method, is essential to the attainment of the ends proposed in the preceding paragraphs, as well as in many that are to follow.

"5. To endeavor to banish, from the treatment of acute and dangerous diseases at least, the ancient axiom, 'Melius anceps remedium quam nullum;'* and to substitute in its place the safer and wiser dogma, that, where we are not certain of an indication, we should give nature the best chance of doing the work herself, by leaving her operations undisturbed by those of art.

"6. To endeavor to substitute, for the monstrous system of Polypharmacy now universally prevalent, one that is, at least, vastly more simple, more intelligible, more agreeable, and, it may be hoped, one more rational, more scientific, more certain, and more beneficial.

"7. To direct redoubled attention to hygiene, public and private, with the view of preventing diseases on the large scale, and, individually, in our sphere of practice. Here the surest and most glorious triumphs of medical science are achieving and to be achieved.

"8. To inculcate generally a milder and less energetic mode of practice, both in acute and chronic diseases; to encourage the Expectant preferably to the Heroic system, — at least where the indications of treatment are not manifest.

"9. To discountenance all active and powerful medication in the acute exanthemata and fevers of specific type, as small-pox, measles, scarlatina, typhus, &c., until we obtain some evidence that the course of these diseases can be beneficially modified by remedies.

"10. To discountenance, as much as possible, and eschew the habitual use — without any sufficient reason — of certain powerful medicines, in large doses, in a multitude of different diseases; a practice now generally prevalent, and fraught with the most baneful consequences.

"This is one of the besetting sins of English practice, and originates partly in false theory, and partly in the desire to see manifest and strong effects resulting from the action of medi-

---

* A doubtful remedy is better than none.

cines. Mercury, iodine, colchicum, antimony, also purgatives in general, and blood-letting, are frightfully misused in this manner.

"11. To encourage the administration of simple, feeble, or altogether powerless, non-perturbing medicines, in all cases in which drugs are prescribed *pro forma*, for the satisfaction of the patient's mind, and not with the view of producing any direct remedial effect.

"One would hardly think such a caution necessary, were it not that everyday observation proves it to be so. The system of giving and also of *taking* drugs capable of producing some obvious effect — on the sensations, at least, if not on the functions — has become so inveterate in this country, that even our *placebos* have, in the hands of our modern doctors, lost their original quality of harmlessness, and often please their very patients more by being made unpleasant!

"12. To make every effort, not merely to destroy the prevalent system of giving a vast quantity and variety of unnecessary and useless drugs, — to say the least of them, — but to encourage extreme simplicity in the prescription of medicines that seem to be requisite.

"Our system is here greatly and radically wrong. Our officinal formulæ are already most absurdly and mischievously complex, and our fashion is to double and redouble the existing complexities. This system is a most serious impediment in the way of ascertaining the precise and peculiar powers (if any) of the individual drugs, and thus interferes, in the most important manner, with the progress of therapeutics.

"We are aware of the arguments that are adduced in defence of medicinal combinations. We do not deny that some of these combinations are beneficial, and therefore proper; but there cannot be a question as to the enormous evils, speaking generally, resulting from them. Nothing has a greater tendency to dissociate practical medicine from science, and to stamp it as a *trade*, than this system of pharmaceutical artifice. It takes some years of the student's life to learn the very things which are to block up his path to future knowledge. A very elegant prescriber is seldom a good physician.

"13. To endeavor to break through the routine habit, universally prevalent, of prescribing certain determinate remedies for certain determinate diseases or symptoms of diseases, merely because the prescriber has been taught to do so, and on no better grounds than conventional tradition.

"Even when the medicines so prescribed are innocuous, the routine proceeding impedes real knowledge, by satisfying the mind, and thus producing inaction. When the drugs are potent, the crime of mischief is superadded to the folly of empiricism. In illustration, we need merely notice the usual reference, in this country, of almost all chronic diseases accompanied with derangement of the intestinal functions, to 'affection of the liver,' and the consequent prescription of *mercury* in some of its forms. We do not hesitate to say, that this theory is as far wrong as the practice founded on it is injurious; we can hardly further enhance the amount of its divarication from the truth.

"14. To place in a more prominent point of view the great value and importance of what may be termed the physiological, hygienic, or natural system of curing diseases, especially chronic diseases, in contradistinction to the pharmaceutical or empirical drug-plan generally prevalent. This system, founded as it is on a more comprehensive inquiry into *all* the remote and exciting causes of disease, and on a more thorough appreciation of *all* the discoverable disorders existing in all the organs and functions of the body, does not, of course, exclude the use of drugs, but regards them (generally speaking) as subservient to hygienic, regiminal, and external means, such as the rigid regulation of the diet, the temperature and purity of the air, clothing, the mental and bodily exercise, &c., baths, friction, change of air, travelling, change of occupation, &c., &c.

"15. To endeavor to introduce a more comprehensive and philosophical system of Nosology, at least in chronic diseases, whereby the practitioner may be led less to consider the name of a disease, or some one symptom, or some one local affection in a disease, than the disease itself; that is, *the whole* of the derangements existing in the body, and which it is his object to remove, if possible.

"16. To teach teachers to teach the rising generation of

medical men that it is infinitely more *practical* to be master of the elements of medical science, and to know diseases thoroughly, than to know by rote a farrago of receipts, or to be aware that certain doctors, of old or of recent times, have said that certain medicines are good for certain diseases.

"17. Also to teach students, that no systematic or theoretical classification of diseases or of therapeutic agents, ever yet promulgated, is true, or any thing like the truth; and that none can be adopted as a safe guide in practice. It is, however, well that these systems should be known, as most of them involve some pathological truths, and have left some practical good behind them.

"18. To endeavor to enlighten the public as to the actual powers of medicines, with a view to reconciling them to simpler and milder plans of treatment. To teach them the great importance of having their diseases treated in their earliest stages, in order to obtain a speedy and efficient cure; and, by some modification in the relations between the patient and practitioner, to encourage and facilitate this early application for relief.

"19. To endeavor to abolish the system of medical practitioners being paid by the amount of medicine sent in to their patients, and even the practice of keeping and preparing medicines in their own houses.

"Were a proper system introduced for securing a good education to chemists and druggists, and for examining and licensing them, — all of easy adoption, — there could be no necessity for continuing even the latter practice; while the former is one so degrading to the medical character, and so frightfully injurious to medicine in a thousand ways, that it ought to be abolished forthwith, utterly, and for ever.

"20. Lastly, and above all, to bring up the medical mind to the standard necessary for studying, comprehending, appreciating, and exercising the most complex and difficult of the arts that are based on a scientific foundation, — the art of Practical Medicine. And this can only be done by elevating the preliminary and fundamental education of the Medical Practitioner."

THE PARADISE OF DOCTORS.

A FABLE.

READ AT THE ANNUAL DINNER OF THE MASSACHUSETTS MEDICAL SOCIETY, MAY 26, 1858.

It happened, once, that a general awakening took place among the physicians, druggists, and citizens of the quiet old State of Massachusetts; during which it was discovered, that a great and culpable neglect had long been prevalent throughout the community, in regard to the important duty of taking physic. A conviction fell upon all, that it was now imperatively necessary that every man, woman, and child should proceed at once and habitually, in sickness and in health, to take three times as much medicine as they had taken before. This new revelation, explained and enforced by competent authorities, quickened into sudden activity every department of industry connected with the preparing, prescribing, and dispensing of drugs. The repose of cities was disturbed in a manner not before known, by the rattling of doctors' carriages, and the braying of apothecaries' mortars. Messengers were seen rapidly traversing streets and roads in all directions, bearing prescriptions and compositions. Nurses' wages were doubled, and cooks were transformed into nurses. All things gave evidence, that a great and portentous reform had come over the land.

In all places of business and amusement, in the street and in the drawing-room, physic was the paramount subject of conversation. Newspapers neglected to announce the arrival of steamers and the brawls of Congress, that they might find place for the last astonishing cures, and the most newly-discovered specifics. Sympathetic intercommunications and experiences were imparted, and listened to with untiring avidity. Many luxuries unknown before found their way into society, dinners were regularly medicated, wines scientifically sophisticated, and desserts were made up of conserves, electuaries, and dinner-pills. The atmosphere was redolent with the incense of aloes and myrrh.

Clergymen and moralists forgot that men were sinful; it was quite enough that they were bilious. Bile was regarded as the innate and original sin, which was to be extirpated with fire and physic, even from the new-born child. Nobody was aware that bile is necessary to life; no two persons were agreed as to what the term *bilious* meant; it was something insidious, mysterious, and awful. Some held that it consisted in having too much bile;

others in having too little. According to some, the bile was held back in the blood; according to others, it was absorbed ready formed into the blood. Fierce schisms and sects were generated on the question, who, and whether any, were exempt from its contaminating presence. The *bon vivant*, after his night's carouse, furnished abundant demonstrations of its existence on the following morning. A healthy laborer, who had had the temerity to boast of his freedom from bilious taint or suspicion, was convicted and brought to his senses by the ordeal of a dozen grains of tartar-emetic.

On the exchange, brokers postponed their stocks and bonds, that they might publish daily lists of the prices of drugs. Fortunes were made and lost in drug speculations. A man grew rich by a patent for manufacturing Peruvian bark out of pine saw-dust. Gilded pills, of various weight and potency, passed as a circulating medium, and were freely taken at the shops in payment for better goods. Finally, the physicians did not attempt to eat or sleep, but barely found time to enter their daily professional charges. They were worshipped and run after, by both sick and well, as the legitimate vehicles of medicine, and were ignominiously deserted if in any case they ventured to pronounce medicine unnecessary.

The fame of these doings went abroad, and Massachusetts acquired the enviable celebrity of being the Paradise of medical men. The doctors in New Hampshire, and the druggists in New York, hearing of the success of their professional brethren in this quarter, began to abandon their establishments and remove into Massachusetts. The example was followed in other States ; new recruits were drawn from the counter and the plough ; and in a short time the country and city were inundated by swarms of medical practitioners of all denominations. Agreeably to the acknowledged law of commerce and political economy, that demand and supply necessarily regulate each other, the business of many persons, which had undergone an undue exaggeration, was at length found rapidly to decline under increasing competition, and the aggregate receipts of the year were found, to the cost of not a few disciples of Esculapius, to be less than they had ever been before. Medicines became drugs, and the Paradise of Doctors became an excellent place for doctors to starve in. Nevertheless, although the market was as much glutted as the people, still a large surplus, both of zeal and physic, remained to be worked off in some way.

Meanwhile, the revival went on, and its effects began to tell upon the faces and movements of the people. There was a deficiency in the will to undertake, and the power to execute, even common enterprises. Men went languidly to their respective places of business, or stayed at home if it was their day to take a purgative or an emetic. Purses were found to be lightened, and the contour of persons grew sensibly less. In one thing only the economy of living was promoted: owing to the decline of appetite, the consumption of food was much diminished. Under this order of things, it was noticed that labor and exercise were little in vogue, and people betook themselves in preference to the occupation of doing nothing. A small number, it is true, made a desperate effort to effect a change by doubling their doses of physic; but the result did not encourage a repetition of the experiment. At last a cholera came; and, although a forty-drug power was promptly brought to bear upon it, the mortality was greater than it had ever been known to be before.

Nevertheless, weak-minded men and strong-minded women failed not to harangue audiences in the streets, on the astonishing powers of medicine. Spirit-rappers were summoned to evoke from their rest the heroic shades of Rush and Bouillaud, Sangrado, Morrison, and Brandreth. These distinguished worthies exhorted their followers not to shrink or falter under the trials to which they were subjected, but rather to redouble their perseverance, until the truth of the faith which they held should be established by the testimony of their martyrdom in its cause.

At length, a meeting accidentally took place

between two old shipmasters, one of whom had lost overboard his barrel of beef, and the other his medicine-chest, in a gale of wind, at the commencement of their passage. On examination and comparison of their respective crews, the contrast was so marked between the ruddy faces of the latter, and the lantern jaws of the former, that a general mutiny sprang up in both crews against the further tolerance of the physic-taking part of their duty. The contagious insurrection spread from Fort Hill to Copp's Hill; and, on the following night, several medicine-chests were thrown overboard by men in the disguise of South-sea Islanders.

The spark which had struck the magazine caused the whole population to explode. A universal mass meeting was called upon Boston Common, and protracted through several days and nights. Agitators, reformers, and stump-orators delivered their harangues and defined their positions. Many speakers advocated an immediate application to the Legislature, calling on them to prohibit, by an especial act, all further traffic in drugs. One, more violent than the rest, demanded that the meeting should resolve itself into a committee of vigilance, for the purpose of making a descent upon the apothecaries' shops, and emptying the contents of their bottles into the streets. He was willing to allow to offenders themselves the option to quit within twenty-four hours, or swallow their own medicines. A more moderate citizen said he rose in support of the general sentiment; but would offer an amendment, that, in the contemplated destruction, an exception should be made in favor of Bourbon whiskey. A few of the advocates of the policy lately prevalent attempted to make themselves heard; but their voices were so attenuated, by the long use of jalap and salts, that they failed to produce any considerable impression.

An old lady, whose shrill voice drew immediate attention, protested against violent measures of all kinds, and moved, as a middle course, that resort should be had to homœopathy. It never did any harm, and was very comforting, especially when well recommended by the physician. It cured her child of the measles in six weeks, and herself of a broken leg in six months, during which time she had two hundred and ninety-five visits, and took more than fifteen hundred globules. She had walked to the meeting on her crutches, to exhibit to the assembly the astonishing powers of the Hahnemannic system. Here she was interrupted by a bluff marketer, who somewhat rudely pronounced homœopathy to be a great humbug, since, but a short time before, his child had eaten part of a raw pumpkin, and was seized with convulsions; and the physician who was sent for, instead of taking measures to dislodge the offending cause, took out a little book, and, remarking to the bystanders that "like cures like," proceeded to prescribe the hundred millionth part of another pumpkin. The next person who rose was a manufacturer, who had calculated that the homœopathic profit on the cost of the raw material was altogether unreasonable. He had himself expended seventy-five dollars in a quarter of a grain of belladonna, so divided as to keep off scarlet fever; but found, after all, that he had not bought enough, for his children had the disease a little worse than any of their neighbors.

At last an old gentleman, moderately endowed with common sense, got up, and inquired if there was no such thing in the world as *rational medicine*, and whether nothing could be made acceptable to the public but extremes of absurdity. He asked if it was necessary that every theologian should be a Papist or an atheist, or every voter at the polls an abolitionist or a fire-eater. He had had the good fortune to know several very sensible, straightforward physicians, who gave medicine where it was necessary, and omitted to give it where it was unnecessary or detrimental. He deprecated the routine practice, which, without understanding the nature of a disease or the necessities of the existing case, inflicted a daily or hourly dose of medicine, sometimes actual, and sometimes nominal, but always at the cost of the patient. Medicine, in its place, was a good thing, but proved a bad thing when we got too much of it. He had himself had the misfortune to be several times sick; and, during the continuance of his disease, felt much more gratified on those days in which it was announced that he was to take no medicine, than when tartar emetic was replaced by calomel, and calomel by colchicum, aconite, and the last new remedy. If patients and their friends were ignorant and unreasonable, it might sometimes be necessary to deal with a fool according to his folly; but he believed that sensible men and women were gratified by being regarded and treated as reasonable beings. It was a mistake in medical men to suppose, that their influence or social position could be improved by the mystery which they observed, and the activity with which they harassed their patients. In Great Britain, an island where the people subsist largely on blue pills and black draughts, the doctors were never known to attain the high aristocratic rank which was occasionally accorded to successful bankers, jurists, and generals. On the contrary, the country was overflowed with starved apothecaries and physicians advertising for situations as travelling servants. He thought one of the greatest misapplications of human industry was in the production of superfluous drugs and drug dispensers. He did not believe in the transmutation of metals, but was a great believer in their transportation. In the form of calomel, the city of New Orleans alone had swallowed up some hundred tons of the quicksilver of Spain and South America. Palaces were being built in various cities alike from poisonous arsenic and harmless sarsaparilla. A century hence, the mines of gold will be sought for, not in California, but in the cemeteries of the old cities, where it has been geologically deposited under the industry of dentists.

He believed that the experienced and intelligent part of the medical profession had long since arrived at the conclusion, that many diseases were self-limited, and that time and nature had quite as much to do as art in the process of their cure. Skilful physicians were always wanted to inform the sick of the character of their diseases, and of the best mode of getting through them; and their skill consisted not in the abundance of their nominal remedies, but in the judgment with which a few remedies were administered or withheld, and in the general safe conduct of the patient. Some diseases are curable by art, and others are not; yet, in the treatment of all diseases, there is a right method and a wrong, and too much activity is quite as injurious as too little. A good shipmaster or pilot could often navigate his vessel in safety, though he could not cure the storm by which its safety was endangered. He believed that medicine would have fulfilled its true mission when doctors should have enlightened the public on the important fact, that there are certain things which medicine can do, and certain other things which it cannot do; instead of assuming for it the power to do impossibilities. Among the good effects which must ensue from this diffusion of light would be the disappearance of quackery from the world; for quackery consists almost wholly in medication. And the more physicians lend themselves to formal, superfluous, and mysterious drugging, the more nearly do they approach to being quacks themselves. He considered physicians an important and necessary class, to whose charge the sick always had been, and always would be, committed. He would gladly cleanse the profession from the fanaticism of heroic doctors on the one hand, and of moonstruck doctors on the other; and would replace these forms of delusion by a discriminating, sincere, intelligent, and rational course of treating diseases.

The old gentleman sat down, and his speech seemed good in the eyes of his audience. Resolutions were moved and adopted, to the effect, that it was unbecoming a free and enlightened people to be drug-ridden or globule-ridden, and recommending recourse to temperance, exercise, regularity, and rational medicine, whenever it happened that medical treatment was necessary.

The meeting quietly dissolved, and its members returned to their respective homes, most of them satisfied that the revival was passed, and that medicine was not altogether the one thing needful.

In a short time the price of drugs fell in the market, while that of provisions advanced. The New-Hampshire doctors and the New-York druggists, finding their occupations gone, returned to the places from which they respectively came. The surplus of indigenous medical men went off to California, or retired to cultivate the earth in the interior counties. Faces assumed a more vigorous and healthy aspect; and the country once more resounded with the music of the axe and the hammer, and the cheerful rattling of knives and forks. Steam-engines, which had been erected for the pulverization of drugs, were attached to saw-mills and spinning jennies. Last of all, a noble and useful art, which had long been depressed under the effects of its own exaggeration, was enabled once more to raise its respectable head, and to regain the confidence of society, under the name of RATIONAL MEDICINE.

PRACTICAL VIEWS ON MEDICAL EDUCATION.*

The undecided state of public opinion in regard to some of the fundamental points in a course of medical education, including among other things the portion of the term of pupilage proper to be spent in attendance on lectures, is thought to justify a further consideration of the subject. In some of its relations, this subject has already been discussed, in the "Transactions of the American Medical Association for 1849," in two reports, pages 353 and 359, to which the reader is particularly referred. The following condensed but more general view of the subject of medical education is now respectfully submitted to the members of the Association.

Medical instruction should be adapted to the power of students to receive and retain what is communicated to them, and should be confined to what is important to them in their subsequent life.

---

* Published by vote of the Medical Faculty of Harvard University in 1850.

In modern times, the constituent branches of medical science are so expanded, that they are not acquired by any physician in a lifetime, and still less by a student during his pupilage. The same is true even of many individual branches. It is not, therefore, to be conceded, that " a scheme of scientific instruction should embrace the whole science, and no part should be omitted;" nor that " a well-digested plan of lectures embraces all that is to be known and taught." Medical science has at this day become so unwieldy, and contains so much that is unnecessary, at least to beginners, that the attempt to explain to students the whole is likely to involve the result of their learning but little.

In Chemistry, at the present time, a thorough adept is unknown. No man living knows all the recorded facts, or all that is to be known and taught, in that science. Organic chemistry alone fills large volumes, though yet in its infancy.

In Materia Medica there are some thousands of substances and their compounds, which possess what is called a medicinal power. Yet it is not probable that any physician effectively reads the one half, or remembers one quarter, or employs in his yearly practice one tenth, of the contents of the common dispensatories.

In Pathology, so complicated and various are the conditions attendant on the individual forms of disease, and their relations with idiosyncrasy, temporary condition, and external agency, with organic lesions and functional disturbances, that few of the most experienced pathologists can be said to understand their whole science, or to be always competent to its successful application.

In Etiology, the theoretical literature of causes has spread itself out to an extent which is burdensome and unprofitable. It is true that "man, from his nature, is subject to suffering, disease, and death;" but it is not equally apparent that " the causes by which these conditions are produced are ascertainable." We know nothing of the vehicle of cholera or influenza; nor is it probably in the power of any physician, by any art or application of his knowledge, to produce, in a given healthy man, a case of common pneumonia or of acute rheumatism, of diabetes or Bright's kidney, of hypertrophy or of cancer, or even of a common boil or wart.

In Therapeutics, many hundred volumes exist, such as would not have existed could a knowledge of the cure of diseases be made so easily tangible, that it could be spread before the student in the three or five years of his pupilage.

In Anatomy, general and special, microscopic and transcendental; in physiology, with its intricate ramifications; in Surgery, of which several subordinate specialities constitute distinct living professions,—it is not to be admitted that the means or time of any ordinary course of lectures can furnish full and complete instruction. Certainly it must be difficult to arrange a course of lectures on any of the extensive sciences which now constitute medicine, if it be indeed true that "the teachers are not justifiable in suppressing any portion."

It is the business of lecturers in medical schools to condense and abridge the sciences which they respectively teach, to distinguish their essential and elementary principles, to sift carefully the useful from the superfluous, and to confine the scope of their teachings, as far as possible, to what is true and profitable, and likely to be remembered and used by their hearers. It is unfortunately too true, that, "in an extended system of instruction, there is much that the student will not master, much that will have escaped his attention, much which he ought to know that he has not learned." The remedy appears to be, to teach him well what he can and should master, and briefly to point out to him the sources, fortunately abundant, from which he may obtain the rest.

Much injury is done to the cause of true learning by medical assumption, amplification, and exaggeration, by premature adoption of novelties, and by tenacity of theories, personal or espoused. Students, in all former years, have expended much time in learning what it afterwards cost them both time and trouble to unlearn,—in acquiring, not merely the truths of science, but the crude announcements and plausible doctrines of sanguine or ingenious men. How much time has been wasted, in some of our distinguished seminaries, in acquiring the visionary and now neglected theories of Rush and Broussais!

The most commonly exaggerated branch of medical science is therapeutics. Enlightened physicians well know that many diseases are incurable, and that others are subject to laws of duration which cannot be interrupted by art. Yet students sometimes return from medical schools, persuaded that their instructors know how to cure a large part of these diseases; and that, if others are less fortunate, it is attributable to their own fault.

Medical teachers should keep pace with the progress of their respective sciences. Yet, in their haste for the promulgation of novelties, they should not omit to give the proper consideration to the older and more settled principles of science. Medical men are liable to commit the error of adopting premature opinions, unsound practice, and inconvenient changes of language and nomenclature,—sometimes from a love of display, and sometimes from a want of self-reliance, and a fear of being thought behind the literature of their time.

The length of a course of lectures is not the measure of its value to the student. A course of lectures should not outlast the curiosity of its hearers, nor their average pecuniary ability to attend. Custom in this country has generally fixed the limits of these things at about four months. A comprehensive and judicious course, confined to the enforcing of necessary points, is far more profitable than a more discursive course to a wearied and diminishing audience.

Lectures are chiefly wanted to impress, by demonstration, the practical branches of science; and they are most effective in places where the facilities for such demonstrations can be commanded. Anatomy requires extensive exhibitions by the teacher, and personal dissections by the student. Chemistry and Materia Medica require illustrations by specimens and experiments. Pathology needs the aid of autopsies, museums, and the clinical demonstrations of large hospitals. A knowledge of Obstetrics is not perfected without apparatus and practice. Surgery is acquired by witnessing numerous operations, surgical diseases, illustrated explanations, and by personal practice on the dead body. Physical exploration is wholly demonstrative. A knowledge of auscultation can no more be acquired from books, or abstract lectures, than a knowledge of music or of individual physiognomy.

The intermediate period between lectures should be spent by students in active and original study, approved and confirmed by regular recitations, and by such opportunities as can be commanded for practical, personal experience. Private schools for small classes, and the private teaching of individuals who are suitably qualified and situated, are more advantageous, for two thirds of the year, than either the fatiguing jostle of overcrowded rooms, or the listless routine kept up by the survivors of a passive class.

The usefulness of a medical school depends, not so much on the length of its session, as upon the amount of education, preliminary and ultimate, which it requires, the fidelity with which it exacts its own professed requisitions, and the train of healthy exertion, active inquiry, and rigid, methodical, self-regulating study, to which it introduces its pupils. The longest lectures are of little use to students who want a common education, and whose medical education does not qualify them afterwards to observe, to inquire, and to discriminate. The exacted evidence of three years of well-conducted study is better than the exhibited ticket of a six-months course.

The subjects most important to be well taught in medical schools are the elementary principles which constitute the framework of medical sciences, and the mode of thought and inquiry which leads to just reasoning upon them. After these, most attention should be given to selecting and enforcing such practical truths as will most certainly be wanted by the young practitioner in his future career of responsibility.

The things to be avoided by medical teachers are technicalities, which are unintelligible to beginners; gratuitous assumptions, and citations of doubtful authorities; prolix dissertations on speculative topics; excessive minuteness in regard to subjects which are intricate and but little used, and therefore destined to be speedily forgotten. To these may be added controversies, superfluous personal eulogiums and criminations, and all self-exaggeration, personal or local.

ON THE EARLY HISTORY OF MEDICINE.*

It is commonly understood, that the history of medicine has already been traced, with sufficient accuracy, in all ages and countries where authorities for its elucidation are extant. The labors of Le Clerc, Friend, Haller, and Cabanis seem to have left very little to be wished in this department of science. But, although a general history of medicine is by no means a desideratum at the present day, yet there are undoubtedly parts of it which are still susceptible of correction or enlargement. Dr. Edward Miller, the author of the present " Disquisitions," apprises us that he has been induced to attempt them, partly from some singular traits which he thought he had discovered in the medicine of the early Greeks, and partly from the extraordinary advancement made of late years in Sanscrit literature. By means of this last we are informed, that, long previous to its introduction into Europe,

---

* From a Review of Miller's Disquisitions on the History of Medicine, published in the New-England Journal of Medicine and Surgery, April, 1812

the science of healing had made very considerable progress in Hindostan; yet to commemorate its details, or appreciate its merits, has never yet been the task of any historian in medicine. This new field of research Professor Miller has attempted to cultivate, and the fruits of his oriental inquiries are to constitute a second volume of "Disquisitions." In the mean time, the present volume, containing general archæological remarks, with speculations on the primitive physic of Greece and Egypt, is submitted to the ordeal of the public.

It must be exceedingly obvious, that, prior to the introduction of letters, no very definite information can be expected with regard to the state of medical practice in any country. If the traditionary account of the most important and notorious events, such as battles and sieges, the rise and fall of heroes and of empires, is involved in necessary uncertainty, we cannot expect that a complex science, closely interwoven in early ages with mystery and superstition, should reach us in a state capable of affording much satisfaction. The few traditions handed down to us from the primitive ages afford matter for speculation to the curious, but yield no certainty to the accurate.

Dr. Miller, seemingly aware of the difficulties attendant on this part of his subject, has thought it proper to commence the present undertaking with a sort of history *à priori*, or *presumptive his-*

tory, of medicine in its primeval state. He begins with stating the progress of observation and reasoning, which would naturally be made by the early and rude nations, in regard to the phenomena of life, health, disease, and death. He details the manner in which a gradual acquaintance would be formed with the nutritious, medical, and deleterious effects of the various productions of nature; and from hence assigns to the Materia Medica the supreme honors of antiquity. Afterwards comes the knowledge of practical physic, of anatomy, and of surgery, in proportion as men became habituated to watch the progress and cure of diseases, to butcher and dissect brute animals, to sacrifice, eat, or embalm their own species, and to inflict or remedy the wounds and injuries occasioned in war or elsewhere.

After this we are presented with an interesting account of that tract of territory, which we have reason to believe contained the earliest tribes of our species. To this region, composed chiefly of Egypt, Ethiopia, Turkey, Arabia, Persia, and India, Dr. M. gives the collective name of the *Primæval Chersonese.** He expatiates on the exuberance of its soil, the variety and value of its productions, its inducements for agriculture, and facilities for commercial intercourse. He represents that six

---

* This application of the term *Chersonese*, we think, rather stretches its ancient signification.

races or stems have, from time immemorial, occupied this ample and favored portion of the earth's surface. These are the Chinese, the Hindus, the Tartars, the Iranians (or Assyrians), the Arabs, and lastly the Nilotic tribes, or those of Egypt and Ethiopia. Among these he assigns an undoubted claim for priority of civilization to three nations, the Hindus, the Iranians, and the tribes inhabiting the banks of the Nile. The individual claims of these three he compromises, by endeavoring to prove, from tradition and history, from identity of language, &c., from conformity of religious and philosophical opinions, and, lastly, from similitude of corporeal structure, that they were only separate branches of one and the same individual family or race of men. In this investigation the author gives proofs of extensive and assiduous research.

Before quitting the general subject of the Primæval Chersonese, we are made minutely acquainted with its natural productions, or those articles which must have constituted the earliest food and medicine of man.

We now come to the particular history of medicine in early Greece, as it existed during the traditionary ages. On collecting the scattered rays of information respecting this period, chiefly from the poets, our author alights on a curious circumstance, which he makes the basis of this chapter; viz., "That, for its first discoveries and improvements, medicine in Greece appears indebted almost wholly to two orders of men, from whom such benefit was not likely to be derived, viz.: —

"1. The chiefs or sovereigns of its different small communities.

"2. The priests or ministers of religion."

Upon this ground the author proceeds to give us two dissertations on the heroic and the priestly medicine of Greece. And, first, of "heroic medicine."

On this subject we are told, that scarcely a royal or distinguished personage, during the traditionary period, can be named, to whom some degree of medical skill has not been accorded. The ascription of this honor is traced to several causes, such as the obscurity which hangs over the beginning of all arts; the veneration which savage tribes entertain for the character of their leaders; and the policy which would lead these chiefs to maintain their ascendency by the display of every species of personal merit or skill, that of medicine being not the least imposing. The practice of these heroic physicians, which the author believes to have been chiefly surgical, is illustrated by various accounts of the therapeutic exploits performed by several individuals. These are Chiron, Esculapius, Machaon, Podalirius, Achilles, Teucer, &c., &c., &c. The claims for medical distinction are, indeed, so numerous, that they may be said to amount to no distinction at all; since every man whose name has been handed down to us as holding a rank in a tolerable degree above the vulgar, would seem entitled to enrolment among the faculty. Chiron the Centaur is stated to have been preceptor to nearly all the heroes who figured in the Argonautic and Trojan expeditions. Now, as Chiron was one of those universal geniuses, who was competent to exercise the arduous and multiform functions of warrior and necromancer, of horse-breaker, musician, and doctor, it must be supposed that those who received the supreme honors of his school were not ushered into the world without a smattering of these various accomplishments. Hence the crew of the "Argo" might, on emergency, be considered a crew of the faculty; and the council of warriors in Agamemnon's camp required only a change of occasion to resolve them into a jury of doctors.

We have already intimated, that any accounts now extant respecting the medicine of the *early* Greeks must be extremely unsatisfactory. We may now add, that, from the few authorities we have, it may be doubted whether any proficiency in medicine was ever made among them, beyond what a rude individual would naturally attain in the science of self-preservation. The boasted achievements performed by their distinguished personages apparently consisted in some trifling and obvious operations, or else in such exaggerated and miraculous performances as distance all possibility of belief. The heroic or surgical practice among them was confined chiefly to the extraction of weapons and the dressing of wounds. The highest praise which Homer has bestowed on the medical or surgical profession is contained in the following lines:—

'Ιητρὸς γὰρ ἀνὴρ πολλῶν ἀντάξιος ἄλλων.
'Ιούς τ' ἐκτάμνειν, ἐπί τ' ἤπια φάρμακα πάσσειν,—

which amount to simply this, that "one doctor is worth a host of other men, to cut out arrows, and apply mild dressings." And, indeed, whenever he tells us of such a man being actually engaged in practice, it is commonly in one or the other of the above processes. Now, it could require no great depth of intellect to discover, that, if a barbed arrow stuck in the flesh, it could most easily be removed by excision; and that, if a wound became dry and painful from exposure to the air, it might be made more comfortable by covering it with emollient applications.

But, with such humble and obvious operations as these, the ancient physicians could not have sustained their elevated rank in society, and substantiated their claims upon immortality. It became necessary, in order to secure complete ascendency over the public mind, that they should profess an intercourse with the gods, a knowledge of mysterious charms and incantations, and other special gifts peculiar to jugglers in all nations since their time.

Very surprising stories are told of Melampus, Polyidus, and Chiron. These, however, are small when compared with the feats of Esculapius, the prince of physicians, and the deified inventor of medicine. Esculapius, in addition to many other astonishing powers, was gifted with a very remarkable faculty, peculiar to himself, of raising at pleasure the dead to life. Not less than six or seven instances are on record of distinguished corpses that were benefited by the exertion of this happy talent. It is impossible to say how far the bounds of science might have been enlarged by so mighty a genius, had not Pluto taken alarm at his progress, and presented a memorial to Jupiter, humbly showing, that, if a stop was not put to the career of this officious mortal, people would soon cease to die, and hell would become a desert; whereupon Jupiter interposed, and killed the wonder-working doctor with his thunderbolts.

There is reason to believe, from what has been said, that the cures effected by these medical worthies were either inconsiderable and real, or else preternatural and counterfeited. We have additional ground for this belief, on finding that frequently, when emergencies occurred opening a fine field for medical practice, the champions of physic were totally idle or inefficient. When a pestilence broke out among the Greeks at the Trojan war, we find them, with all their heroic and priestly medicine, resorting, not to their drugs and preparations, not to any regular system of practice, but simply to superstitious prayers, rites, and atonements. The Argonauts, with Esculapius at their head, required the aid of a sorceress, before they could administer an opiate to the dragon that watched their fleece. Chiron died of a wound or ulcer in the leg, and Achilles of one in the heel. Such disasters as these last were not to be expected, after what Dr. Miller tells us in his account of Chiron: "So celebrated was he in tradition for the cure of ulcers, as we are informed by Galen, that, when a sore was obstinate and could not be healed up, it was customary in later times to call it a *Chironian ulcer;* intimating, by the expression, that it was an ailment of such malignity as to baffle the skill even of Chiron himself."

Now, we conceive, it was no compliment to the Centaur to name only incurables after him. We also conceive that, between Galen and Dr. Miller, the origin of the term *Chironian ulcer* may have been mistaken; and that it may be derived, not from the skill of Chiron in curing malignant ulcers, but from the circumstance of his having languished and died under a malignant ulcer. Galen informs us, on this subject, that of the phagedæna, or eating ulcer, there were different species, called the Chironian and Telephian: "Harum species quædam sunt, quæ Chironia et Telephia dicuntur." In another place he tells us that the Telephian ulcer was so called from Telephus, who was afflicted with it. Now, the case of Chiron was not dissimilar to that of Telephus, as both their maladies were occasioned by the wound of a spear; only Telephus got well, whereas Chiron, after languishing with his lame leg for nine days, either died, or was made into a constellation; for all which the reader may consult Ovid. Fastorum V., 379–414.

Machaon, the son of Esculapius, when wounded at the siege of Troy, retired with Nestor to his tent, where they took from the hands of a woman a farrago of onions, cheese, meal, honey, and wine. From Pope's translation of this account in the Iliad, which Dr. M. has quoted, we are led to suppose that this potion was a *prescription* of the physician himself for his own case. Witness the following lines: —

"The draught *prescribed* fair Hecamede prepares."

And again,

"This *for the wounded prince* the dame prepares."

Unfortunately, however, there is no sort of authority in the original for the above expressions; and it appears that Hecamede prepared the draught, probably of her own invention, to treat her master Nestor, as well as his guest Machaon, and this, too, for the sole purpose of assuaging their thirst.

Τοῖσι δὲ τεῦχε κυκειῶ ἐϋπλόκαμος Ἑκαμήδη. Π. λ. 624.
Τὼ δ' ἐπεὶ οὖν πίνοντ' ἀφέτην πολυκαγκέα δίψαν.* 642.

---

* The translations of this passage by Cowper and Dacier are correct Chapman has the same inaccuracy with Pope.

It is a little remarkable that the learned professor should copy out the whole Greek passage for his book, and overlook such words as τοῖσι, σφῶϊν, σφὶ, and τὼ; or imagine them to be meant for Machaon individually. We are much inclined to suspect that he placed undue reliance on the translation, when we find him leaving off his Greek in the middle of a sentence, and observing that "it might be difficult in English poetry to discover a translation more distinguished for a happy mixture of *precision* and elegance, than the above version of Pope."

One more of these worthies, and then we have done with "heroic medicine." We presume that the name of Achilles will not yet descend to oblivion, even though our author should fail in his attempts to dub him also a doctor of medicine. Nevertheless, Achilles, it seems, was a pupil of Chiron. He cured the wound of Telephus with the rust of his spear; and the plant Achillæa, or yarrow, had the honor to be named after him. But it ought not to be forgotten, that the circumstance of his pupilage was common to most of the pre-eminent heroes of his time, and that, in the cure of Telephus, he had scarcely any merit. Telephus consulted the oracle, and was told that his wound could be healed only by the same *spear* which had occasioned it. Accordingly he applied to Achilles, whose spear had done the mischief, and requested his medical assistance. Achilles at first refused, saying that he was no physician; but afterwards was prevailed on to scrape the rust of his spear into the wound, which, in due time, got well. With regard to the plant Achillæa, we presume its name has as much to do with medicine as that of the plant Jeffersonia.

We now come to consider the second department which Dr. Miller has made in the physic of Greece, namely, his Priestly Medicine. As he has shown that the medicine of heroes was chiefly surgical, he now makes it equally clear that that of priests and conjurers was mere "practical physic." For this he gives us all the presumptive evidence which can arise from the natural ascendency of priests and wizards over the public mind, and from the analogy of customs in all the barbarous nations in the world. He gives us, however, only two instances of priest-physicians in Greece, namely, Melampus and Orpheus; of whom Melampus appears to us to have been only a fortune-hunter, who cured the daughters of Prœtus of real or pretended madness, that he might gain the hand of one of his patients, together with her kingdom, in marriage; while, with regard to Orpheus, there is very little authority for his having practised physic in any particular instance, and his high reputation is sufficiently supported by the established fact, that

"He *played* so well, he moved Old Nick."

On considerations like the foregoing, we are disposed to ascribe to the ancient Greeks the credit of very little real proficiency in the art of healing. From similar motives, we doubt the correctness of Dr. Miller's belief, that Greece was indebted for its first discoveries and improvements in medicine solely to two classes of men, namely, the chiefs or sovereigns, and the priests or ministers of religion. Unwilling, however, to interfere with the doctor's ardor for classification, we only suggest, for a second edition of his work, the propriety of adding a new class or department in primitive physic, to be called the department of *old women*, or of *female medicine*. These early practitioners of physic, we think, he has treated with unmerited neglect; for we will engage, where he produces one instance in Greece of a priest skilled in medicine, that we will furnish two of females possessing the same accomplishment. It is sufficient now to mention only the names of Circe, Medea, Angitia, Agamede, Helen, and Œnone.*

The last portion of our author's work embraces the history of medicine in Egypt and the East; and on this subject our limits compel us to be more brief. The advantages possessed by the Eastern countries over European Greece for the early cul-

---

* "In these early ages, all the knowledge of the tribe formed a common stock; and their imperfect arts might be exercised by all those who were endowed with a certain portion of intelligence. Medicine, therefore, existed before there were any regular physicians." — *Cubanis's Revolutions of Med. Science.*

tivation of science, are said to have been the coalition of their inhabitants into large and mighty empires, instead of petty states and communities; and also the peculiar nature of their ecclesiastical institutions, in which an hereditary priesthood was placed in possession of all the facilities and inducements for scientific speculation. The invention of letters, or alphabetic characters, was among them an early auxiliary to the cultivation of the sciences; and medicine was not the last to profit by so signal an advantage. Some of the earliest lettered productions contained copious treatises on the healing art as an integrant portion of their contents.

The very ancient and celebrated personage *Thoth*, or, as he is called by Dr. Miller, *Tot*, and who is the same with Hermes or Mercury of the Greeks, seems to have been the founder of medicine in Egypt. His writings, afterwards held sacred, were divided into forty-two books, six of which treated of medical subjects, namely, one of anatomy, one of diseases, one of instruments, one of medicaments, one of disorders of the eyes, and one of diseases of women. While the higher orders of Egyptian priesthood were employed in the study and execution of religious and philosophical offices contained in the former books, a second or inferior class were busied in the study and practice of healing. The Pastophori — for so the cultivators of physic were called — were bound to make themselves intimately acquainted with the medical scriptures of Thoth; and, so long as their practice was strictly conformable to these, no blame was incurred by them. On the contrary, if any practitioner ventured to deviate in the least from these sacred rules, he became responsible with his own life for the safety of his patient. This circumstance must have furnished a powerful check to improvement, and kept the science of medicine long in a state altogether stationary.

Of the other peculiarities in Egyptian practice, the following are among the most remarkable: The art was made altogether hereditary, so that "he who was born a physician was prohibited equally by Heaven and by law from abandoning the occupation of his ancestors." The profession was also subdivided into minute departments, so that each particular disease had a separate healer. Some took charge of disorders of the eyes, some of the head, some of the teeth, some of the abdomen, &c. The vast number of individuals who were engaged in some branch of medical practice led to the assertion of Homer and Herodotus, that in Egypt every man met with was a physician.

What were the particular modes of practice enjoined by Thoth it is impossible now to know; for the books of the Pastophori have long since been lost. Dr. Miller, however, has industriously attempted to glean whatever authorities were afforded respecting them, from their successors in art and science, the Greeks. He has told us, that the Pastophori, and even the kings, were wont to immolate and dissect beasts and human victims, but with what proficiency in anatomy it is not known. In the science of diseases they appear to have had some idea of critical days, to have divided disorders into acute and chronic, and to have ascribed their pestilential distempers to a morbific principle in the air. In the Materia Medica, they seem to have been acquainted with many efficacious articles, together with their most useful forms of composition.

Having now run through the contents of this volume, we would observe that, in general, it is far from being an uninteresting production. The extent of the author's researches, and the ingenuity of his deductions, will afford some novelty and instruction to most readers. His predominant fault is a disposition to annex an undue consequence to circumstances which are doubtful or unimportant. We think he might profit by the observation of Cabanis, that, in a subject where materials to compensate inquiry are wanting, "the friends of truth should not lose their time in forming vain conjectures, however *learned* they may happen to be."

WHETHER CHOLERA IS CONTAGIOUS.*

WITHIN the present century, cholera, a disease indigenous in hot climates of the East, has, at various intervals, made its appearance in the temperate latitudes of Europe and America. It is now again exciting interest, from its possible and perhaps probable approach to this country.

The experience of the last thirty or forty years has led a majority of medical men who had observed the disease to believe, that, as a general law, it is not contagious. In this belief I must individually remain, until evidence more satisfactory than any which has yet appeared shall justify an opposite conviction.

The great epidemics of 1830 and 1847 had a remarkable coincidence in the path which they pursued, and in the order and dates of their arrival in different cities. They seem to have followed certain great routes of travel, and to have avoided others equally frequented. According to Leségue, they both visited consecutively, and in correspond

---

* From the Boston Medical and Surgical Journal, March 1, 1866.

ing months, Tiflis, Astrachan, Moscow, Petersburg, and Berlin. In 1831, cholera did not take the most frequented route from Berlin to Paris, but passed along the shores of the Baltic, crossed over to Sunderland, went down to London, and again crossed the channel and arrived in Paris about six months after its appearance at Berlin. A disease propagated by contagion of any kind would hardly have avoided the most frequented thoroughfares from Berlin to Paris, while it occupied half a year in going round by England.

The epidemic now or lately prevailing in Europe appears to date back at least nine months, at which time it existed among the caravans of pilgrims visiting or returning from the city of Mecca. In the middle of May last, it was at Alexandria and Cairo; in June at Constantinople, Ancona, and Marseilles; and in November at Paris, Havre, and other European cities.

Thus it appears that cholera has now existed in Europe from three to eight months, among cities having constant commercial intercourse with seaports of the United States, during which time thousands of passengers, and tens of thousands of bales and packages, have been landed in our maritime cities. If cholera were as contagious or portable as many believe it to be, it ought to have begun and perhaps finished its work in many of our seaports before this time.

WHETHER CHOLERA IS CONTAGIOUS. 289

Epidemics require two things for their introduction and extension. These are, first, predisposition in the inhabitants of the place visited; and, second, the arrival or presence of an exciting cause. This cause in some epidemics, such as small-pox, is contagion. In others it is an occult influence, not yet discovered nor understood, nor known to be controlled, except in some instances, by hygienic agencies. No country, I believe, has succeeded in keeping out cholera by quarantines; and no country, as far as we know, can produce it artificially, or retain it after the predisposition has disappeared. In its own time, it moves on thoroughfares where men are travelling, and spreads in cities where they are stationary, for no better known reason than that mankind are its necessary food, and that, where there are no people, there can be no cholera. But why, of two frequented roads or cities, it selects one and avoids the other, investigators have not yet been able to satisfy us.

The credit of having introduced the present epidemic into Europe is, by a sort of popular acclamation, assigned to the hosts of squalid devotees who perform an annual pilgrimage to Mecca. Yet we are told that "the cholera exists every year among the caravans of Mussulmans arriving at the holy cities," so that their supposed mission of forwarding the cholera to Europe in most years fails to be performed.

Cholera, like influenza and some other migratory diseases, has usually, but not always, advanced from east to west. Of the vehicle in which it travels, or the course it is next to take, we know about as much as mankind knew of the cause of lightning before the discovery of electricity. Its conveyance and propagation have been ascribed to air, to water, to material foci, to electricity, to ozone or to the want of it. Of late, in consequence of the vast development by the microscope of the existence everywhere of minute living organisms, it has become more common to ascribe the arrival of this and other like epidemics to certain unseen "germs" which are called seeds or ova, cryptogamic or animalcular, according as the fancy of the theorist inclines him to adopt a vegetable or an animal nomenclature.

But in this, as in many other cases, it is easier to trace an analogy, or to assume a cause, than it is to prevent an effect. Although inquirers have been indefatigable in their attempts to enlighten the world on the means of ridding ourselves of the presence of the various offensive cotenants of our globe, yet no crusade has yet succeeded in banishing from our fields and houses the unwelcome swarms of mosquitos, worms, grubs, and flies, which molest us with their annual presence; nor in suppressing the blight of grain, the potato-rot, or the peach-tree disease. Happily, some if not most of these have their periods of abatement or disappearance, and this rather through the order of Providence than the agency of man. Cholera seems to abide in the same category. We know little of its exciting cause, and not much of its prevention; except that, by following in our personal habits the dictates of reason and experience, we diminish both the frequency and danger of its occurrence.

Whatever may be the cause or vehicle of cholera, credulous and excitable persons are impatient of suspense, and are prone to cut a knot which they fail to untie. When an epidemic disease first appears, some coincidence is always brought to light which is supposed capable of accounting for it. The arrival of a ship, the opening of a trunk, or the washing of a garment, are among the most frequently accepted causes. But, as these events have happened a thousand times before, and apparently under like circumstances, without any known results, it has been thought necessary by some of our later writers to narrow the compass of actual exposure down to the reception of the morbid excretions of one individual into the digestive canal of another. The first impression made by this anouncement must, if true, be one of relief, the danger not seeming likely to happen very often. But to the possibility of such danger we can never oppose an absolute negative, so long as we persist in eating smelts and flounders caught about the mouths of our drains, or even turnips, salads, and strawberries raised at Brighton. The risk, however, is so small, that most persons will prefer to take it, rather than to deprive themselves of food or luxuries.

A great part of the logic which has been used to prove the contagiousness of cholera might equally well be applied to prove that gun-shot wounds are contagious. The part of a battle-field in which men are falling fastest is the most dangerous for survivors to frequent. Secondary cases are almost sure to follow primary ones. Men who inhale the breath, or are sprinkled with the blood, of their wounded comrades, are much more liable to get the prevailing disease than those who remain quietly at home.

Of the many sensation tales printed and reprinted about cholera, and the supposed instances of remarkable communication or arrestation, it is sufficient to say that they are frequently interesting, being fully as dramatic as they are probable.

In the same regard we cannot help noticing, that credulity, and perhaps private cupidity, have caused much stress to be laid on the supposed preventive efficacy of what are called "disinfectants;" a mysterious word, which implies a thing assumed but not proved to exist. We have deodorizers, such as chlorine, charcoal, &c., which, by their combinations, render certain effluvia imperceptible to our senses. But that these are not *disinfectants*, there is most abundant evidence. The narrative, then, of the physician at Malta, who covered certain surfaces in vessels with oil, and had them " disinfected by chlorine gas," after which " no new cases occurred," is to be classed with other like results, with which the medical press always abounds at the close of epidemics.

In clean and well-regulated cities of temperate climates, cholera is far from being the most formidable of epidemics. A greater part of its victims are the miserably poor, the worn out, the ill provided, and the intemperate, in whom this disease only anticipates the date, but does not greatly increase the annual or biennial number, of deaths. Its mortality in our northern Atlantic cities rarely amounts to one per cent of the population in a given place or year; so that a man may reside through an epidemic in one of these cities with less risk than he can take a pleasure voyage to Europe. After having witnessed many cases of cholera in this and other cities, I am farther satisfied that it affords one of the easiest modes of exit from the world.

People who would avoid or prevent cholera should cultivate equanimity, regularity of life and habits, cleanliness, salubrious exercise, temperance, and avoidance of all excesses. When they have done their duty in providing for the care of the sick, allaying public panics, and abating public nuisances, they may safely dismiss their apprehensions. Little good and some harm is always done by the indiscreet agitation of a subject which is to a great extent beyond our control. A single or sporadic case of cholera occurring in a village of a thousand inhabitants may attract little notice, and perhaps pass without record; but a hundred cases in a city of a hundred thousand inhabitants make an aggregate which generally causes some panic, though the proportion is exactly the same, and the panic equally unnecessary. It is possible that the supposed immunity of country districts in comparison with cities may be accounted for by the fact, that, in the sparse population of country towns, cases are less liable to be detected and published.

I may be excused for repeating the following remark from among some "Aphorisms" published by me about thirty years ago, when the disease was new and little known among us.* "Should the cholera continue to prevail for three years throughout this continent, it would cease to interrupt either business or recreation. Mankind cannot always stand aghast; and the wheels of society at length would be no more impeded by its presence than they now are by the existence of consumption, of old age, or of drunkenness."

TESTIMONY ON THE CATTLE DISEASE IN MASSACHUSETTS.*

DURING the prevalence of a disease called Pleuropneumonia, among cattle, in 1859, many animals were slaughtered at the expense of the State, from fear of contagion. A Committee of the Legislature collected the testimony of various witnesses as to the expediency of further continuing the slaughter. The result was, that no more cattle were killed, and the disease disappeared spontaneously. This disease was quite different from the Rhinder-pest of Europe, lately prevalent in that quarter of the globe.

DR. JACOB BIGELOW CALLED.

MR. ANDREW. Have you given to this subject of malignant pleuro-pneumonia, — by whatever name it might be called, — in neat cattle, any special attention of your own, outside of that which you have given as an auditor of this testimony?

A. I have no experimental knowledge on this subject, having never seen a case of the present epidemic. But I have seen something of former

---

* Legislative Documents, 1859.

epidemics, among men and cattle. I have attended to a part of the testimony, which I have happened to hear, and have read some other things in the newspapers and elsewhere.

Q. Be kind enough to give the Committee the result of your reflections upon the subject.

A. I have bestowed some thought upon the subject, and have arrived at the general conclusion, that, although the investigation now going on has elicited many useful facts in regard to the disease, yet the most important points to be learned are not yet arrived at. There are certain fundamental considerations which should govern any investigation of this sort, and which I believe remain yet to be settled. And one of the first and most important of these is the great question of the contagiousness of the disease. I am aware that most of the world are now reported as believing that the disease is contagious; and I am aware that most of those who have started on the present inquiry, and most of the witnesses whom I have had the pleasure to hear, have begun, not so much an inquiry whether the disease is contagious, as with the foregone conclusion that it is contagious. Some gentlemen, I do recollect, stated that they began with an unbiassed mind, and have gone on with their inquiry until they have arrived at the conviction that this disease is contagious. But I find, from the course that the investigations have generally taken, that the inquirers have started by taking it for granted that the disease is contagious. And as the weight of arguments, and of supposed proofs, has hitherto been on the side of contagion, I will, without committing myself to any opinion, — for I do not know any more than any gentleman here knows, as to whether the disease is contagious or not, — venture to suggest a few inquiries, which may be put for what they are worth, in the opposite scale to that of the contagion of the disease.

In the first place, the inquiry, in regard to the new outbreaks of the disease, has generally been, to trace what I may perhaps be allowed to call its pedigree, to ask where it came from, and not to inquire into the previous and more important question, whether it came at all, — in other words, whether it did not spring up and originate on the spot. Now, we well know that epidemics, and among them some of the most formidable, the most extensive, and most deadly epidemics, are not contagious at all. Contagious diseases are those which are communicable from one individual to another. Non-contagious epidemics are those which are communicated to a large number of individuals, either simultaneously or consecutively, from some cause, irrespectively of each other. To make this plain, I will suppose that one or several wells in a place have been poisoned. The people who drink the water of those wells will be sick; but they do not make each other sick, nor will they make others sick by communicating the poison to them. Now I conceive there are some reasons which may go toward showing, that this disease, supposed to be communicated by importation from other countries, is not so communicated in reality. The inquiry seems to me to have been, thus far, a one-sided inquiry. Investigations have been made, and facts noted, in regard to the few animals that have been imported, and which have been taken sick in this country afterwards, and happened to be, or were, among the first cases. But in the same inquiry a multitude of other cases have been overlooked and ignored. Cattle have been imported from the most infected countries in Europe, and have brought with them no disease whatever. I am not in possession of statistics to enable me to say how many cattle are imported into the United States. I do not know whether, in a year, there are hundreds or thousands, but I presume the number is very large; yet, of the number which come from England or Holland, and other infected countries, the proportion of cattle which remain healthy is immeasurably greater than of those which become diseased. The disease, we are told, now exists all over the world, in every quarter of the globe. And among the cases existing there must have been first cases; for, even if the disease be contagious, it must have had a beginning,—it must have sprung up in England, in Holland, Germany, or somewhere. And if it may spring up once spontaneously, why may it not spring up twice, or a dozen times? And why may it not spring up in Belmont, or in Brookfield, as well as in any other now infected part of the globe?

In times of popular panic, all widely spread epidemics are believed, by the populace at large, to be contagious. This has been the case in regard to cholera in modern times, in regard to leprosy in old times, in regard to certain pestilential fevers in various times. And the public have acted upon this persuasion, and sick individuals have been avoided, neglected, and fled from, as prolific fountains of contagious disease. And yet these epidemics are now known and admitted, by the intelligent part of the medical profession, to be not contagious.

Two things are necessary to the spreading even of a contagious disease. One of these is the presence of contagion; and the other is the presence of what physicians call predisposition, or susceptibility on the part of the community, to take the disease. And unless both these conditions are present, the disease cannot spread. The most contagious diseases with which we are acquainted, — for example, small-pox and measles, — are always present in all large cities. And they do not extend so as to be considered in the character of epidemics, except once in a certain number of years; and the reason that they do not thus spread at one time as well as another, is that the predisposition to take the disease is wanting.

Every epidemic disease has its rise and climax and decline, after which it goes out for the time, and becomes matter of history. And such, I presume, will one day be the case with the cattle disease now prevailing here. This is the fact in regard to the epidemic prevalence of cholera, of influenza, of the murrain among cattle, and the rot among sheep. They all have their rise, climax, and decline; and, after the susceptible individuals have had them, and died or got well, they then go out for want of fuel, precisely as a conflagration in a city sometimes goes out after it has burnt up the wooden houses, leaving the brick houses standing. As to the epidemic diseases which are not contagious, such as the cholera and influenza, as I have just mentioned, they travel across continents and across oceans, in some vehicle with which we are not acquainted, and of which mankind now know as little as they did of the cause of lightning and thunder before the discovery of electricity. Perhaps this cause will one day be discovered. All I have now to say is, that, to my knowledge, it has not been discovered.

It seems to me, that the question of the contagiousness of this disease, which is all-important, for it certainly lies at the foundation of all useful practice, and of the great question connected with the arresting of the disease, — it seems to me that the question of contagiousness may be tested by an experiment of the following kind. Not by collecting public rumors, and sudden impressions or convictions of credulous individuals, but by taking a certain number — say, ten or twenty — of healthy cattle, placing them in a healthy district, and then turning in among them a certain number of diseased cattle. That will lead, I think, to a useful result. If the exposed cattle shall all take the disease, and die of it, we may then infer that the epidemic is contagious, and deadly in its character. If, on the contrary, it shall turn out that none of them get the disease, then we shall be justified in drawing exactly the opposite conclusion. And, lastly, if a part of them shall get the disease, and the rest shall not, we shall have a gauge and index, by which we may judge of the average risk and danger of the disease. And if it turns out that only ten per cent of the exposed cattle shall get the disease, surely we have no reason to kill off twenty per cent, for fear they should get or give it.

I do not think of any other suggestions at present to make, but shall be happy to answer any questions which gentlemen may propose.

I will merely state, in regard to the management and treatment of this epidemic, which I think has got to go out by and by, as its predecessors have done, — so far as I can learn, that the question at issue is as to the propriety of slaughtering the infected and suspected individuals among the cattle of the Commonwealth at large. I have not made up my mind in favor of the propriety of this measure. No doubt, if all the cattle in the State are slaughtered, the disease will stop for a time. But, as we must have beef, and must have milk, we shall immediately go to importing other cattle; and then, if contagious, we may get the disease again, as we got it before. And, moreover, if it should turn out that half the cattle in the State are slaughtered, and only the remaining moiety left, I should not consider, even if the disease should then stop, that it was proved to be contagious: for, in the first place, the remaining cattle might still get a similar disease from an epidemic cause, such as I have already stated, independent of contagion; and, lastly, if it did stop, I should not infer that, necessarily, the result had any thing to do with the supposed cause. If I were to state an instance in illustration of this point, I would say, that in the dark ages, when men were ignorant and credulous, they attempted to arrest epidemics, by hanging Jews and burning witches; and, if this practice did not prove effectual in stopping the disease, they proceeded to execute more Jews and witches, until it did stop. But I believe it does not follow, and would not in the mind of any reasonable man now-a-days follow, that these two events stood to each other in the relation of cause and effect.

Q. Have you ever seen, yourself, either now or at previous times, any cause of disease in animals, corresponding to this malignant pleuro-pneumonia?

A. I have seen cases of disease in animals, and sometimes where the disease was prevalent among the animals of a great farm. I have known herds of cattle to have numbers affected, and droves of swine also; but I have never made a study of such disease, inasmuch as it never has prevailed, within my knowledge, to such an extent as to excite particular curiosity in regard to a minute examination of its symptoms and anatomical character.

Q. Then are you able to say, Doctor, whether these symptoms of disease, both in the living and dead subject, which have been disclosed in the testimony, are new to New England, or not?

A. I am not able to say. I have no knowledge on that subject. What are called sporadic cases, single cases, may have occurred, for all that I know, for all time. But they have not been subjected to a systematic examination so as to identify them, and to know whether they are the same or different.

Q. Have you examined the accounts of this malignant disease, as it has appeared in England and on the Continent?

A. I have not.

Q. Are you able to pass an opinion as to this question, — whether the facts thus far disclosed from the examination made here in Massachusetts are numerous or exact enough to enable any one to draw a satisfactory inference as to the real character of the disease, touching its contagiousness or infectiousness?

A. They have been numerous enough to justify one in drawing inferences in regard to its pathological character; that is, in regard to its symptoms and morbid appearances after death. As to its contagiousness, I have already stated that I do not think the observations sufficiently extensive.

Q. Can you give the Committee any opinions which would be needful to them touching the probability of this disease, — whatever it may be, — being liable to substantial reduction by medical treatment. I am aware this is entirely outside of your practice, — but as a student of natural science generally?

A. I think that, like other epidemics, it could be alleviated, palliated, and rendered more safe, by what I should call a natural, salutary treatment; but I know of no very violent or heroic measures that would be likely to arrest or lessen its intensity or extent.

Q. To make a practical application, I will suppose a case. Supposing that the disease itself is a contagion, and supposing the contagion to be present in a herd of thirty cattle, so long that you know all of those cattle to have been subjected to the possible influences of the contagion. You would infer, I suppose, as to some percentage of that thing, that the susceptibility of the contagion was also present. Then what would be your advice to the proprietor of the thirty cattle as to what he should do with all of them, before there has been any appearance of active disease in any one of them? And then, in the next place, what would you advise to be done for those who began to manifest symptoms?

A. I should pursue the same course, if it were practicable, with cattle, that I should pursue with men, or that men would pursue in regard to themselves. I would remove, if possible, those that had been exposed, to a healthy district. I am not sure that this would be practicable, in view of the supposed conflicting interests of the owners of the cattle and their neighbors. I do know that if a man is in Norfolk or New Orleans when the yellow fever breaks out, he comes, if he can, to Boston or some other healthy district. So a man who resides in a fever-and-ague district, if he has got the disease, or expects to get it immediately, leaves the place, and goes into a non-malarious country, a country where he is not subject to the influence which brought it on where he was.

Q. That would not apply to contagious diseases like measles or smallpox. Suppose that this disease is contagious in animals, as measles or smallpox are in men, and a man's herd had been subjected to contact with diseased animals, so that, if a susceptibility was present in the herd, the inference would naturally follow that some of them would be sick, — is there any course of treatment which would seem to you to be wiser, so far as you know, than any other?

A. The first course would be to get the animals into another locality. If that could not be done, I should put them in some situation where they would enjoy free air. I should keep them upon a very moderate diet, such as would neither overfeed nor underfeed them, and I should let them take their chance. I do not know of any medication which would be relied on to stop the progress of individual cases.

Q. What should you think of the slaughter of all of them, on the ground that they had been subjected to disease?

A. I should infer that there would be no case of the disease left, if they were all slaughtered. But it would do no certain good to wait until some were taken sick, and then slaughter them.

Q. There is then no medium ground, if you adopt any system of killing, between where you begin and where you stop, until you have killed all?

A. I cannot give positive information on that point. My presumption is, that it would be a very difficult thing to carry a middle course into profitable execution; because most contagious diseases are contagious from beginning to end, and to slaughter an animal affected with disease, after the actual symptoms of that disease have shown themselves, is to shut the door after the steed is stolen, — premising that the disease is contagious.

Q. Suppose the disease is contagious, the only logically consistent system would be to slaughter every animal which had been possibly exposed to the contagion, — would it not?

A. If that theory is adopted as a rule of practice, I should say that, to be thorough, the only way is to kill all animals showing symptoms of disease, and all which by exposure had become candidates for it.

Q. Whether you have any means of forming an opinion as to the probable effect of isolation; supposing you draw a cordon around a certain space, called an infected district, — whether it is reasonable, that, keeping up non-intercourse between animals outside and inside, the contagion could be stopped, — assuming it to be contagion?

A. I think it would have a good effect. It would satisfy the requirement of public opinion. I do not know of any way of isolating cattle so as to keep them from some communication. An infected herd may be shut up from danger; but, as the disease may appear in other places, I do not know how the legislation of one town can produce a non-intercourse with another town or State. Suppose, for example, that Massachusetts should pass laws as stringent as possible, to cut off all intercourse between the cattle of this State and those of Rhode Island and Connecticut, what is to hinder the cattle from going to the boundary fence, and putting their noses together?

Q. Suppose you made a neutral line?

A. That may be done if you produce the co-operation of other States; and I think that would be very satisfactory to public opinion.

Q. Don't you think it worth while, now we have got this disease among us, to ascertain whether it be curable or not?

A. By all means.

Q. Would you advise that as a medical man?

A. I would advise, as a medical man, that squads or small herds of cattle should be made the subjects of different experimental treatment; that half a dozen be treated in one method, and half a dozen in another method, and another half dozen in a third method; and that the result be observed.

Q. You think it would be advisable to have a commission appointed for the purpose of making this investigation or inquiry?

A. I should think it might result in very useful information, provided it is made by individuals qualified to judge, and of impartial character, so that their minds might not be settled upon any thing beforehand.

Q. How, in your opinion, is this disease communicated to the animal? through the blood or directly from the lungs?

A. That I am wholly unable to say. I have formed no opinion upon it. If it is a contagious disease, it is conveyed by something received from the cattle: if it is not a contagious disease, it is produced by some morbific influences derived from elsewhere. What part it invades first is of secondary consequence.

Q. Suppose it to be in the air, what part of the animal would be likely to be first affected, — the blood or the tissues?

A. That I am utterly unable to answer. Nobody knows. It is easy to answer questions on conjecture. If you produce proof, the answer would be on a very different ground.

Dr. LORING. Doctor, if you had two herds of cattle, consisting of ten each, and they were half a mile apart; and, to improve your stock, you purchased during the last year a creature of Mr. Chenery, and that creature should have become sick in the herd with which you herded it, and you soon found that the rest of that herd were becoming sick, — would you remove these sick ones to your well herd half a mile off, to give them a chance to recover?

A. Considering the question of contagion still open and unsettled, I might, as a precautionary measure, to cover a possible risk, make such removal. If it were a matter of indifference or mere curiosity, I do not know that I would.

Q. Have you heard the testimony relative to the

sale of calves by Mr. Chenery, and their removal to Brookfield?

A. I have heard something about it.

Q. I mean the testimony, that in every case the disease has been traced to one origin. On the supposition that you can confide in that testimony, would you call it epidemic or contagious?

A. I should suspend my opinion until I got further evidence; knowing that cholera and yellow fever, and many other epidemics not known to be contagious, were traced with as much minuteness and exactitude from family to family, and from man to man, as these cases of the cattle now are.

Q. Is that so, — that epidemics are traced? Do they not rise with exposure?

A. Some epidemics do, and some do not.

Q. Is it not the common history of epidemics, that they rise irrespective of connection with the disease.

A. Smallpox is an epidemic supposed to be communicated only by contagion. Cholera is an epidemic communicated by other causes than contagion.

Q. I understood you to make that distinction, — that epidemic diseases originated from other diseases aside from contact.

A. The term epidemic is a general term, including both contagious and non-contagious diseases. Epidemics are diseases that spread over a whole community. One class is contagious, and another class is not contagious.

Q. Can there be any more conclusive evidence that a disease extending over quite an extent of territory originated in contagion, these being traced distinctly to one origin in every case?

A. No better than to subject it to a new and decisive experiment, such as I have suggested, to see whether the converse of the rule will operate or not.

Q. If you find that calves from the same herd are sent in other directions, and the disease is not communicated?

A. I should entertain the same views, and want more evidence.

Q. If twelve well cattle should be placed with twelve diseased ones in a healthy location, and all the well ones should take the disease, would it be proof that the disease was contagious?

A. As I have already said, I should think it strong presumptive proof. There are two things necessary to prove a contagious affection: one is the existence of contagion, and the other is that the animals were so susceptible as to take it.

Q. I suppose these animals were susceptible, and did not take it, — would that prove it was not a contagious disease?

A. We cannot tell in advance whether they are susceptible; but, if we could, such facts on either side would be strong presumptive evidence of the contagion or non-contagion of the disease.

Q. You think, Dr. Bigelow, that this question of contagion is entirely open?

A. I am aware that the preponderating opinion of the world seems to be in favor of the contagion; but, to my mind, this opinion does not prove the contagion any more than that multitudes of prevalent erroneous doctrines may be considered as proved.

Q. I suppose, in modern times, — especially in our enlightened community, — it is not deemed necessary, in scientific investigation, to set aside all the testimony of creditable witnesses, is it?

A. Not to set it aside, but to give it all the examination it deserves; and, whether it comes from one or a hundred persons, I should say that every man has a right to form his own opinion from the intrinsic merits of the case itself.

Q. Well, when you say there have been panics and superstitions in regard to epidemics, originating in former times, you don't mean that the intellectual condition of mankind is the same, and that disease is less understood than it was then?

A. As a general fact, the intellectual condition of mankind and their information are improved, and disease is in some respects better understood; but in others, I am sorry to say, it is not better understood.

Q. I suppose, that, if this disease has prevailed for a great number of years, and been submitted to scientific investigation, as far as science can apply to the diseases of animals, the testimony of those who have investigated it would be considered worthy of considerable weight?

A. It is, of course, worthy of receiving a certain amount of candid attention; but it is well known that there is as much error in medical science as there is in theological or political science. A great deal of it is matter of opinion, and not of positive, demonstrable fact.

Q. I suppose you are aware that some very interesting experiments in certain parts of Europe, in regard to the contagious character of this disease, were made by scientific persons there, somewhat analogous to the proposition made by yourself, with regard to shutting up diseased animals in healthy places?

A. I am not acquainted with satisfactory experiments made in any part of the world. If the experiments have been made which I suggested, I should take the result of it as leading to pretty strong presumptive proof.

Mr. BIRD. Nothing of the kind has been proved here, however.

Dr. LORING. I am simply endeavoring to ascertain what scientific experiments have been made anywhere.

Mr. BIRD. I do not think, Mr. Chairman, it is

fair for any one to bring in knowledge which he may have of matters elsewhere: they are not before the Committee.

Dr. LORING. In speaking of this question of contagiousness, Doctor, you suggested that there were importations constantly to this country, and that it was very extraordinary that cases of this disease should be so rare under those circumstances. I suppose you are aware that the number of cattle imported from Holland to this country is small, — that the Dutch animal is not a favorite of American importers?

A. I stated that I am not in possession of statistical facts, to enable me to say how many animals are imported from one country or another. But, since I came into this room, I have asked the opinion of half a dozen gentlemen supposed to have, and whom I found to have, more or less knowledge of the amount and the number of cattle introduced by importation; and I have found that they all of them seemed to express an opinion that the number was quite large, and that they were imported from various countries; I do not know how many from one country or another. But I understand that the disease has existed in all quarters of the globe, and all countries, from here to the antipodes, although I did not take the trouble to single out any particular country from the rest.

Dr. Loring. Some interesting facts might be given as to the importation of cattle into this country, showing that the cattle which are favorites with breeders and importers seldom come from infected districts.

[*To Dr. Bigelow.*] Have you any knowledge that the disease does exist in every quarter of the globe?

A. No further than I have read in the newspapers, and heard in this room. It exists in America, in Great Britain, Holland, Denmark, Africa, and Australia, and I know not how many other countries. I presume there can be little doubt that it has existed in intermediate countries, and in Asia, the remaining quarter of the globe.

Q. Are you aware of the knowledge which we have had here in regard to the instances in Africa of this disease, that the testimony shows that it was carried into Africa from a distant and infected district, and, so far as any stop has been put to it, it has been by burning it out, by isolation?

A. I do not know of any other or different facts, in regard to the introduction of the disease into Africa, than those which at one time were believed to exist in regard to the introduction of the cholera into the United States. We know that that disease was a subject of great alarm. Passengers were prohibited from landing from New York, and in some of the New-England States; and, as that procedure was founded in error, the other may also prove to be

Some of the statements that I have seen or heard in the course of this hearing appear to me not very probable. I noticed that it was stated, that the disease prevailed at one time in Denmark, and then it stopped, — how and when, and in what manner, I am unable to say, — and that it afterwards broke out in consequence of a cow being brought from Hungary that had the disease. It appeared to me more probable that the disease had remained in Denmark all the while, or was indigenous there.

Dr. LORING. I made the statement that the bringing of one hundred and eighty oxen from Hungary caused the re-appearance of the disease in Denmark. The application of stringent laws in Denmark had satisfied the farmers that the disease was nearly eradicated. In regard to Australia, Doctor, are there any statements with regard to the existence of the disease in Australia that you are aware of, other than those in the newspapers? Is it not a fact, that all the knowledge we have of that country goes to show that the seed of the disease got into Australia, but was destroyed so soon that it never spread?

A. When I read the newspaper account, the only thing that struck me was the extreme improbability that this disease could have been carried in the body of a cow, on a three-months' passage from Europe to Australia, and that it could then be communicated from that animal.

Q. Did you ever hear of the disease in South America?

A. I never did.

Q. You referred to the analogy between hanging witches and Jews in times of superstition to cure distempers. Do you think there is any analogy between such a piece of barbarous superstition as that is, and an intelligent and enlightened attempt to remove disease by killing the disease-breeding cattle?

A. The question whether any proceeding is enlightened or intelligent depends not so much upon the qualifications of the individuals to judge rightly, as upon the manner in which they apply their knowledge to practice. I believe it to be a fact, that people are as much terrified in the most civilized times, in regard to epidemics, as they were in the most ignorant and unenlightened age of the world. If I may be allowed to relate an anecdote, I will do so. When the cholera first broke out in New York, where it destroyed some three thousand people, in the height of the epidemic, the city government of this city despatched a commission, consisting of three physicians, to investigate the disease, and report what they thought expedient to be done. I was one of the commission. After residing in New York three days, we returned in a steamboat, the last which came from New York that season, to Providence. When we arrived a mile below Providence, a boat came to us with orders from the Board of

Health of Providence to hold no communication with the shore.

We sent repeated applications to be permitted to land and get home, for we were impatient and tired: but we were kept there against our will the whole day, at anchor in the stream below the town of Providence; and, about once in an hour, a boat came down to tell us, that the Board of Health were still in session in the court-house, and that the court-house was surrounded by a mob, and that the Board of Health was disposed to allow us to land, but the mob kept sending in petitions not to permit this pestilential epidemic to enter into their State. At length a despatch came to us, that we might land at Seekonk, in the State of Massachusetts, but that we should not land in Rhode Island. I do not know of any thing in the dark ages much less intelligent than that.

Q. Then you think there is some analogy between hanging Jews and witches who do not communicate disease, and killing cattle which are spreading disease in every direction?

A. Both are expedient, only so far as it gratifies popular excitement.

Q. If you had a herd of animals, and introduced among them a diseased one, and you found by experience that that disease passed from that animal into others, you would not hesitate to distribute your animals about the community?

A. In obedience to the popular will and a desire to accommodate it, and not to outrage any strong prejudices of the community, I should not.

Q. I am not speaking of popular prejudices; but, as a man and good citizen and a good farmer, what would you do if you had a disease brought into your herd, and it went from one animal to another, step by step, and you saw that the disease went by contagion, — without the application of the nicest scientific principles, — should you consider it a barbarous prejudice to shut up your cattle?

A. If I was convinced that the disease was brought there by contagion, I should not allow them to go elsewhere. If not, I should endeavor to get at such evidence as I might, to settle the question.

Q. I suppose you would be unable to say whether animals would be fit for breeding, — for the purposes of reproduction, — in this diseased state?

A. I am not clear on that point: we know that children are sometimes born of parents in their last illness, and those children grow up to be healthy, useful citizens.

Dr. LORING. That point has been put here once before, and a comparison made between men and animals; and it has been stated that there were men who had but one lung, and were useful for all the practical purposes of human life. That may be true. The question arises, whether there is any difference between an intellectual and accountable being and a simple animal, who is good for nothing except the service he will render to man. It seems to me that there is; and I don't want to ask any question on that point.

Mr. BIRD. I want to ask the Doctor whether, in his opinion, a cow or bull is affected by an acute attack, so that one lung is destroyed, leaving the other entirely healthy, — whether the progeny of such animals would or would not be healthy?

A. That involves further inquiry. Among mankind, we know that there are certain diseases that are hereditary.

Q. Well, in case of an actual attack of pleuro-pneumonia, what would be the effect in that respect?

A. If the animal had the disease and was recovered, I do not see why he is not entitled to have as healthy progeny as any other animal. If I understand the disease, it is capable, in some instances, of recovery. After he gets well, with one half of a lung or a whole lung disabled, then what remains to him is an infirmity, and not a disease. He is like a man with one limb gone: he is good for various purposes, though he may not walk very well.

Q. Do you think it would be practicable or safe to remove any animals diseased with a contagious disease. That is, if you had a suspicion that animals had a contagious disease, do you think it would be safe to remove them to some other district?

A. I think it would be safe to remove them into a healthy district, providing their disease is contagious, if all other cattle are removed from the same locality.

Q. You don't imagine that private enterpris could do this thing?

A. I should think it proper that the Commonwealth should institute experiments that might throw light upon the epidemic.

Dr. LORING. You thought that free air and a moderate diet might have a beneficial effect upon the disease?

A. Nothing strikes me as more probable, with a removal of the diseased animals into as different a situation as possible.

Q. Suppose you were to enter a country barn, that reminded you of the once-fashionable "ventilation gossamer hat," filled with meadow hay, you would conceive that there was free air and moderate diet; and suppose you found the disease very extensively in such a barn as that?

A. I should be inclined to try another barn; for example, a colder after a warmer one.

Q. Well, suppose you were in a warm and tight, well-clapboarded barn, with plenty of good English hay, and you found the disease still worse, what would you do under the circumstances?

A. I should either give it up and let the cattle die, or should try a new experiment.

Dr. LORING. Well, we did try a new experiment: we killed them; because those were the facts we found, to a remarkable extent, in North Brookfield.

Mr. ANDREW. Doctor, I think I have heard it stated that no pulmonary disease in the human system is contagious. Is that true?

A. I know of no disease of the lungs, or generally speaking of the chest, which is contagious. There are some diseases — a very few in number — which have appeared to be epidemic to a small extent, such as what was once called typhoid pneumonia. But I do not know of any evidence that such diseases are contagious, or that there is any evidence that there is any analogy between these and pleuro-pneumonia, which occurs in mankind.

Q. Supposing it to be true that no disease of the lungs or chest in man is contagious, is it, or is it not, possible to draw any inference from that fact touching the contagiousness of lung or chest diseases in neat cattle?

A. I should consider the evidence to be very strong evidence. As far as it goes, the analogy leads to the justification of the belief, that what is not contagious in one race of beings may not be in another. You have to jump too wide a gap between the human being and the brute creation to suppose otherwise. No such inference could be justified with certainty: it is at most a probability.

Dr. LORING. When you were speaking of the question of contagiousness, you thought it might be decided by taking ten or twenty diseased cattle, and putting them into a healthy place. It occurred to me that precisely that experiment had been tried at Brookfield; otherwise, how do you account for the jump of the disease from Belmont to North Brookfield?

A. I am not qualified to give decisive information nearer than this. I see two methods by which it could have appeared at North Brookfield. One of these is contagion; the other is indigenous origin, arising in North Brookfield as it has done in some other places.

Q. It seems to be possible that it may have been indigenous in Belmont and North Brookfield?

A. Yes.

Mr. BIRD. Dr. Bigelow, is it, or is it not, safe to place any material reliance upon supposed analogies between this disease and similar diseases in foreign countries?

A. If, upon accurate comparison of the accounts given and reports made of the two diseases, they closely resemble each other, I should say it was justifiable. Not otherwise.

Q. What diseases, within your knowledge of the medical world, are regarded to be contagious other than cutaneous diseases?

A. Smallpox, measles, hooping-cough, the ship fever or typhus fever. The typhoid fever we do not commonly consider as contagious. Ship fever is; and, as an example of it, the late Dr. Moriarty, brother of the present Dr. Moriarty, physician on Deer Island, took the disease and died, having had communication with patients there.

Q. Are not cases of ship fever transferred from ships to Deer Island?

A. They are; and, if there is a predisposition existing to take the disease, it will spread. If not, it will not spread. I have known cases of ship fever, to the number of seventeen, to be taken at one time to the House of Industry at South Boston, and not a secondary case occurred there.

Q. Does not that pretty nearly destroy the theory of its contagiousness?

A. It shows that there was no predisposition there. It is pretty generally acknowledged that ship fever has a contagious element, and may be communicated to predisposed persons.

Q. Well, as a general rule, it is only eruptive diseases that are contagious, is it not?

A. No, sir: I am not prepared to say so. The hooping-cough is considered contagious, and I think I might add, mumps; and perhaps some others.

There are various diseases in regard to which the medical profession are not agreed whether they are contagious or not. I have said that these diseases are generally conceived to be contagious: I do not positively assert myself that they are.

Q. Then it is very difficult to say positively how far the contagious virus is affected by susceptibility, or by other conditions, so as to determine that in given cases it will absolutely be communicated.

A. There are causes in existence which we cannot measure, and do not know at the time; and we cannot foretell the result in certain cases of exposure.

Dr. LORING. Ship fever is considered contagious, generally, is it not?

A. Yes.

Q. Well, now, ship fever requires susceptibility. Would you consider that an argument against its contagion; or was the fact that I never took ship fever when attending it in the hospital, an argument against its contagiousness?

A. That would be no argument against its contagiousness?

Q. Would not the law that applies to ship fever apply to all contagious diseases? Is there any reason to doubt that?

A. I presume it does.

REPORT ON HOMŒOPATHY.

MADE TO THE COUNSELLORS OF THE MASSACHUSETTS MEDICAL SOCIETY IN FEBRUARY, 1854.

THE Committee appointed by the Counsellors of the Massachusetts Medical Society, to consider the resolution of the Essex North-District Society,* and also that of Dr. Spofford, in relation to the subject of Homœopathy, beg leave to report:—

That the Massachusetts Medical Society was incorporated mainly for the purpose of establishing a proper standard of medical education, and of insuring a competent degree of knowledge among those who should be authorized to practise the profession of medicine in this Commonwealth; and they are not aware that the Society possess any power to coerce men, after they have been thus educated and qualified, to embrace or renounce any theoretical opinions or modes of practice which they may innocently believe, or which, not believing, they may think it proper to profess.

---

* These resolutions contemplated dissolving the connection of homœopathists with the Society.

In medical science there are certain fundamental laws relating to the structure and functions of the body, and the morbid changes to which it is subject, also regarding the signs by which those changes are discovered, — upon which all well-educated physicians are agreed. But, in certain provinces of medical science, such fundamental laws, owing to the imperfection of our means of knowledge, cannot at the present time be established. This is the case with Therapeutics, or the art of treating or curing diseases, in which the evidence required by science is difficult to obtain; and in regard to which writers and teachers, sects and individuals, and even the same individual in the course of an ordinary lifetime, may without dishonesty entertain great diversities of opinion.

The tendency of modern observation is such as to lead us to the belief, that disease is less frequently under the control of remedial treatment than it was formerly supposed to be. Where observations are impartially made by competent persons, it is found that people recover, and also that they die, under all the ordinary modes of treatment. And the evidence collected from sources which are worthy of reliance is not so abundant or satisfactory as to convince a reasonable man, that any general system of practice can be relied on for the cure of all cases. Hence it is not surprising, that diversities, contrasts, and even extravagances in practice, are embraced by the sanguine, the credulous, the uninformed, and the interested, frequently based upon no better authority than accident, imperfect observation, or defective power of judgment, in the party who adopts them.

The broadest division which has been recognized for centuries, in the treatment of disease, is that which resolves the whole subject into the active and the expectant modes of practice. The first employs various interfering agencies in the management of the sick, — the last waits more on the unassisted course of nature, — and both have long had their exclusive advocates.

To the last of these divisions Homœopathy really, though not avowedly, belongs. Its character is, that, while in reality it waits on the natural course of events, it commends itself to the ignorant and credulous by a professed introduction into the body of inappreciable quantities of medicinal substances. Now, the nugatory effect of such quantities is demonstrated by the fact, that in civilized life every person is exposed to the daily reception, in the form of solution, dust, or vapor, of homœopathic quantities of almost every common substance known in nature and art, without any appreciable consequences being found to follow. And the pretended exactness with which such nominal doses are administered by homœopathic practitioners is doubtless a fallacy, capable of producing in the living body no other effects than those which charlatanry has in all ages produced in the minds and bodies of imaginative patients.

It is a fact much older than the institution of this Society, that visionary systems of practice have replaced each other in the faith of multitudes, at least several times in a century. And this will probably be the case so long as practical medicine continues to be, what it now is to a great extent, a theoretical and conjectural science. At the present period, among the sects usually called irregular, the homœopathic sect prevails to a considerable extent in this country and in Europe. In the United States it is exceeded only by the sect called Botanic or Thompsonian practitioners, which at the present time appears, of the two, to number most disciples. It is not probable that the faith of either of these sects will be displaced by a return of their followers to any more enlightened or rational creed. Nevertheless, it is safe to predict that they will both be superseded, in the course of time, by other systems not more rational or probable in themselves, but possessing the attraction of greater novelty, or urged upon the credulous with greater adroitness. When the world, and especially the unenlightened part of it, shall be settled in their opinions on other sectarian subjects, we may anticipate unanimity of opinion among them in the science of practical medicine.

But it is not only to expectant medicine, in the form of its counterfeit, homœopathy, that the censure of prejudice and credulity is to be attached. The opposite system of active practice, carried to the extreme usually called heroic, is alike chargeable with evil to the patients, whenever it becomes the absorbing and exclusive course of the practitioner. Physicians are too often led to exaggerate the usefulness of the doctrines in which they have been educated, and especially of those by the exercise of which they obtain their daily bread. In such cases, habit gets the ascendency over enlightened judgment; and the man of routine or of narrow views asks himself, from day to day, what drug or what appliance he shall next resort to, instead of asking the more important question, whether any drug or any appliance is called for, or is properly admissible in the case.

In Medicine, as in the other inexact sciences which deeply concern the welfare of mankind, enough has been learned to show, that extreme measures, either of omission or of commission, are not, when systematized as a whole, productive of benefit or safety to mankind.

It is quite probable that the prevalence, at times, of eccentric and ultra-sectarian doctrines in medicine, is attributable to the exaggerated value attached by physicians themselves to incessant activity in practice, and an assumption of credit for particular modes of medication, to which, as such, they are not entitled. There is often a want of openness in the intercourse of physicians, both enlightened and ignorant, with their patients, who are requested to believe that their cure depends not in any degree on the salutary influences of nature and time, but in the rigid enforcement of a prescribed routine of practice, either active or formal, as the case may be. And, when opposite modes of treatment are urged upon the public by different practitioners with reasonings equally specious, it is not surprising that patients should sometimes adopt that which is least troublesome in its operation. Neither is it surprising that they should sometimes embrace even a deception, which absolves them from their allegiance to an unnecessarily severe or troublesome course of treatment.

An honest and independent practitioner, and especially a member of the Massachusetts Medical Society, should never be induced to give his counsel or his aid, in any shape, to empiricism and dishonesty, whether it occur among those who are within or without the pale of its membership. And no consideration of gain or notoriety should induce those whose age or standing causes them to be resorted to for consultation, to lend their influence or countenance to encourage either the delusions of those who are honest, or the practices of those who are not.

If quackery, individual or gregarious, is ever to be eradicated, or even abated, in civilized society, it must be done by enlightening the public mind in regard to the true powers of medicine. The community must be made to understand, that there are certain things which medicine can do, and certain other things which it cannot do.; that some diseases are curable by active interference, and others by time and nature alone; that true medical skill lies in discrimination and prognosis, and judicious adaptation of management, more than in assumed therapeutic power, in regard to special agents; and that he who professes to cure by medicine a self-limited fever is as much an impostor, or deluded man, as he who pretends to do the same thing with a fractured bone or incised wound. Nothing so much shakes the confidence of mankind in the medical profession as unfulfilled promises; nothing so much strengthens this confidence as fair dealing, exhibited in an earnest requirement and fearless expression of the truth. Such a course, by commending itself to the sensible and enlightened, may be expected, sooner or later, in some measure to influence the unreasonable and ignorant, — much sooner, indeed, than a warfare carried on in the arena of empiricism with its own weapons.

ADDRESS DELIVERED BEFORE THE AMERICAN ACADEMY OF ARTS AND SCIENCES,

AT THE OPENING OF THEIR COURSE OF LECTURES, OCTOBER 27, 1852.

At a meeting of the American Academy of Arts and Sciences June 22, 1852, —

Mr. Agassiz, in behalf of the committee appointed to consider the best means of increasing the Academy's Publication Fund, reported, that the committee were unanimous in recommending that a course of public lectures, of a popular character, be given by Fellows of the Academy during the ensuing winter; that the President be requested to commence the course, by an Address setting forth the objects and aim of the course; and that each section of the Academy appoint one of its number to deliver one lecture upon some special subject belonging to, and prominent in, the section's sphere of research.

IT has been a serious question whether, amid the general sadness which hangs as a cloud over our city, which has seemed to check the ordinary current of affairs, and to darken the very atmosphere of social intercourse,* the pre-arranged exercises of this place should not be suspended in solemn and silent respect to the unusual occasion. But we are bound by circumstances to perform that which, at

---

* The death of Daniel Webster.

this time, we would not have wished to do. And, leaving to the public voice the expression of that general emotion, to which no limited occasion can afford utterance, we shall proceed in the attempt to execute the more humble duty that has been set before us.

I am instructed, in behalf of the American Academy of Arts and Sciences, to report to you this evening on the character and condition of that institution, and the objects of the present course of lectures. If it were possible that a society which has existed in your midst for two or three generations, and which from time to time has numbered among its members many of the most enlightened and valuable of our citizens, could be in any measure unknown, I might safely rely on the more gifted laborers who are to follow me in this field, for the vindication of its character and name. And, if the present occupation of this lecture-room were a question of doubtful propriety, I might briefly say, that the Academy needs, nay, more, that it deserves, your countenance and support; and that this is the place and the manner in which your kind regards have been solicited towards the encouragement of its labors. But as the quiet operations of science have not that wide-spread notoriety which attends the more absorbing questions of peace and war, of property and privilege, of safety and of danger, there is reason for attempting a more detailed consideration of the objects and results of our Academic Incorporation.

Academies in the higher use of the term, philosophical and learned societies, exist, and have long existed, in every country of civilized Europe. In common with colleges and universities, they are designed to cultivate and disseminate scientific truth; but, unlike those institutions, the usual province of the modern academy is to investigate, rather than to teach; to bring together experts from the various walks of science, literature, and art; to accumulate, for the benefit of the whole, the researches and observations of all; to aid and to encourage the different inquirers on their respective tracks; and to furnish vehicles for what is true, and ordeals for what is unsettled, in the progress of human knowledge.

One of the early fruits of the restoration of arts and letters in Italy was the perception of the great advantage attending the combination of effort in academic institutions. In that country were the first efficient examples of learned bodies co-operating for their common good, and bringing their united efforts to bear in the promotion of the arts and sciences. From Italy, the principle of academic association spread to England, Germany, and France; and, in all those countries, noble institutions, having their foundation in the earnest quest of truth, and supported by the zeal and learning of the best men of their times, have been sent down to the present age, marking their way by many high developments of human intellect, and noble achievements of human science. Some of them, which for two centuries have enjoyed the sunshine of royal and public patronage, now find themselves intrenched in ample halls, surrounded by the machinery of modern science, dispensing rewards with princely prodigality; offering seats, of which the prospective vacancy fills with ambition the learned of foreign countries; throwing lustre on the cities of their respective establishment; and connected by little resemblance, save that of etymology, with the simple preceding groves of Plato and Arcesilaus.

Academic institutions have differed widely from each other in the object, as well as the comprehensiveness, of their pursuits. Not only does the history of literature furnish many examples of academics of sciences and the arts, but there are well-known like institutions of belles lettres, of language, of inscriptions, of painting, sculpture and architecture, of music, of antiquities, and of many subordinate branches of useful and of elegant learning. Of course, the value of membership in any of these bodies has depended on the character of the institution itself, and the principles on which it is conducted. The Royal Academy of France, often known *par excellence* as *the Academy*, not only under its original name, but under the subsequent appellations of National and Imperial Institute, has, during a long period of years, sustained an almost uninterrupted pre-eminence in the republic of letters. The labors of this body have cast a flood of light on modern science; and its assembled savans have formed a tribunal, from whose scientific sentence there seemed no appeal. Yet even this institution, under the occasional supineness of its members and the influence of royal favoritism, has more than once been a mark for the shafts of cotemporaneous criticism. The poet Piron, affecting to define his own humble position by an epitaph, says, "Here lies Piron, who was nothing at all, not even an Academician."

In the year 1779, in the midst of the exhausting and yet unfinished contest of our Revolution, with humble resources, but with confidence of future promise, the American Academy of Arts and Sciences was founded by an association of citizens of Massachusetts. The fathers of our Commonwealth, well aware that the lights of liberty and learning are jointly conducive to the stability of free government, gave their sanction, and in many cases their individual efforts, to construct the foundation of an ample edifice. Among the constellation of worthies enrolled as the first members, we find the names of the two Adamses, of Bowdoin and Cushing, of Chauncey and Cooper, of Hancock, of Lowell, of Sedgwick, Strong, and Sullivan, and about fifty others,—all of them names already registered in the annals of their country's service, or distinguished as proficients in the learning of their time.

The preface to their first publication states, that the Legislature was called on to sanction the society on a liberal and extensive plan, and to establish it on a firm basis. "And to the honor of our political fathers," say they, "be it spoken, that, although the country was engaged in a distressing war,—a war the most important to the liberties of mankind that was ever undertaken by any people, and which required the utmost attention of those who were intrusted with our public concerns,—they immediately adverted to the usefulness of the design, entered into its spirit, and incorporated a society with ample privileges."

But the approval of the Legislature was but a small offset to the difficulties against which the new association had to contend. "The country being young," say they, "few among us have such affluence and leisure as to admit of" our "applying much time to the cultivation of the sciences." And in another place, "Many important European discoveries have been in a great measure useless to this part of the world, in consequence of a situation so remote from the ancient seats of learning and improvement. And of such publications as have reached this country, the smallness of the number has greatly limited their usefulness, as but few have had the opportunity for perusing them."

Under such disadvantages, so unlike the state of things now, well might our courageous predecessors solace and assure themselves by a prospective view of the harvests they were sowing for their descendants. "Settled," say they, "in an extensive country, bordering upon the ocean, and opened to a free intercourse with all the commercial world, — a country comprehending several climates and a rich variety of soils, watered and fertilized by multitudes of springs and streams, and by many grand rivers, — the citizens have great opportunities and advantages for making useful experiments and improvements, whereby the interests and happiness of the rising empire may be essentially advanced. At the same time enjoying, under a mild but steady government, that freedom which excites and rewards industry and gives a relish to life, — that freedom which is propitious to the diffusion of knowledge, which expands the mind and engages it to noble and generous pursuits, — they have a stimulus to enterprise which the inhabitants of few other countries can feel."

Such were the principles and the auspices under which was kindled the small, dim light of our Academy. Although it was not often overfed with fuel, nor at all times watched with vestal vigilance, it has at least never been suffered to go wholly out; and, after glimmering with uncertain, yet increasing rays, for two thirds of a century, it has at length grown to be an acknowledged beacon in science, a light to the philosophic of our own country, a western star, to whose unshadowed brilliancy and true monitions the European world now looks with interest and respect.

The early labors of the Academy were in keeping with its early professions. They did not trench deeply on fields appropriated by foreign explorers, but rather turned their inquiries to the capacities of their own country, to the improvement of its practical advantages, and the knowledge of its natural history. With the exception of a few limited papers in mathematics and astronomy, the first volumes of the Transactions are occupied with such objects as the cultivation of corn and the engrafting of trees; examination of springs of water, and reports on diseases of cattle; speculations on natural caves, recorded earthquakes, and conjectured volcanoes. Narratives are given of the appearance of waterspouts, and of remarkable devastations of lightning on trees, rocks, and dwelling-houses. Fossil frogs, "that under the cold stone" were believed to have passed monotonous ages of incomprehensible existence, are presented, in these memoirs, living and jumping before the reader. Flocks of swallows, blackening the air with their numbers, abandon the joyous, twittering, feather-chasing career of their summer life, and, with ominous solemnity, assemble on the banks of some stagnant pool, rendered famous perhaps with the tradition of former engulfments of their species, and then are seen no more. A cloud settles on the mystery of their wintry existence; and the wonder was, that, when they appeared in the following spring, their sleek and glossy plumage bore no traces of the deep mud under which they were believed to have slept out their hybernation.

The riches of our vegetable kingdom, and the importance of establishing a more thorough and practical knowledge of its different portions, did not escape the attention of the pioneers of our natural history. Great difficulties beset the early botanists in the prosecution of their inquiries, from the novelty of the subject, the paucity of books, and the difficulty of maintaining correspondence with foreign scientific authorities, in those cases where books are insufficient, and knowledge, to a certain extent, must be ocular and traditionary. Yet the Rev. Dr. Cutler, of our State, has culled for himself an enduring garland from a field in which it would appear that the harvest was plenteous, but the laborers were few.

The valleys of New England are not the seat of antiquities and hieroglyphic records; yet, in the earlier volumes of the Transactions, there is more than one account of the memorable inscription on our far-famed Dighton rock. This curious relic of the scattered and now fast disappearing aboriginal inhabitants of our country, is copied and described by various persons, and hypothetically explained by the late excellent Judge Davis, of this city. Whatever be the mystery it involves, a hunting scene or a religious rite, an achievement of war or of conquest, the pages of the Academy offer a faithful facsimile for the use of foreigners and of posterity, who may happen to find themselves called and competent to its perusal.

But by far the most ambitious among the early speculations of the Academy is the theory of Governor Bowdoin, then President of the Institution, on the existence in the universe of an all-surrounding orb. That distinguished gentleman and scholar, after various speculations on the supposed waste of material light from the surface of the sun, and the danger to all material bodies from their own unresisted gravity attracting them towards each other, published an elaborate memoir, entitled "Observations tending to prove, by phenomena and Scripture, the existence of an orb which surrounds the visible material system, and which may be necessary to preserve it from the ruin to which, without such a counterbalance, it seems liable, by that universal principle in matter, gravitation."

The author satisfies himself, by a train of ingenious reasoning, of the sufficiency of his theory to prevent the apprehended catastrophe. He deals not only with the necessities of such an arrangement to produce stability in our universe, but draws supernumerary arguments from the presence of the Milky Way, the blue color of the firmament, and lastly from various corroborative texts of Scripture.

History is silent in regard to the extent of the impression made upon the world by the promulgation of this comprehensive theory. The orb is supposed to have been standing several years after the announcement of its character and office; and, when it fell, the Academy, nothing daunted, proceeded to prosecute its celestial investigations with a zeal and tenacity of purpose prophetic of its future more elevated destiny.

"————— tenacem propositi —————
————— si fractus illabatur orbis
Impavidum ferient ruinæ."

Should any one incline to disparage the labors of our predecessors, on account of their honest and earnest, though sometimes misdirected, inquiries for truth, he will find parallel examples in the early history of every learned body in Europe of a century's standing. The first publications of the oldest philosophical societies contain speculations on the transmuting of metals, projects for perpetual motion, schemes for raising water without power, and for flying in the air by machinery, credulous inquiries about secret poisons and fabulous natural productions. They did not think it beneath them to investigate extravagant rumors; and they often propounded interrogatories, with this view, to foreign ambassadors, missionaries, merchants, and navigators. The Royal Society of London sent many grave inquiries to Sir Philberto Vernatti, then resident in the Indies, in hopes to solve some of the difficulties which were weighing upon them. The first of these was, "Whether diamonds and other precious stones grow again after three or four years in the same places where they have been digged out?" The categorical answer to this question is, "Never." Another inquiry is, "Whether, in the island of Sombrero, there be found such a vegetable as Master James Lancaster relates to have seen, which grows up to a tree, shrinks down when one offers to pluck it, and would quite shrink unless held very hard?" Sir Philberto replies, that he "cannot meet with any that ever heard of such a vegetable."

Again they inquire, "Whether the Indians can so prepare that stupefying herb Datura, that they may make it lie several days, months, years, according as they will have it, in a man's body, and at the end kill him without missing half an hour's time?"

The twenty-ninth question is, "Whether there be a tree in Mexico that yields water, wine, vinegar, oil, milk, honey, wax, thread, and needles?" The answer here is more encouraging: "The cocos-trees yield all this, and more."

In the inquisitiveness and credulity which marked these early stages of scientific inquiry, we have at least the gratifying assurance, that our philosophic fathers did not close their ears against the reception of knowledge, from whatever quarter it might proceed. They were just emerging from the deep intellectual darkness which for long ages had brooded over the world. They were the survivors of many generations, among whom to inquire had been a crime, to reason had been a heresy, and to experiment a satisfactory evidence of intercourse with the powers of darkness. Secretly, and by stealth and stratagem, the germs of science had here and there been nourished into visible life; but the air and the sunlight of heaven were denied to their upward expanding tendencies. And when at length, with the Reformation, the revival of letters, and the introduction of the printing-press, a veil was lifted from the moral and material world, no wonder that inquiring eyes were dazzled, and strong heads were turned, with the startling developments of the solar system, the circumnavigation of the globe, and the practicable intercourse of men and nations with each other.

The comparatively short period during which the American Academy has existed, has been one of advanced and rapid progress in the history of science throughout the world. It has been the era of the Herschels and Laplace, of Lavoisier and of

Davy, of Cuvier, of Watt, and a host of gigantic minds, whose conquests over unknown regions will never be obliterated from the map of science. During this period of progress, the small number and limited opportunities of the scientific men of our own hemisphere have been such as to render them lookers-on, recipients and dispensers, rather than originators, of new discovery. For many years, the publications of this Academy were so sparse and inconsiderable as to induce serious question from some foreign scientific bodies, whether the usual exchange of printed Transactions were worth keeping up. There was a long period, during which the late venerated Bowditch seemed to be the almost solitary pillar on whose support the Academy relied for its character and position in the philosophic world. And to his praise be it said, that, while engaged in the surpassing labors which have constituted the monument of his living and posthumous fame, he never shrunk from identifying his name with a small, and then almost obscure, institution of his native country. Punctual in his attendance on its meetings, earnest in his appeals to the lagging industry of its members, foremost in every movement for its prospective welfare, pouring into its vacant pages the overflowing of his own exuberant mind, he was not only a centre, but a central fire; not only attracting, but exciting, warming, illuminating, all within the circle of his influence. By his side walked the accomplished Pickering, laborious, erudite, modest; a votary of learning for its own sake; whose capacious and cultivated mind, affluent in various lore, seemed poor only to his own aspiring and comprehensive genius.

By these men, more than all others, in the day of its obscurity, was this Academy cherished and upheld. They did not feel authorized to boast much of its history, nor of its existing performances. They were not vainglorious of their own share in whatever of reputation it might have happened to acquire. But they felt and expressed that in it was contained the germ of future development; that to a certain extent it had books, and endowments, and position; that it was their duty and that of their cotemporaries to cultivate its capacities, to improve its condition, and at least to preserve it unimpaired, until the increasing population and wealth in our country, and correspondent increase of the men and means of science, should impart to it a vigorous vitality, like that which sustains the older institutions of Europe.

We do not assume too much in saying, that this period has at length arrived. The thinly attended meetings, few and far between, in which a quorum was with difficulty convened, perhaps only to spend an hour in debating a by-law or electing a foreign fellow, have been replaced by monthly and semi-monthly gatherings, in which the time is often too short to give utterance to the accumulated researches of the members. The demand for publication of new and important matter outstrips the limited resources of the treasury, and now brings the institution before the public of this city, a solicitor for the hearing of its claims. What is it that this Academy, through its members, is now performing? What is it that it asks the means of publishing to the world? Not the meagre and uninteresting record of every-day phenomena. Not the premature speculations of unqualified reasoners on more expanded subjects. Not the repeated lessons received, with unquestioning docility, from the higher sources of transatlantic wisdom. It now rather sits in judgment on unsettled questions of European science, and pushes its own unaided investigations beyond the previous bounds of human knowledge. Its researches during the last five or six years have been such in magnitude and importance, that they may without disadvantage be brought into comparison with those of many of the time-honored institutions of the Old World. Closely connected with our distinguished University, numbering among the teachers of that seminary a large portion of its most accomplished and efficient members, making the pages of its publications a vehicle for the light which emanates from the observatory, the apparatus, the collections of that venerable seat of learning, aided moreover by the naturalists, the philosophers, and the annalists of other societies among us, — it has established an influence which could not well be now spared from the republic of science.

We may say, without fear of contradiction, that there are few branches of physical knowledge which have not been illustrated or enlarged by the members of this body; and when difficult labors are to be performed, or difficult problems to be solved, no source of information in our country has been deemed more reliable, or more frequently been put in requisition, than the authority of this Academy. The plants of California and New Mexico have repeatedly come here to be named and described. The late exploring expedition sent to this city a large portion of its collected treasures, for investigation and judgment. The fossil bones of gigantic quadrupeds are accumulated in our midst with a completeness and abundance such as is found in no other place; and they are presented to the world with an amplitude of scientific delineation, seldom, if ever, surpassed. Huge limbs and heads of undescribed troglodytes, exceeding those of man which they counterfeit, and whose race is now living in African forests, have received their first description in this city.

The pages of our Transactions offer the faithful impress, not elsewhere found, of the footprints of colossal birds and mysterious reptiles, transferred from the banks of our own rivers, where, awaiting the perusal of the naturalist, they have lain for unknown ages, stereotyped in stone. It is fresh in our recollection, that, when the credulity of the popular voice, not without the assent of men of science, had given a fictitious reality to a monster compounded of contributions levied from many individuals, and when this deception gained foothold not only in our own greatest city, but afterwards in one of the enlightened capitals of Germany, the doubt was removed and the deception made manifest by the scientific sentence of one of this Academy.

A few years ago, a call was made by the Legislature of this Commonwealth for researches into the various departments of its indigenous natural history. This call was promptly and ably responded to; and the reports returned on the geology, the forest-trees, the fishes, the insects, and the other invertebrata of Massachusetts, were in the highest degree creditable to those Academicians from whose labors they emanated. Some of these subjects are yet waiting the results of this course of lectures, to give their illustrations to the public.

The incipient mysteries of organic development, the structure and transformations of the animalcular world, the scarce visible organisms which fill our waters with busy and effective life, the unknown generations which have written with their own remains the history of preceding nature, have often been drawn from obscurity, their laws and limits studied, and many of their new and unknown forms for the first time described and arranged by one of our adopted members, whom we may well place in the foremost rank of living naturalists. And, as if to indicate the claim to notice of what might seem a humble department of zoology, we have been taught, from the same indefatigable source, that, since the period of man's existence on this globe, a vast peninsula, constituting nearly an entire State of this Union, has been raised from the bottom of the ocean, and added to the previous continent, by the silent conspiring agency of coral polypes.

When we turn our inquiries in another direction, we find that the study and knowledge of the electric power has not deserted the country of Franklin. This mighty agent, before which men trembled in former ages, — believing, in their alarm, that Jove was wielding his bolts, or "that spirits were riding the northern light," — has become, in philosophic hands, the docile messenger of thought over our vast country, and the faithful monitor of danger in our cities, and seems about to reveal the very measure of its velocity to the persevering interrogations of members of this Academy.

I should weary you with detail, were I to recount the various contributions made among us to mathematical, chemical, economical, mechanic, and microscopic science, and to the natural history of the globe and of its inhabitants. I might say, that the tornado which last year swept over a neighboring district has left on our pages an impress more minute than ever whirlwind left before. I might say, that the forthcoming nautical almanac, the joint and arduous production of our mathematicians, will stand in the foremost rank of similar authorities. I might bring before you the perfected turbine wheel, and the elaborate cordage machinery, as examples of the mechanical ability and inventive genius of our Academicians; and I might cite many instances of energetic co-operation with other bodies, in the magnetic observations, in meteorology, in the coast survey, and in the general advancement of geographical and philosophic knowledge.

Conspicuous above other sciences, for the vastness of its objects, and the amount of intellectual effort which it has called into being, stands astronomy, one of the earliest, the most difficult, and most successful studies of the human mind. For many years, the discoveries of its observers, and the results of its analysts, have, by the common consent of Central and Northern Europe, been chronicled in one place, in the city of Altona, in the astronomical journal of the eminent Professor Schumacher. But Schumacher is dead, and his divided mantle has fallen upon the shoulders of more than one competent successor. The only journal in the English language now devoted to pure astronomical science, regularly reporting, with discriminating exactness, the advances made in that department of knowledge, and enriched by contributions from both sides of the Atlantic, as well as from its own editor, is now published in this country, and issues periodically from the press of Cambridge in Massachusetts.

It has not been in vain that public liberality has provided our University with instruments capable of penetrating the depths of space. It has found in that place eyes adequate to perceive, and minds competent to analyze, the abstruser revelations of astronomical science. The meetings of this Academy have heard the announcement of new celestial bodies, and the assignment of unexpected laws to others already familiar to the European world. Who is there, from the schoolboy to the sage, who has not dwelt and gazed and speculated on the mysterious ring that surrounds the planet Saturn? Who has not wondered at this exceptional feature of the known universe, and planted himself, in imagination, on the surface of that distant sphere, that he might seem to contemplate the radiant arch which spanned its unknown firmament? Yet this remaining anomaly of the visible creation, this marvel and study of modern astronomy, has been destined to reveal its structure at our own observatory. And the probability of its fluid nature, and the laws by which it is sustained, have been deduced from the observations, and established by the profound analysis, of our own astronomers.

Need I call up before this audience the recent fame of that far ulterior planet, which, since the creation of the world, has held its dim and undetected course around the verge of our solar system, until at length its remote presence so weighed upon the instructed sense of the Parisian philosopher, that it was felt and known even before it was seen? And need I say that this object of absorbing interest, this wonder of its time, after justifying, in some measure, the rival claims to its discovery of the three most enlightened nations of Europe, came at last to receive the determination of its true orbit, position, mass, and motion, from the geometers of our own Academy?

I have said enough to show, that the American Academy of Arts and Sciences has earned for itself a position among similar institutions of the world; and although, from the necessary limits of the occasion, I have not been able to take fitting notice of other investigations made here for the advancement of knowledge and other worthy achievements in the parallel walks of literature, yet without arrogance I might assert, that, in the different sections of this Academy, embracing the great departments of modern research and cultivation, men are now found competent to perceive truth, and qualified to return light, on the varied objects of human science.

It is not necessary to say, that the meetings of such a body afford a nucleus, around which are attracted and concentrated the contributions of most of our scientific men. And the regularly published proceedings of this body are the vehicle through which are given to the world the results of their labors.

It ought not then to be said, that, in this enlightened community, the efforts of so active and efficient an institution should be embarrassed by financial deficiencies. Yet such is the uniform excess of its expenditures over its limited income, that the Academy is not able to procure the books wanted for the information of its members, or to issue the publications which should give utterance to its own investigations. So far from enjoying the promptness and amplitude of appearance which attend the productions of similar institutions abroad, it has happened, more than once, that the discoveries of our scientific men have had to wait, until they were actually superseded by the same discoveries abroad, because the printed pages and the illustrations of the engraver could not be commanded at the requisite time.

As a nation, we are proud of whatever contributes to our national glory. We are boastful of our growth, our political progress, our victories, our annexations. We are proverbially sensitive, even in small matters, to questions of precedence and subordination; and we give our undivided sympathy even to a national contest of locksmiths. The triumph of nautical skill in a distant boat-race binds this Union more firmly together, by the common thrill of exultation which vibrates from Maine to Texas.

Have we, then, no place for the rising star of science? Shall we avert our eyes from the dawning light, because its rays do not fall on us from the accustomed east? Have we no encouragement for those, our countrymen, to whom the Old World is beginning to yield its reluctant honors? Are we incapable of appreciating the value of scientific progress, and the importance that our own country should not be last in the general march of improvement which characterizes the present age? Such has not been the character and usage of this our city. Such could not have been the expectation of those who, in adverse times, planted and nourished among us seeds capable of a redundant harvest.

I have thus, ladies and gentlemen, endeavored to present to your favorable notice the character and claims of the Academy of Arts and Sciences. In the course of lectures which is to follow, the Academy will speak for itself. I am aware that it is presumptuous for one absorbed in the cares of a responsible profession, who has added little to the common storehouse of indigenous science, to appear as the advocate and representative of so distinguished a body. But I am impressed with the importance of the occasion, and obey the commands which have been laid upon me; and I will shelter myself under the belief, that it may sometimes be permitted, even to the drone in the hive, to cause the air to vibrate in honor of the labors of his more efficient colleagues.

APHORISMS ON THE WAR.*

I.

TO THE EDITORS OF THE BOSTON DAILY ADVERTISER:

It would be an anomaly and a disgrace, if the United States, with more than twenty millions of loyal inhabitants, affluent, powerful, and warlike, should not be able to put down the insurrectionary movement of an impoverished and restricted people, of scarcely half their numbers.

The war which we are waging, vast as its evils are, may be said to be popular in the United States. Soldiers desire to fight, contractors to operate, citizens to assist, — all are impatient of delay. The nation looks with absorbing interest on the grand drama which is advancing to its *denouement*. The blood and the treasure are forgotten. The spectacle is magnificent, the stake is beyond calculation, and the price is not grudged.

Incumbrances by debt and taxation are the common burden of all countries. We alone have hitherto enjoyed an immunity greatly exceeding that of other nations. And, now that our turn has

---

* From the Boston Daily Advertiser, Feb. 8, 1862.

come, we may safely repose on the unquestioned vigor and vitality of our country to carry us through the trial.

If a friendly nation could be found, equal in power and population to our own, who would generously assume half our debt, and relieve us in twenty-five years from half our liability, we should probably think our burden a light one. Such a nation is to be found in the mere increment of our own population, which doubles once in twenty-five years.

An impoverished and declining people, such as the South now is, cannot long carry on an expensive war. When soldiers are neither fed nor clothed nor paid, they are apt to mutiny and disband, and, as in Spanish America, to form guerillas, and plunder friends and foes for subsistence.

We hear much of the implacable and deadly hatred of Southerners for the North. This will not be cured by concessions and smooth speeches. When the landholders and slaveholders and excited ladies of the South shall find themselves left in the hands of an unscrupulous and lawless soldiery, they may perhaps think of invoking from the Union flag a protection which nothing else can afford them.

Virginia is already ruined. With a debt exceeding forty millions before the war began; with her soil alternately threatened or overrun by opposing armies; compelled to support a standing army of her own, and at the same time to feed a host of gratuitous auxiliaries; exhausting herself in erecting forts and batteries for the United States hereafter to occupy; deserted by the population of nearly half her counties; rich only in neglected fields and unmarketable negroes,—what is she to expect short of regeneration, by the transfer of her soil to more suitable and loyal owners?

South Carolina is ruined. Originally inconsiderable in importance; her slender resources early crippled by the prodigious effort to take Fort Sumter; overrun by a negro majority in her population, so that every black man cannot find a white man to guard him; the unburnt remnants of her principal city cut off from intercourse with the civilized world; her best ports and islands in the hands of the enemy,—she seems not destined to occupy a large space in future American history.

The great wars of history have not often been ended in a year. We may yet have victories to encourage us; we may need disasters to unite us; foreign interference may complicate our struggle But foreign nations have more interest in the attitude of their near neighbors than in that of a remote people like ours, with whom they know that a collision involves no ultimate good.

When this war is ended, we must probably become for some time a military nation. We shall have to manage anomalous communities of straggling Indians, of refractory Mormons, of emancipated slaves and their emancipated masters. And this will be a tax on the resources of our growing nation, but not greater than that which has been required to control either British India or French Algeria.

APHORISMS ON THE WAR.*

II.

To the Editors of the Boston Daily Advertiser:

In the war of the American Revolution, we were defeated at Bunker Hill, at Long Island, White Plains, Brandywine, Germantown, Camden, Guilford, and various other places. Yet our brave fathers fought manfully for seven years, and in the end conquered a glorious peace.

In the war of the Revolution, we had generals of various abilities and fortunes, mostly without education or experience, among whom no one was defeated so many times as General Washington. Yet our brave fathers persevered manfully until they conquered a glorious peace.

In the present century, all the great nations of Europe — France, England, Prussia, and Russia — have encountered many defeats more extensive, disastrous, and humiliating than any which we have suffered. Yet these nations are now the most powerful and prosperous in Europe. The last of

---

* From the Boston Daily Advertiser, May 18, 1862.

them is at present, like ourselves, engaged in the struggle of emancipation, a labor which the others have fortunately brought to a termination years ago.

In the common acceptation of the terms, an army is said to conquer which retains possession of the field of battle, while the party which leaves it is said to be defeated. Yet it often happens that the results in slaughter and starvation preponderate greatly against the victors. The battles of Bunker Hill, Eylau, and Borodino left the victorious party worse than it found them. A dozen victories like that of Chancellorsville would destroy the rebel army and the rebel cause.

The capital of a nation consists of its men and its property. In an active war, if every battle were a drawn battle or a barren victory, the weaker party and not the stronger would perish from inanition.

At the beginning of the present war, there were about thirteen slave States, properly so called. Of these we now hold four, if not five, through conquest or loyal adhesion. We also hold a large number of their most important cities and seaports, including Baltimore, Norfolk, and New Orleans. Considering the magnitude of the war, this is pretty good success for two years. Another two years of proportionate success will annihilate the rebellion.

It is probably necessary that the war should continue two years longer, to cause the world to supply itself with cotton from other sources, and to open the eyes of the South to the insignificance and ruin brought on by their suicidal labors.

DIALOGUE BETWEEN NAPOLEON THE FIRST, AND JEREMIAH, A LATE CITIZEN OF THE UNITED STATES.*

NAPOLEON. Well, citizen Jeremiah, glad to see you established at the Court of Rhadamanthus. What news do you bring from the outer crust?

JEREMIAH. Dismal enough, please your majesty; all going to destruction, — Union split, rebels not beaten nor like to be, business quashed, manufactures and commerce annihilated, crops short, stocks down, amusements done for ever, and people groaning and starving from one end of the continent to the other. I had just made up my mind to emigrate to France or Kamschatka, when I found myself suddenly drafted and marched into Pluto's army.

N. Why, man, I thought you called your country the model of creation, overflowing with men and money, food and raiment, and nothing to do but squat where you please, and enjoy yourselves as long as you please!

J. So it was, till the outbreak of this accursed

---

* From the Boston Daily Advertiser, Aug. 11, 1862.

rebellion; but now a quarter of the people have gone off, and are going to cut the throats of the other three-quarters.

N. It did not use to be so in my time. I generally thought that such questions were settled in favor of the most men, the most guns, and the most money. If it were not that my jailor Pluto is more inexorable even than Sir Hudson Lowe, I should like to contract to put your "gigantic rebellion," in one year, into a quart measure.

J. Alas, sir! haven't they got a million of men in arms, and four million of niggers to keep them supplied with food, fodder, and clothing, all without expense, and all of them inhabiting the most delightful and salubrious country in the world?

N. And haven't you three or four millions of men to their one, and fifty ships to their one, and five hundred gold eagles to their one? Why, man! you must fight till you have killed off a million on each side, and then you will have two millions left, and they will have nothing. Or, what is equivalent, you must let them see that you mean to do it, and have set about it.

J. Ah, sir! think of the tremendous bloodshed and slaughter of going to war in that style.

N. Tut, man! I left twelve thousand of my brave fellows on the field at Austerlitz, and fourteen thousand at Jena, and thirty thousand at Eylau. A most humane policy it was, too, on my part; for, if I had dawdled away a week in fighting the same battles, I should have had three times the number killed, and perhaps been beaten myself. And then, Jeremiah, *on meurt par tout*, these men might all have been dead in their beds in less than a generation.

J. What is to become of our ships and commerce when the terrible iron-clads are infesting every part of the Atlantic, and likely to be soon in the Pacific? And what is to be done, when the Yazoo is full of rams, and the "Nashville" runs daily into every port in the South, and keeps them supplied with the necessaries and luxuries of the earth, which we so sadly want?

N. Blockade them, catch them, sink them; or, at least, don't whine about them.

J. It is discouraging to think that we have now been at war more than a year, and have accomplished nothing. On the other side, they threaten to take Washington, and make a diversion on Bunker Hill. And the sickness, too, appears to be increasing, and all on our side.

N. You incorrigible *bête*. Have you not taken Norfolk and Newbern, Pulaski and Pensacola, New Orleans and the Mississippi, and twice as much more? I never made so much progress in one year in my conquest of Europe. And as for disease, — was I stopped by the plague at Cairo, or prevented by the marsh fever from driving **the** British out of Walcheren?

J. But it seems that foreign intervention has at last become inevitable.

N. There you have touched the thing with a needle! Foreign intervention in your quarrel! I should like to have a finger in that pie myself. Let us see. France and England make joint war upon you. Grand expedition planned to your coast. Sea covered with your privateers. Bread riots at home. Disturbance among the makers of lace, broadcloth, rails, linen, hardware, and rat-traps. Suddenly I make a little private peace of my own, and open my ports to Yankee cruisers, who bring me in British manufactures, China tea-chests, India saltpetre, Australian gold, and — oh! ah! — what was I dreaming of? — I was beginning to jump for joy; and here I am, deep under Pluto's hatches, and powerless as my royal brother, Cotton.

J. King Cotton is burning himself like a Phœnix, expecting to rise with a singed tail from his own ashes. But his subjects hate us worse than yours ever hated the English: they will never agree to live with us again, — never, never. Would that the good old Constitution were strong enough to hold us all together!

N. Hark'ee, Jeremiah! you have tried Constitution on them long enough: they repudiate it, kick it, spit upon it. They don't want the Constitution, but the "institution." What if they do hate you? Just observe, man, — a few strong garrisons and camps of observation have a wonderful effect in nourishing the affections of such people.

J. But the niggers, the everlasting niggers.

N. If you want my opinion, Jerry, it is, that the negroes make good slaves, but better soldiers. Did not they drive my fine army of thirty thousand men, under General Le Clerc, into the sea at St. Domingo? At Magenta and Solferino, the most desperate fighters were the Turcos, a set of double-dyed darkies from the rear of Algeria. Did not your General Jackson thank the blacks for their bravery at New Orleans? Look ye! If I wish to conquer a country, give me one that is half filled with a disaffected population.

J. But you would not inaugurate the horrors of a servile war.

N. There was a time when they could have kept their slaves under the Constitution. But it begins to look too late for that. A part will be emancipated, a part perhaps exported, or a part perhaps left in the hands of their masters if it should be necessary to save them from idleness and starvation. A restraint will no doubt be put on their excesses. But, in the mean time, the grander question, which involves the peace and happiness of twenty-seven millions of your free white men, has received a decision which now rings as a watchword from Maine to Kansas, " Crush the rebellion." And the mountains and valleys of New Hampshire and of California alike echo the resolute response, "Put it through." Depend on it, they will do it, Jerry, in spite of your croaking.

J. I think I feel better.

THE DARK SIDE, THE BRIGHT SIDE, THE PRACTICABLE SIDE.*

We are discovering at last that the South are a dangerous people. Warlike, audacious, needy, unscrupulous, individually disinclined and disqualified for industrial pursuits, but both inclined and qualified for war, rapine, and conquest, their separate existence is incompatible with the peace of the world. Such men, in former times, inaugurated the dark ages, and now control the miserable destinies of Spanish America. There is no safety for civilization, liberty, or human progress, but in their absolute suppression.

This suppression can be effected by a united North and a war of moderate continuance, such as those to which other nations have been accustomed to submit. History tells of wars of ten years' and of thirty years' duration; but our war has not yet lasted two years. The tremendous struggle of England against France, beginning in 1793, and lasting (with the brief exception of the peace of Amiens) till the battle of Waterloo, in 1815, occu-

---

* From the Boston Daily Advertiser, 1862.

pied more than twenty-one years. And this was a war of fluctuating fortunes, of fruitless and ruinous expenditures, of disheartening failures and defeats; nevertheless manfully carried on, under different and adverse administrations, with the unwelcome accompaniments of the press-gang and the tax-gatherer, of grinding imposts and unfathomable debt, until England came out of it at last, perhaps the most wealthy and powerful nation of the globe.

We have yet to learn, what every nation in Europe has had to learn, that war, if not the normal state of mankind, is nevertheless an endurable state. It can be indefinitely borne by a nation, conscious of its own power, the justice of its cause, and the slow but sure decline of its adversary. The South began this contest with abundance of food and clothing, with ships and trade, with flourishing commercial cities, and a great staple which was indispensable to the civilized world. How many of these things have they left to enjoy or to use at the present time? Certainly, if the progressive impoverishment of the next year shall bear its due proportion to that of the last; if there is any thing reliable in the bodings of their own newspapers; if the supporting of an immense army is ruinous to a cramped and exhausted country; if drawn battles, or even victories, shall leave them worse off than before, — then the end of their career must be only a question of time.

Meanwhile the North is relatively rich, progressive, and prosperous. The cities are busy, the crops abundant, the markets prompt and remunerative, the wages of labor high, the inducements for immigration great; manufactures, commerce, and agriculture all actively and profitably pursued; the taxation by no means excessive, when compared with that of other nations; and the national debt, if it becomes large enough to reach posterity, sure to constitute a firm, cementing bond of the Union.

The importance of the South has been overrated. If the Southern States were swallowed up by an earthquake, the world would be again supplied with cotton in a few years. Cotton, as we know it, is an annual plant, requiring for its production only seed, soil, and necessity. The seed is always to be had; the soil constitutes a zone round the earth of some seventy degrees; the necessity is furnished by starving Europe, and by the high price of cotton, which now makes it by far the most profitable crop that can be anywhere raised.

Two years more of vigorous war and blockade will cause the world to supply itself with cotton, without an earthquake. The hundred new places which are now struggling to raise cotton, will be five hundred next year. And, whenever the production shall have once more overtaken the demand, cotton will become a drug; and, if it shall ever happen that the pacified South shall be able to return as before to the cultivation of cotton, it will only be to render it still more a drug, exceeding in that character all other kinds of property except negro property, which will then not pay for keeping.

It now seems probable that the future acts in the drama of this war will be better adapted to our own character and power, as well as to those of the enemy, than they have hitherto been. We shall make it a question of relative endurance, rather than of enormous invasion and illimitable bloodshed. There is no doubt that a Napoleon or a Pelissier might take Richmond by the sacrifice of a hundred thousand men; but the prize would not be worth the cost. On the other hand, how long can the devastated fields and exhausted granaries of Virginia hold out in supporting the army of locusts which now, in the character of defenders, infests and devours them? Yet such an army must be kept up in every Southern State to protect its vulnerable points from the inroads which are made, at comparatively little expense, on every coast and river.

The policy, which under Washington carried us through the Revolution, will again carry us through this war. The hot blood of the South may at times prove more than a match for us in the onset of the battle-field; but it poorly bears the weary and consuming influence of passive warfare, of labor wasted on trenches instead of crops, of starving families deserted by drafted men, and left to the doubtful fidelity of slaves, — of idle and marauding soldiers, driven by hunger to plunder friends and foes, — of factious and desperate parties, and the deferred hope of a military empire founded on the wretchedness of the many for the benefit of the few.

INDEX.

Academic institutions, 336.
Academy of Arts and Sciences, 333.
Achilles, 281.
Agassiz, Professor, 333, 351.
Allopathy, 218.
Amazon, River, 8.
Ambrose Paré, 169.
American Philosophical Society, 98.
American success, 31.
Ancient and modern studies, 37.
Andral, 153.
André, Major, body of, 133.
Animalcular origin, 290.
Aphorisms on the War, 359.
Architecture, 70.
Artificial method, 219, 226.
Astronomy, 18.
Atkinson, Professor W., 20.

Bacon's philosophy, 43.
Bad effect of premature study, 7.
Beautiful and sublime, 28.
Belmont, 323.
Botanic physicians, 329.
Bowditch, Dr. N., 346.
Bowdoin, Governor, 342.
Brain overworked, 7.
Brookfield, North, 323.
Buckle, Mr., 33.
Burial of the dead, 119.

Caligo, what, 117.
Carlo Borromeo, 131.
Cattle disease, 295.
Causes of epidemics, 300.
Cemeteries, rural, 133.
Chance discoveries, 65.

Chemistry, growth of, 10.
Chiron the Centaur, 276.
Cholera, whether contagious, 287.
Cicero on Cataline, 51.
Classical studies, 47.
Classic languages, 22.
Climax of epidemics, 300.
Cochituate water, 137.
Cold, preservation by, 128.
Collegiate education, 19.
Columbia, River, 8.
Contagion, 297, 322, 324.
Contagion of epidemics, 310.
Cotting, Dr. B. E., 245.
Cotton, King, 367.
Cotton, raising of, 372.
Cultivated mediocrity, 35.
Cure of diseases, 223.
Cutler, Dr., 341.

Dark ages, 43.
Dark side, &c., 370.
Dead languages, 54.
Death of Pliny, 111.
Decay of organized beings, 120.
Defeats, effect of, 361.
Destitution of last age, 3.
Dickens, Charles, 245.
Dighton rock, 341.
Disinfectants, 280.
Dryness, preservation by, 130.

Edinburgh Review, 45.
Education, self, 25, 27.
Edward I., King of England, 122.
Egyptian medicine, 285.
Elephant, extinct, 129.
Eloquence, 68.

INDEX.

Embalming, 130.
Empirical remedies, 235.
England, medical men in, 215.
English universities, 81.
Erysipelas, 152.
Esculapius, 278.
Etiology, 265.
Etymology, 73.
Exact sciences, 173.
Excess of classic studies, 78.
Exclusive method, 220, 233.
Expectant medicine, 328.
Expectant method, 219, 230.
Extreme doctrines, 217.

Fallacious practice, 183.
False definition, 177.
Female medicine, 283.
Fiction, 13.
Five thousand years unprogressive, 65.
Forbes, Sir John, 243, 246.
Frogs, fossil, 340.

Geography, growth of, 8.
Geology, growth of, 9.
Gilbert Blane, Sir, 171.
Gladstone, opinions of, 83.
Gothic architecture, 71.
Gould, A. A., Dr., 245.
Grecian architecture, 70.
Greek language, 22, 45.
Greeks, ancient, 21.
Greeks and Romans, 57.
Grotius, 85.
Growth of knowledge, 8.

Hanging Jews, 302.
Henry VIII., King of England, 127.
Hereditary position, 32.
Heroic medicine, 275.
Heroic treatment, 227.
History, greatness of, 11, 13.
History of Medicine, 271.
Hobbes on dark ages, 43.
Homer, estimation of, 59.
Homeric studies, excess of, 85.
Homœopathic method, 219, 231.
Homœopathy, report on, 326.
Hooker, Worthington, Dr., 245.
Hooping-cough, 150.
Horsford, Professor, 136.
Hydropathy, 233.

Iliad, heroes of, 57.
Imperfect former knowledge, 8.
Imported cattle, 298.

Increase of books, 5.
Indian names, 74.
Inflections of language, 51.
Influenza, 290.
Inventions, 4.
Inventions, warlike, 30.

Jeffrey, Lord, 27.

Languages, various, 49.
Laplace, 15.
Lead diseases, 139.
Lead pipes, action of water on, 137.
Learned professions, 17.
Liberal education, 16.
Light and heat, 103.
Living languages, 53.
Locomotion, means of, 3.
London, report on lead in, 141.
Lord Jeffrey, 27.
Louis, 157.

Macaulay on Athens, 76.
Macaulay on the ancients, 41, 42.
Machaon, 280.
Master of Arts, 18.
Materia Medica, 75, 264.
Measles, 150.
Mecca, pilgrims to, 288.
Medical education, 263.
Medical etiquette, 209.
Medical literature, vast, 204.
Medicine, a conjectural art, 164.
Melmoth's Pliny, 114.
Metastatic diseases, 148.
Miller's History of Medicine, 271.
Misdirection of ancient taste 39.
Mitford's Greece, 76.
Modern discoverers, 64.
Modern poetry, 78.
Modern studies, 87.
Modern war enginery, 30.
Moorish architecture, 72.
Mount-Auburn Cemetery, 119.
Mummies, Egyptian, 130.
Mythology, ancient, 56.

Napoleon, 25.
Napoleon and Jeremiah, 364.
Natural gifts, 34.
Natural history, extent of, 10.
Neptune, planet, 354.
New England, 94.
New philosophy, 43.
Niger, River, 9.
Nile, River, 8.
Nineteenth century, 89.

INDEX.

North, strength of, 372.
Numerical method, 244.

Orb, all-surrounding, 342.
Over practice, 217.

Palliation of diseases, 224.
Panic, popular, 317.
Paradise of doctors, 251.
Paroxysmal diseases, 148.
Pathology, 264.
Periodical literature, 15.
Peter the Great, 25.
Pharmacy, 75.
Philberto, Vernatti, Sir, 344.
Philology, 14.
Physical instrumentalities, 63.
Physick, Dr., 207.
Pickering, John, 347.
Pleuro-pneumonia, 295.
Pliny the elder, 111.
Poetry, 68.
Poisoned wells, 297.
Polypharmacy, 242.
Popular panic, 317.
Precocity of Americans, 200.
Predisposition, 289, 299.
Preparatory education, 18.
Present increase of knowledge, 4.
Preservation of organic nature, 121.
Priessnitz, 233.
Priestly medicine, 282.
Primæval Chersonese, 273.
Printing press, 63.
Professions, learned, 17.
Progress of improvement, 4.
Pronunciation doubtful, 55.
Proportion of bulk and strength, 6.
Pseudo-sciences, 13.

Quackery, 210.

Railroad train, 28.
Rational medicine, 238.
Rational method, 220, 236.
Reformation, the, 63.
Renaissance of letters, 61.
Revolution of society, 63.
Reynolds, Dr. Edw., 245.
Robinson Crusoe, 23.
Roman youth sent to Greece, 23.
Royal Institution, 98.
Royal Society, 98, 344.
Rumford, Count, 90.

Safe-conduct of sick, 225.
Saturn, 353.

Scarlet fever, 151.
School system of New England, 7.
Schumacher, Professor, 352.
Sculpture, 69.
Selection and subdivision, 16.
Self-education, 25, 27.
Self-limited diseases, 143, 145.
Semi-barbarism of last age, 2.
Ship fever, 325.
Sidney Smith's opinions, 81.
Slaughter of cattle, 301, 306.
Small-pox, 152.
Smith, Dr. Nathan, 157.
South Carolina, 360.
South, decline of, 371, 373.
Specific remedies, 219.
Steamship, 28.
Street cars, 15.
Subdivision and selection, 16.
Sublime and beautiful, 28.
Success in the world, 25.
Sudden discoveries, 67.
Summary of discovery, 44.
Surgery, 229.
Swallows disappearing, 340.

Tanquerel on lead diseases, 139.
Taste in architecture, 72.
Technology, 1, 2.
Telegraph, 28.
Telephus, 281.
Terminology, 74.
Therapeutics, 265.
Therapeutics, failure of, 144.
Thompsonian physicians, 329.
Thoth, 284.
Three centuries of Christian era, 46
Trade of medicine, 178.
Translation, effect of, 24.
Treatment of disease, 173.
Troy, siege of, 29.
Typhoid fever, 153.

Unity of disease, 236.
Utilitarian studies, 28.

Value of diagnosis, 180.
Vesuvius, eruptions of, 112.
Virginia, 359.

War, endurable, 371.
Wars of history, 370.
Watering-places, 235.
Winthrop, Governor John, 98.
Witches, burning of, 302.

"Young Physic," 243.

www.ingramcontent.com/pod-product-compliance
Lightning Source LLC
Chambersburg PA
CBHW032022220426
43664CB00006B/335

*9 7 8 3 3 3 7 1 7 8 5 5 0 *